W9-CBS-866

Mifflin
Harcourt

GO MATH!

Volume 2

© Houghton Mifflin Harcourt Publishing Company • Cover Image Credits: (Hares) ©Radius Images/Corbis; (Garden, New York) ©Rick Lew/The Image Bank/Getty Images; (sky) ©PhotoDisc/Getty Images

Made in the United States
Text printed on 100% recycled paper

Houghton
Mifflin
Harcourt

GO MATH!

Curious George by Margret and H.A. Rey. Copyright © 2010 by Houghton Mifflin Harcourt Publishing Company. All rights reserved. The character Curious George®, including without limitation the character's name and the character's likenesses, are registered trademarks of Houghton Mifflin Harcourt Publishing Company.

2017 Edition

Copyright © by Houghton Mifflin Harcourt Publishing Company

All rights reserved. No part of this work may be reproduced or transmitted in any form or by any means, electronic or mechanical, including photocopying or recording, or by any information storage and retrieval system, without the prior written permission of the copyright owner unless such copying is expressly permitted by federal copyright law. Requests for permission to make copies of any part of the work should be submitted through our Permissions website at https://customercare.hmhco.com/permission/Permissions.html or mailed to Houghton Mifflin Harcourt Publishing Company, Attn: Intellectual Property Licensing, 9400 Southpark Center Loop, Orlando, Florida 32819-8647.

Printed in the U.S.A.

ISBN 978-0-544-71053-5

12 13 14 15 0607 24 23 22 21

4500817327 D E F G

If you have received these materials as examination copies free of charge, Houghton Mifflin Harcourt Publishing Company retains title to the materials and they may not be resold. Resale of examination copies is strictly prohibited.

Possession of this publication in print format does not entitle users to convert this publication, or any portion of it, into electronic format.

Dear Students and Families,

Welcome to **Go Math!**, Kindergarten! In this exciting mathematics program, there are hands-on activities to do and real-world problems to solve. Best of all, you will write your ideas and answers right in your book. In **Go Math!**, writing and drawing on the pages helps you think deeply about what you are learning, and you will really understand math!

By the way, all of the pages in your **Go Math!** book are made using recycled paper. We wanted you to know that you can Go Green with **Go Math!**

Sincerely,

The Authors

Made in the United States
Text printed on 100% recycled paper

© Houghton Mifflin Harcourt Publishing Company • Image Credits: (bg) ©Sankar Salvady/Flickr/Getty Images; (t) ©Blaine Harrington III/Alamy Images; (c) ©Don Johnston/All Canada Photos/Getty Images; (b) ©Erich Kuchling/Westend61/Corbis

Authors

Juli K. Dixon, Ph.D.
Professor, Mathematics Education
University of Central Florida
Orlando, Florida

Edward B. Burger, Ph.D.
President, Southwestern University
Georgetown, Texas

Steven J. Leinwand
Principal Research Analyst
American Institutes for Research (AIR)
Washington, D.C.

Contributor

Rena Petrello
Professor, Mathematics
Moorpark College
Moorpark, CA

Matthew R. Larson, Ph.D.
K-12 Curriculum Specialist for Mathematics
Lincoln Public Schools
Lincoln, Nebraska

Martha E. Sandoval-Martinez
Math Instructor
El Camino College
Torrance, California

English Language Learners Consultant

Elizabeth Jiménez
CEO, GEMAS Consulting
Professional Expert on English Learner Education
Bilingual Education and Dual Language
Pomona, California

© Houghton Mifflin Harcourt Publishing Company • Image Credits: (bg) ©Russ Bishop/Alamy Images ; (t) ©Richard Wear/Design Pics/Corbis

VOLUME I

Number and Operations

Big Idea Represent, count, write, order, and compare whole numbers to 20. Develop a conceptual understanding of addition and subtraction through 10. Count to 100 by ones and tens.

Vocabulary Reader Fall Festival! 1

1 Represent, Count, and Write Numbers 0 to 5 9

✓ Show What You Know 10
Vocabulary Builder 11
Game: Bus Stop 12
1 Hands On • Model and Count 1 and 2 13
2 Count and Write 1 and 2 19
3 Hands On • Model and Count 3 and 4 25
4 Count and Write 3 and 4 31
✓ Mid-Chapter Checkpoint 34
5 Hands On • Model and Count to 5 37
6 Count and Write to 5 43
7 Hands On: Algebra • Ways to Make 5 49
8 Hands On • Count and Order to 5 55
9 Problem Solving • Understand 0 61
10 Identify and Write 0. 67
✓ Chapter 1 Review/Test 73

2 Compare Numbers to 5 77

✓ Show What You Know 78
Vocabulary Builder 79
Game: Counting to Blastoff 80
1 Hands On • Same Number 81
2 Hands On • Greater Than. 87
3 Hands On • Less Than. 93
✓ Mid-Chapter Checkpoint 96
4 Problem Solving • Compare by Matching Sets to 5. . . . 99
5 Compare by Counting Sets to 5. 105
✓ Chapter 2 Review/Test 111

© Houghton Mifflin Harcourt Publishing Company

Big Idea

GO DIGITAL

Go online! Your math lessons are interactive. Use *i*Tools, Animated Math Models, the Multimedia *e*Glossary, and more.

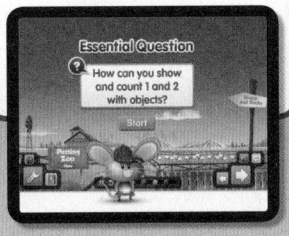

Chapter 1 Overview

In this chapter, you will explore and discover answers to the following **Essential Questions**:

- How can you show, count, and write numbers?
- How can you show numbers 0 to 5?
- How can you count numbers 0 to 5?
- How can you write numbers 0 to 5?

Chapter 2 Overview

In this chapter, you will explore and discover answers to the following **Essential Questions**:

- How can building and comparing sets help you compare numbers?
- How does matching help you compare sets?
- How does counting help you compare sets?
- How do you know if the number of counters in one set is the same as, greater than, or less than the number of counters in another set?

Chapter 3 Overview

In this chapter, you will explore and discover answers to the following **Essential Questions**:

- How can you show, count, and write numbers 6 to 9?
- How can you show numbers 6 to 9?
- How can you count numbers 6 to 9?
- How can you write numbers 6 to 9?

Practice and Homework

Lesson Check and Spiral Review in every lesson

3 Represent, Count, and Write Numbers 6 to 9 115

✓ Show What You Know 116
Vocabulary Builder 117
Game: Number Line Up 118
1 Hands On • Model and Count 6 119
2 Count and Write to 6 125
3 Hands On • Model and Count 7 131
4 Count and Write to 7 137
✓ Mid-Chapter Checkpoint 140
5 Hands On • Model and Count 8 143
6 Count and Write to 8 149
7 Hands On • Model and Count 9 155
8 Count and Write to 9 161
9 Problem Solving • Numbers to 9 167
✓ Chapter 3 Review/Test 173

© Houghton Mifflin Harcourt Publishing Company

4 Represent and Compare Numbers to 10 177

✓ Show What You Know 178
Vocabulary Builder 179
Game: Spin and Count! 180
1 Hands On • Model and Count 10 181
2 Count and Write to 10 187
3 Hands On: Algebra • Ways to Make 10. 193
4 Count and Order to 10 199
✓ Mid-Chapter Checkpoint 202
5 Problem Solving • Compare by Matching Sets to 10 . . . 205
6 Compare by Counting Sets to 10 211
7 Compare Two Numbers 217
✓ Chapter 4 Review/Test 223

Chapter 4 Overview

In this chapter, you will explore and discover answers to the following **Essential Questions**:

- How can you show and compare numbers to 10?
- How can you count forward to 10?
- How can you show numbers from 1 to 10?
- How can using models help you compare two numbers?

5 Addition 227

✓ Show What You Know 228
Vocabulary Builder 229
Game: Pairs That Make 7 230
1 Addition: Add To 231
2 Hands On • Addition: Put Together 237
3 Problem Solving • Act Out Addition Problems 243
4 Hands On: Algebra • Model and Draw Addition Problems. 249
✓ Mid-Chapter Checkpoint 252
5 Algebra • Write Addition Sentences for 10 255
6 Algebra • Write Addition Sentences 261
7 Algebra • Write More Addition Sentences 267
8 Hands On: Algebra • Number Pairs to 5. 273
9 Hands On: Algebra • Number Pairs for 6 and 7. 279
10 Hands On: Algebra • Number Pairs for 8 285
11 Hands On: Algebra • Number Pairs for 9 291
12 Hands On: Algebra • Number Pairs for 10. 297
✓ Chapter 5 Review/Test 303

Chapter 5 Overview

In this chapter, you will explore and discover answers to the following **Essential Questions**:

- How can you show addition?
- How can using objects or pictures help you show addition?
- How can you use numbers and symbols to show addition?

© Houghton Mifflin Harcourt Publishing Company

Chapter 6 Overview

In this chapter, you will explore and discover answers to the following **Essential Questions**:

- How can you show subtraction?
- How can you use numbers and symbols to show a subtraction sentence?
- How can using objects and drawings help you solve word problems?
- How can acting it out help you solve subtraction word problems?
- How can using addition help you solve subtraction word problems?

Personal Math Trainer
Online Assessment and Intervention

6 Subtraction 307

✓ Show What You Know 308
Vocabulary Builder 309
Game: Spin for More 310
1 Subtraction: Take From 311
2 Hands On • Subtraction: Take Apart 317
3 Problem Solving • Act Out Subtraction Problems 323
4 Hands On: Algebra • Model and Draw Subtraction Problems 329
✓ Mid-Chapter Checkpoint 332
5 Algebra • Write Subtraction Sentences 335
6 Algebra • Write More Subtraction Sentences 341
7 Hands On: Algebra • Addition and Subtraction 347
✓ Chapter 6 Review/Test 353

© Houghton Mifflin Harcourt Publishing Company

7 Represent, Count, and Write 11 to 19 357

✓ Show What You Know 358
Vocabulary Builder 359
Game: Sweet and Sour Path 360
1 Hands On • Model and Count 11 and 12. 361
2 Count and Write 11 and 12. 367
3 Hands On • Model and Count 13 and 14 373
4 Count and Write 13 and 14 379
5 Hands On • Model, Count, and Write 15 385
6 Problem Solving • Use Numbers to 15 391
✓ Mid-Chapter Checkpoint 394
7 Hands On • Model and Count 16 and 17 397
8 Count and Write 16 and 17 403
9 Hands On • Model and Count 18 and 19 409
10 Count and Write 18 and 19 415
✓ Chapter 7 Review/Test 421

Chapter 7 Overview

In this chapter, you will explore and discover answers to the following **Essential Questions**:

- How can you show, count, and write numbers 11 to 19?
- How can you show numbers 11 to 19?
- How can you read and write numbers 11 to 19?
- How can you show the teen numbers as 10 and some more?

8 Represent, Count, and Write 20 and Beyond 425

✓ Show What You Know 426
Vocabulary Builder 427
Game: Who Has More? 428
1 Hands On • Model and Count 20 429
2 Count and Write to 20 435
3 Count and Order to 20 441
4 Problem Solving • Compare Numbers to 20 447
✓ Mid-Chapter Checkpoint 450
5 Count to 50 by Ones 453
6 Count to 100 by Ones 459
7 Count to 100 by Tens 465
8 Count by Tens 471
✓ Chapter 8 Review/Test 477

Chapter 8 Overview

In this chapter, you will explore and discover answers to the following **Essential Questions**:

- How can you show, count, and write numbers to 20 and beyond?
- How can you show and write numbers to 20?
- How can you count numbers to 50 by ones?
- How can you count numbers to 100 by tens?

© Houghton Mifflin Harcourt Publishing Company

Big Idea

GO DIGITAL

Go online! Your math lessons are interactive. Use *i*Tools, Animated Math Models, the Multimedia *e*Glossary, and more.

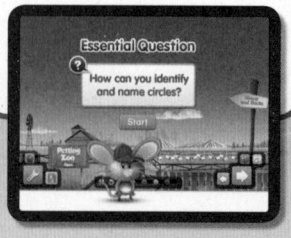

Chapter 9 Overview

In this chapter, you will explore and discover answers to the following **Essential Questions**:

- How can you identify, name, and describe two-dimensional shapes?
- How can knowing the parts of two-dimensional shapes help you join shapes?
- How can knowing the number of sides and vertices of two-dimensional shapes help you identify shapes?

Personal Math Trainer
Online Assessment and Intervention

VOLUME 2

Geometry and Positions

Big Idea Identify, name, and describe two- and three-dimensional shapes. Describe positions of objects in space.

Vocabulary Reader School Fun 481

9 Identify and Describe Two-Dimensional Shapes 489

✓ Show What You Know 490
Vocabulary Builder 491
Game: Number Picture 492
1 Identify and Name Circles 493
2 Describe Circles 499
3 Identify and Name Squares 505
4 Describe Squares 511
5 Identify and Name Triangles 517
6 Describe Triangles 523
✓ Mid-Chapter Checkpoint 526
7 Identify and Name Rectangles 529
8 Describe Rectangles 535
9 Identify and Name Hexagons 541
10 Describe Hexagons 547
11 Hands On: Algebra • Compare Two-Dimensional Shapes 553
12 Problem Solving • Draw to Join Shapes 559
✓ Chapter 9 Review/Test 565

© Houghton Mifflin Harcourt Publishing Company

10 Identify and Describe Three-Dimensional Shapes 569

✓ Show What You Know 570
Vocabulary Builder 571
Game: Follow the Shapes 572
1 Hands On • Three-Dimensional Shapes 573
2 Hands On • Identify, Name, and Describe Spheres . . . 579
3 Hands On • Identify, Name, and Describe Cubes 585
4 Hands On • Identify, Name, and Describe Cylinders . . . 591
5 Hands On • Identify, Name, and Describe Cones 597
✓ Mid-Chapter Checkpoint 600
6 Problem Solving • Two- and Three-Dimensional Shapes 603
7 Hands On • Model Shapes 609
8 Above and Below 615
9 Beside and Next To 621
10 In Front Of and Behind 627
✓ Chapter 10 Review/Test 633

Chapter 10 Overview

In this chapter, you will explore and discover answers to the following **Essential Questions**:

- How can identifying and describing shapes help you sort them?
- How can you describe three-dimensional shapes?
- How can you sort three-dimensional shapes?

Practice and Homework

Lesson Check and Spiral Review in every lesson

© Houghton Mifflin Harcourt Publishing Company

Big Idea

Measurement and Data

Big Idea Develop a conceptual understanding of measurement and data. Classify and count by color, shape, and size.

Vocabulary Reader Plants All Around 637

11 Measurement 645

✓ Show What You Know 646
Vocabulary Builder 647
Game: Connecting Cube Challenge 648
1 Hands On • Compare Lengths 649
2 Hands On • Compare Heights 655
3 Problem Solving • Direct Comparison 661
✓ Mid-Chapter Checkpoint 664
4 Hands On • Compare Weights 667
5 Length, Height, and Weight 673
✓ Chapter 11 Review/Test 679

12 Classify and Sort Data 683

✓ Show What You Know 684
Vocabulary Builder 685
Game: At the Farm 686
1 Hands On: Algebra • Classify and Count by Color 687
2 Hands On: Algebra • Classify and Count by Shape . . . 693
3 Hands On: Algebra • Classify and Count by Size 699
✓ Mid-Chapter Checkpoint 702
4 Hands On • Make a Concrete Graph 705
5 Problem Solving • Read a Graph 711
✓ Chapter 12 Review/Test 717

Science, Technology, Engineering, and Math (STEM) Activities STEM 1

Picture Glossary H1
Index H14

GO DIGITAL

Go online! Your math lessons are interactive. Use *i*Tools, Animated Math Models, the Multimedia *e*Glossary, and more.

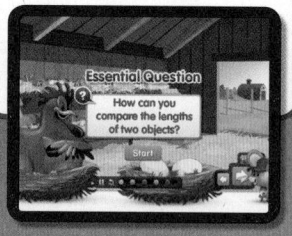

Chapter 11 Overview

In this chapter, you will explore and discover answers to the following **Essential Questions**:

- How can comparing objects help you measure them?
- How can you compare the length of objects?
- How can you compare the height of objects?
- How can you compare the weight of objects?

Chapter 12 Overview

In this chapter, you will explore and discover answers to the following **Essential Questions**:

- How does sorting help you display information?
- How can you sort and classify objects by color?
- How can you sort and classify objects by shape?
- How can you sort and classify objects by size?
- How do you display information on a graph?

© Houghton Mifflin Harcourt Publishing Company

School Fun

written by Ann Dickson

BIG IDEA Identify, name, and describe two- and three-dimensional shapes. Describe positions of objects in space.

© Houghton Mifflin Harcourt Publishing Company

Here is my classroom. Come on in.

Learning time is about to begin.

© Houghton Mifflin Harcourt Publishing Company

Social Studies

Why do we have rules?

These are the book bags
we hang by our names.
Circle the ones that look the same.

Social Studies

Why do we need to take turns?

© Houghton Mifflin Harcourt Publishing Company

Here are the books. We read them all!

Which books are big?

Which books are small?

© Houghton Mifflin Harcourt Publishing Company

Social Studies

Why do we help others?

Here are markers of every kind.

Name all of the colors that you can find.

© Houghton Mifflin Harcourt Publishing Company

Social Studies

Why do we put things away?

Our blocks and toys are over there.

Which shapes are round?

Which shapes are square?

© Houghton Mifflin Harcourt Publishing Company

Social Studies

Why do we share?

Name _____

Write About the Story

Vocabulary Review

alike

different

© Houghton Mifflin Harcourt Publishing Company • Image Credits: (fruit) ©ultimathule/Shutterstock

DIRECTIONS These lunch boxes are alike. In one lunch box draw something that you like to eat. Now circle the lunch box that is different.

Alike and Different

1

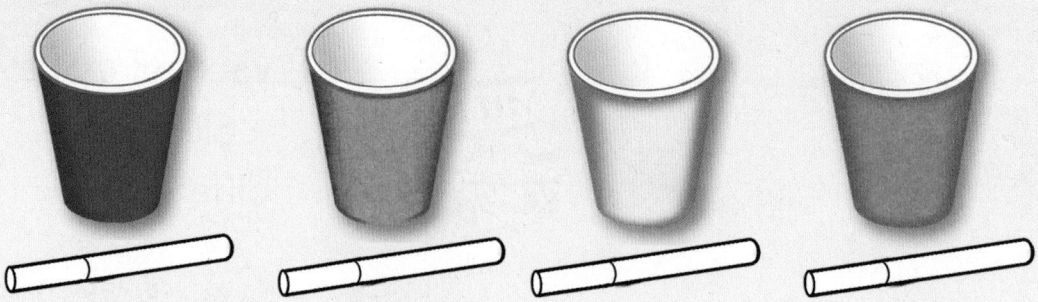

2

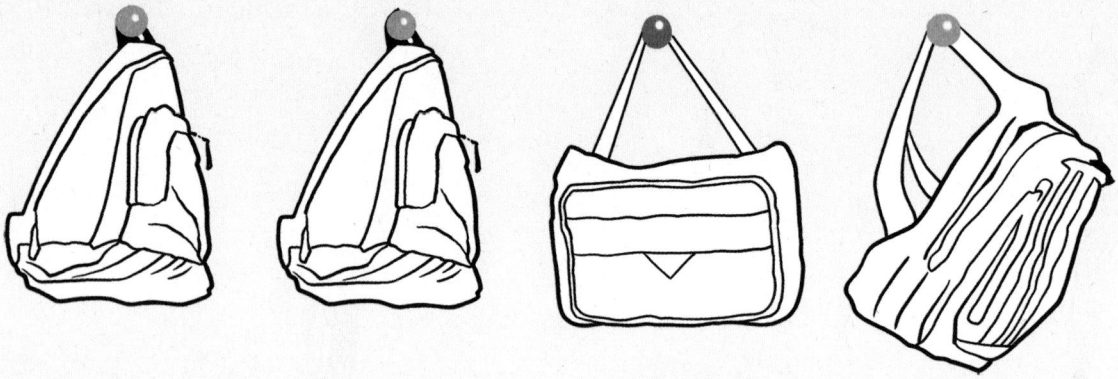

3

DIRECTIONS **1.** Color the markers so that they match the colors of the cups. **2.** Color the book bags that are alike by shape. **3.** This classroom needs some books. Draw a book that is a different size.

© Houghton Mifflin Harcourt Publishing Company

Chapter 9

Identify and Describe Two-Dimensional Shapes

Curious About Math with Curious George

The sails on these boats are shaped like a triangle.

- How many stripes can you count on the first sail?

© Houghton Mifflin Harcourt Publishing Company • Image Credits: (bg) ©LHB Photo/Alamy
Curious George by Margret and H. A. Rey. Copyright © 2010 by Houghton Mifflin Harcourt Publishing Company.
All rights reserved. The character Curious George®, including without limitation the character's name and the character's likenesses, are registered trademarks of Houghton Mifflin Harcourt Publishing Company.

Name _____

Show What You Know

Personal Math Trainer
Online Assessment and Intervention

Shape

1

2

3

Count Objects

4

5

6

This page checks understanding of important skills needed for success in Chapter 9.

DIRECTIONS **1–3.** Look at the shape at the beginning of the row. Mark an X on the shape that is alike. **4–6.** Count and tell how many. Write the number.

© Houghton Mifflin Harcourt Publishing Company

Name _____

Vocabulary Builder

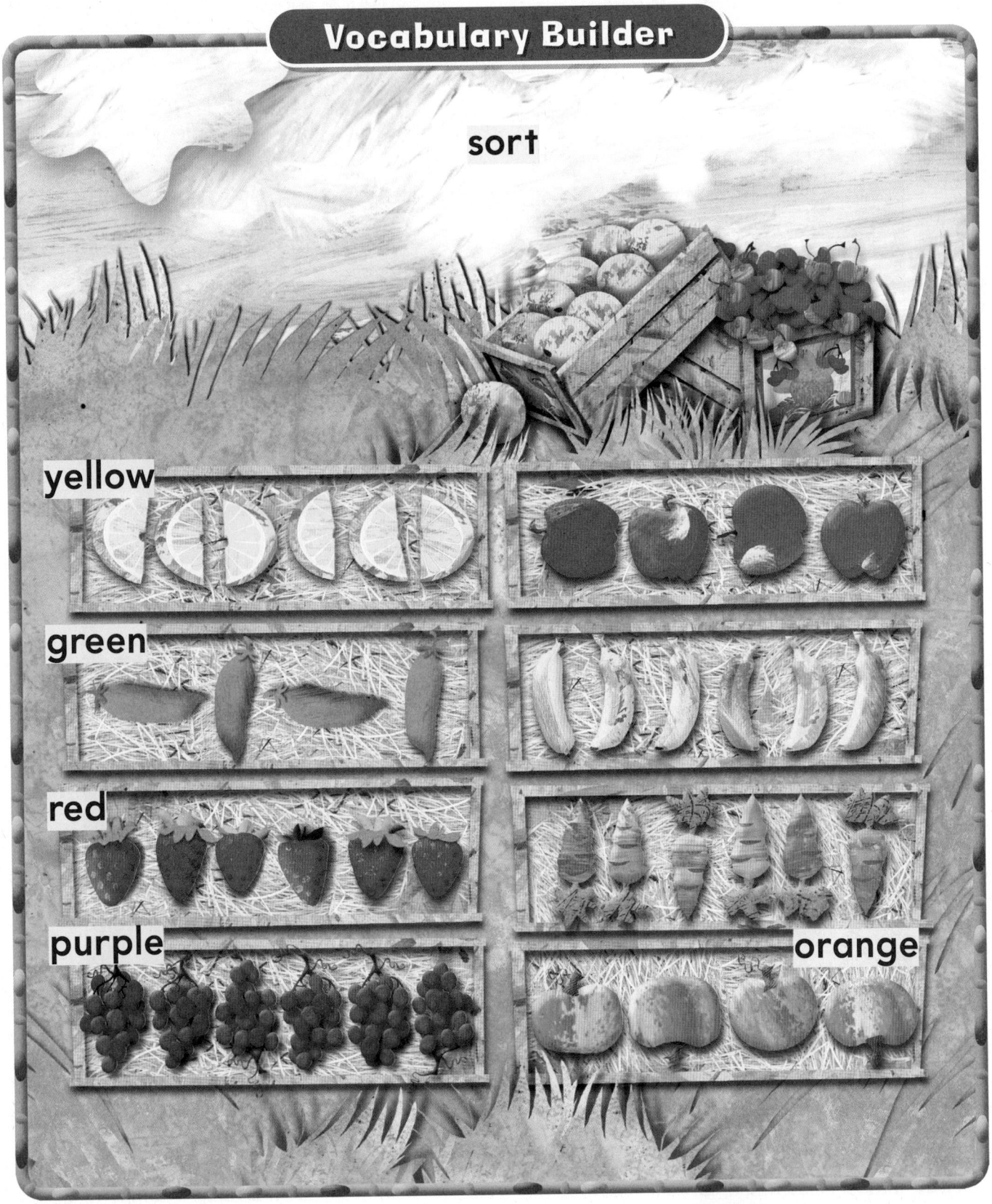

DIRECTIONS Circle the box that is sorted by green vegetables. Mark an X on the box that is sorted by purple fruit.

GO DIGITAL
- Interactive Student Edition
- Multimedia eGlossary

© Houghton Mifflin Harcourt Publishing Company

Game Number Picture

© Houghton Mifflin Harcourt Publishing Company

DIRECTIONS Play with a partner. Decide who goes first. Toss the number cube. Color a shape in the picture that matches the number rolled. A player misses a turn if a number is rolled and all shapes with that number are colored. Continue until all shapes in the picture are colored.

MATERIALS number cube (labeled 1, 2, 2, 3, 3, 4), crayons

Chapter 9 Vocabulary

alike

igual

3

circle

círculo

11

curve

curva

16

different

diferente

19

hexagon

hexágono

34

rectangle

rectángulo

52

side

lado

63

square

cuadrado

70

circle

© Houghton Mifflin Harcourt Publishing Company

alike

© Houghton Mifflin Harcourt Publishing Company

different

© Houghton Mifflin Harcourt Publishing Company

curve

© Houghton Mifflin Harcourt Publishing Company

rectangle

© Houghton Mifflin Harcourt Publishing Company

hexagon

© Houghton Mifflin Harcourt Publishing Company

square

© Houghton Mifflin Harcourt Publishing Company

© Houghton Mifflin Harcourt Publishing Company

triangle

triángulo

79

vertex

vértice

83

vertices

vértices

84

zero

cero, ninguno

86

© Houghton Mifflin Harcourt Publishing Company

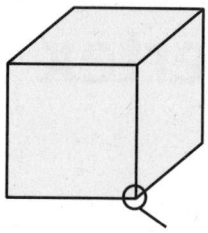

vertex

© Houghton Mifflin Harcourt Publishing Company

triangle

© Houghton Mifflin Harcourt Publishing Company
Credit: ©Artville/Getty Images

six tomatoes

zero tomatoes

© Houghton Mifflin Harcourt Publishing Company

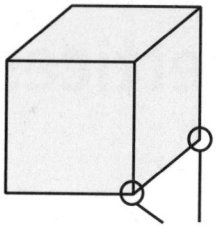

vertices

Game

Shapes

circle

curve

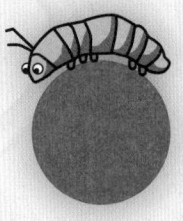

hexagon

rectangle

side

square

triangle

vertex

© Houghton Mifflin Harcourt Publishing Company

DIRECTIONS Say each word. Tell something you know about the word.

© Houghton Mifflin Harcourt Publishing Company

DIRECTIONS Place game pieces on START. Play with a partner. Take turns. Toss the number cube. Move that many spaces. If a player can name the shape and tell something about the shape, the player moves ahead 1 space. The first player to reach FINISH wins.

MATERIALS 1 connecting cube game piece for each player, number cube

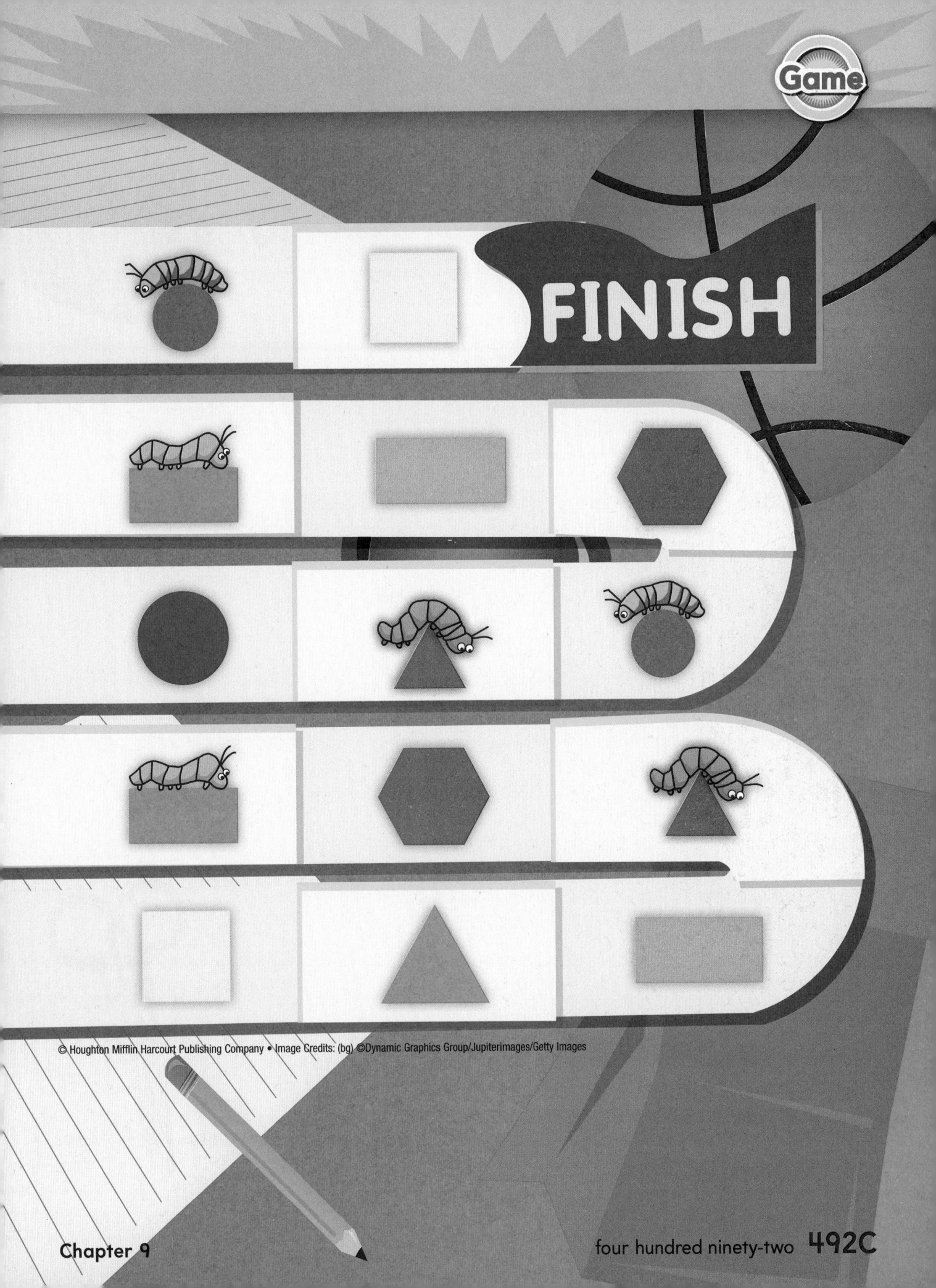

© Houghton Mifflin Harcourt Publishing Company • Image Credits: (bg) ©Dynamic Graphics Group/Jupiterimages/Getty Images

Journal

The Write Way

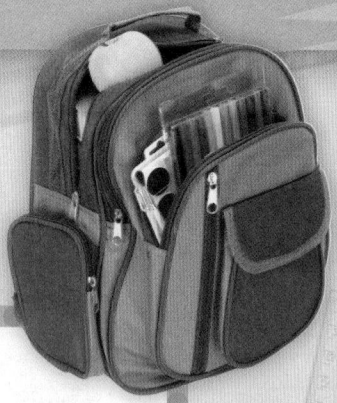

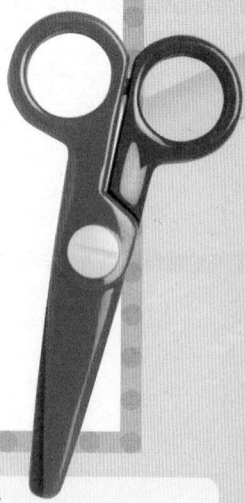

DIRECTIONS Choose two shapes. Draw to show what you know about the shapes.
Reflect Be ready to tell about your drawing.

© Houghton Mifflin Harcourt Publishing Company • Image Credits: (t) ©Podfoto/Fotolia

Name _____

Identify and Name Circles

Essential Question How can you identify and name circles?

Learning Objective You will identify and name circles.

Listen and Draw

Real World

Hands On

circles	not circles

DIRECTIONS Place two-dimensional shapes on the page. Identify and name the circles. Sort the shapes by circles and not circles. Trace and color the shapes on the sorting mat.

© Houghton Mifflin Harcourt Publishing Company

Share and Show

1

DIRECTIONS 1. Mark an X on all of the circles.

© Houghton Mifflin Harcourt Publishing Company

Name _____

© Houghton Mifflin Harcourt Publishing Company

DIRECTIONS 2. Color the circles in the picture.

Problem Solving • Applications Real World

WRITE Math

3

4

DIRECTIONS **3.** Neville puts his shapes in a row. Which shape is a circle? Mark an X on that shape. **4.** Draw to show what you know about circles. Tell a friend about your drawing.

HOME ACTIVITY • Have your child show you an object that is shaped like a circle.

© Houghton Mifflin Harcourt Publishing Company

Name _____

Identify and Name Circles

Learning Objective You will identify and name circles.

1

DIRECTIONS 1. Color the circles in the picture.

© Houghton Mifflin Harcourt Publishing Company

Lesson Check

1

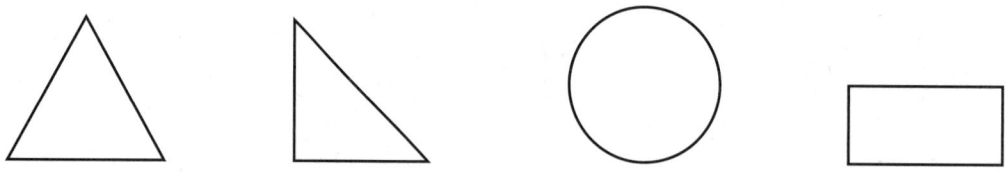

Spiral Review

2

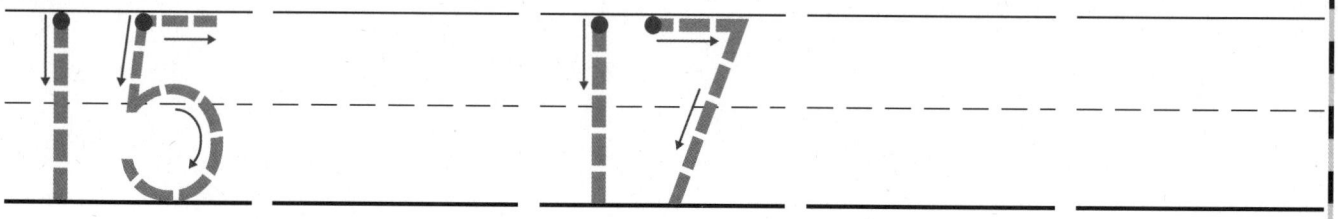

3

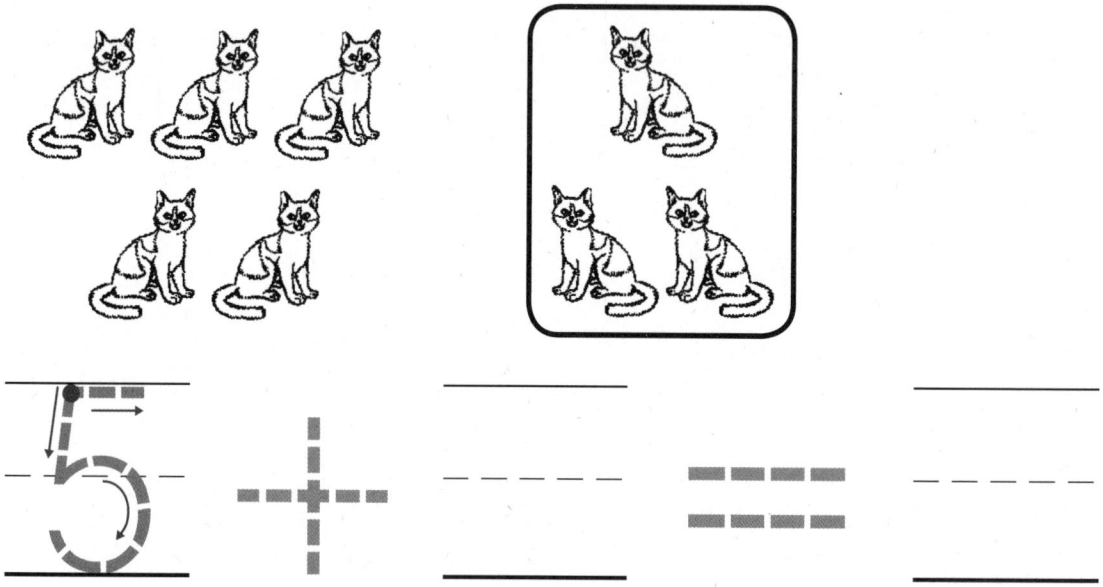

DIRECTIONS **1.** Color the circle. **2.** Count forward. Trace and write the numbers in order. **3.** Trace and write to complete the addition sentence about the sets of cats.

© Houghton Mifflin Harcourt Publishing Company

Name _____

Describe Circles

Essential Question How can you describe circles?

Learning Objective You will use informal language to describe the attributes of circles.

Listen and Draw Real World

DIRECTIONS Use your finger to trace around the circle. Talk about the curve. Trace around the curve.

© Houghton Mifflin Harcourt Publishing Company

Share and Show

1

circle

2

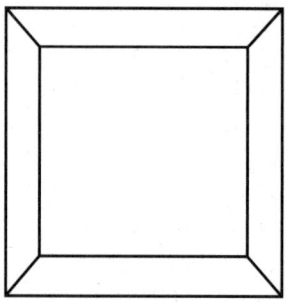

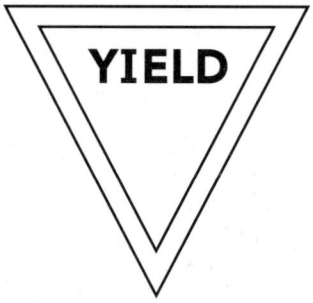

DIRECTIONS 1. Use your finger to trace around the circle. Trace the curve around the circle. 2. Color the object that is shaped like a circle.

© Houghton Mifflin Harcourt Publishing Company

Name _____

3

DIRECTIONS 3. Use a pencil to hold one end of a large paper clip on one of the dots in the center of the page. Place another pencil in the other end of the paper clip. Move the pencil around to draw a circle.

© Houghton Mifflin Harcourt Publishing Company

Problem Solving • Applications

4

DIRECTIONS **4.** I have a curve. What shape am I? Draw the shape. Tell a friend the name of the shape.

HOME ACTIVITY • Have your child describe a circle.

© Houghton Mifflin Harcourt Publishing Company

Name _____

Describe Circles

Learning Objective You will use informal language to describe the attributes of circles.

1

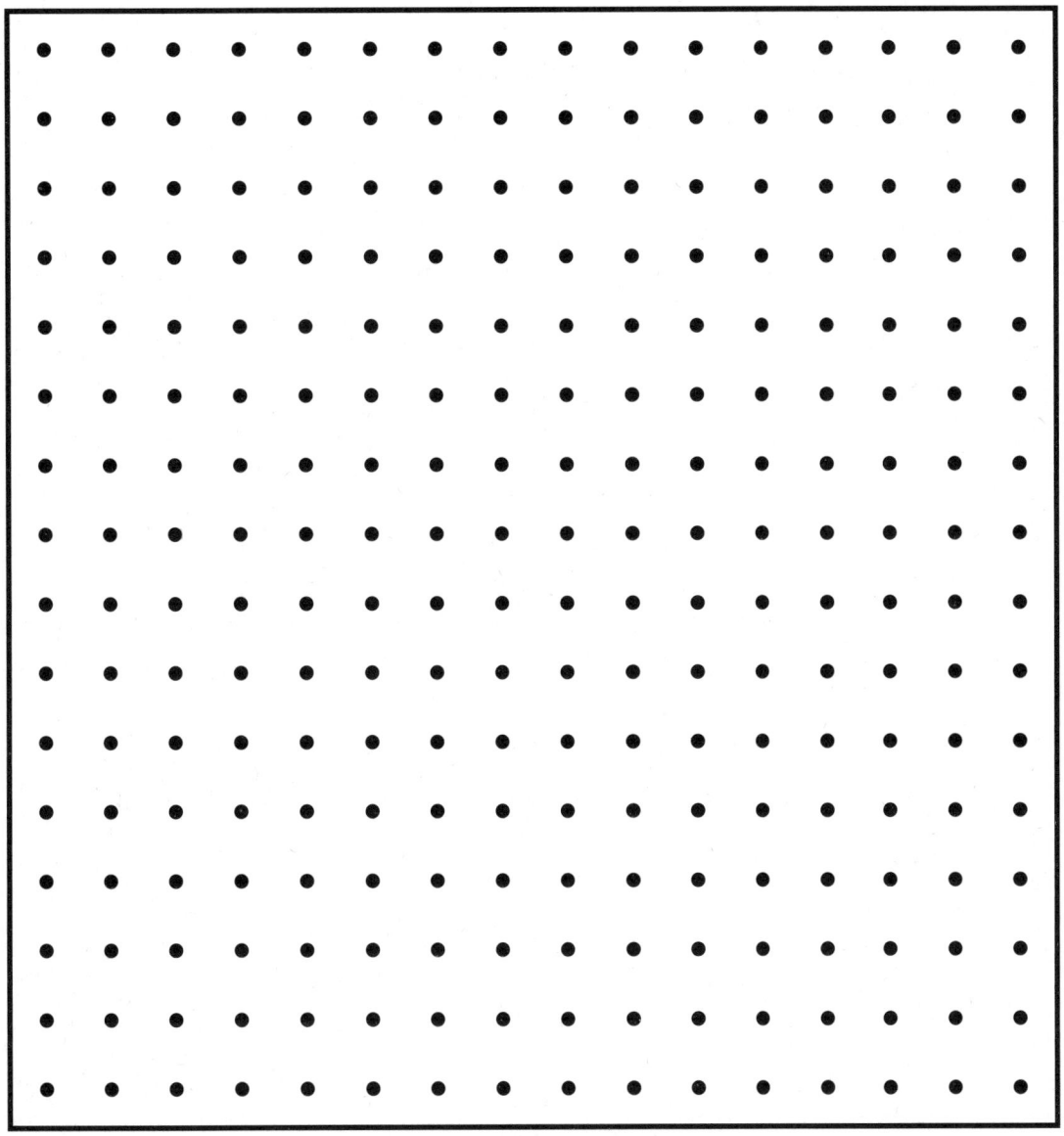

2

DIRECTIONS **1.** Use a pencil to hold one end of a large paper clip on one of the dots in the center. Place another pencil in the other end of the paper clip. Move the pencil around to draw a circle. **2.** Color the object that is shaped like a circle.

© Houghton Mifflin Harcourt Publishing Company

Lesson Check

1

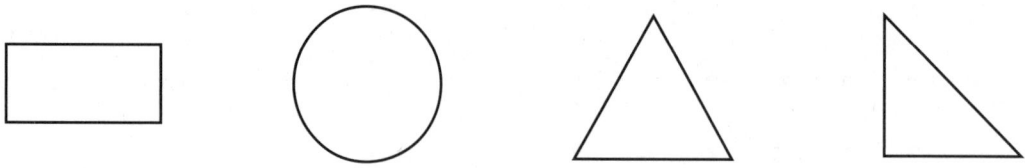

Spiral Review

2

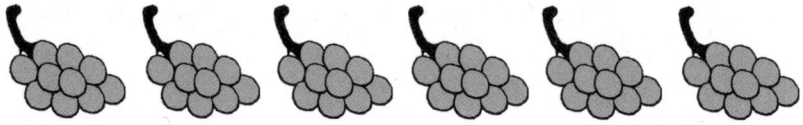

50 60 70

3

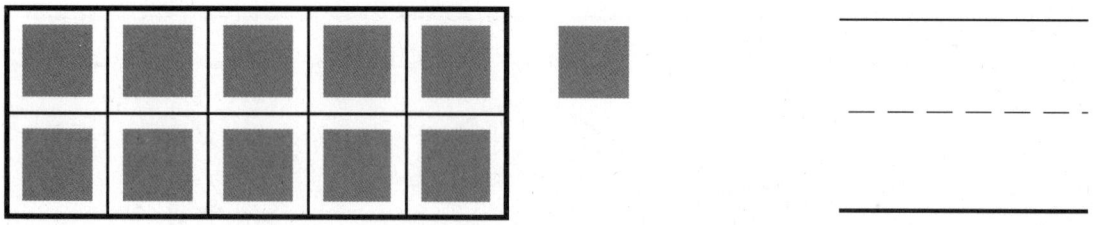

DIRECTIONS **1.** Which shape has a curve? Color that shape. **2.** Point to each set of 10 as you count by tens. Circle the number that shows how many grapes there are. **3.** How many tiles are there? Write the number.

© Houghton Mifflin Harcourt Publishing Company

Name _____

Identify and Name Squares

Essential Question How can you identify and name squares?

Learning Objective You will identify and name squares.

Listen and Draw

Real World

Hands On

squares	not squares

DIRECTIONS Place two-dimensional shapes on the page. Identify and name the squares. Sort the shapes by squares and not squares. Trace and color the shapes on the sorting mat.

© Houghton Mifflin Harcourt Publishing Company

Share and Show

1

DIRECTIONS 1. Mark an X on all of the squares.

© Houghton Mifflin Harcourt Publishing Company

Name _____

© Houghton Mifflin Harcourt Publishing Company

DIRECTIONS **2.** Color the squares in the picture.

Problem Solving • Applications Real World

WRITE Math

3

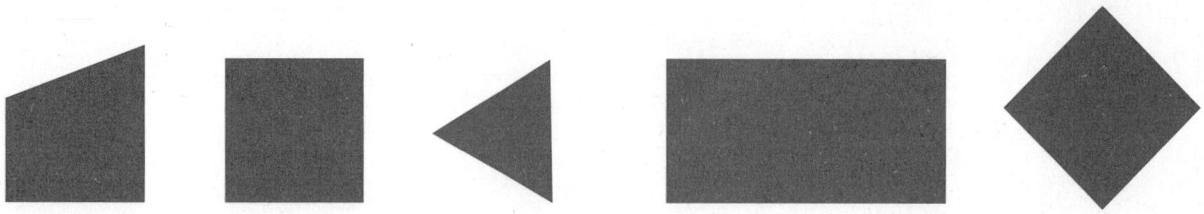

4

DIRECTIONS **3.** Dennis drew these shapes. Which shapes are squares? Mark an X on those shapes. **4.** Draw to show what you know about squares. Tell a friend about your drawing.

HOME ACTIVITY • Have your child show you an object that is shaped like a square.

© Houghton Mifflin Harcourt Publishing Company

Name _____

Identify and Name Squares

Learning Objective You will identify and name squares.

1

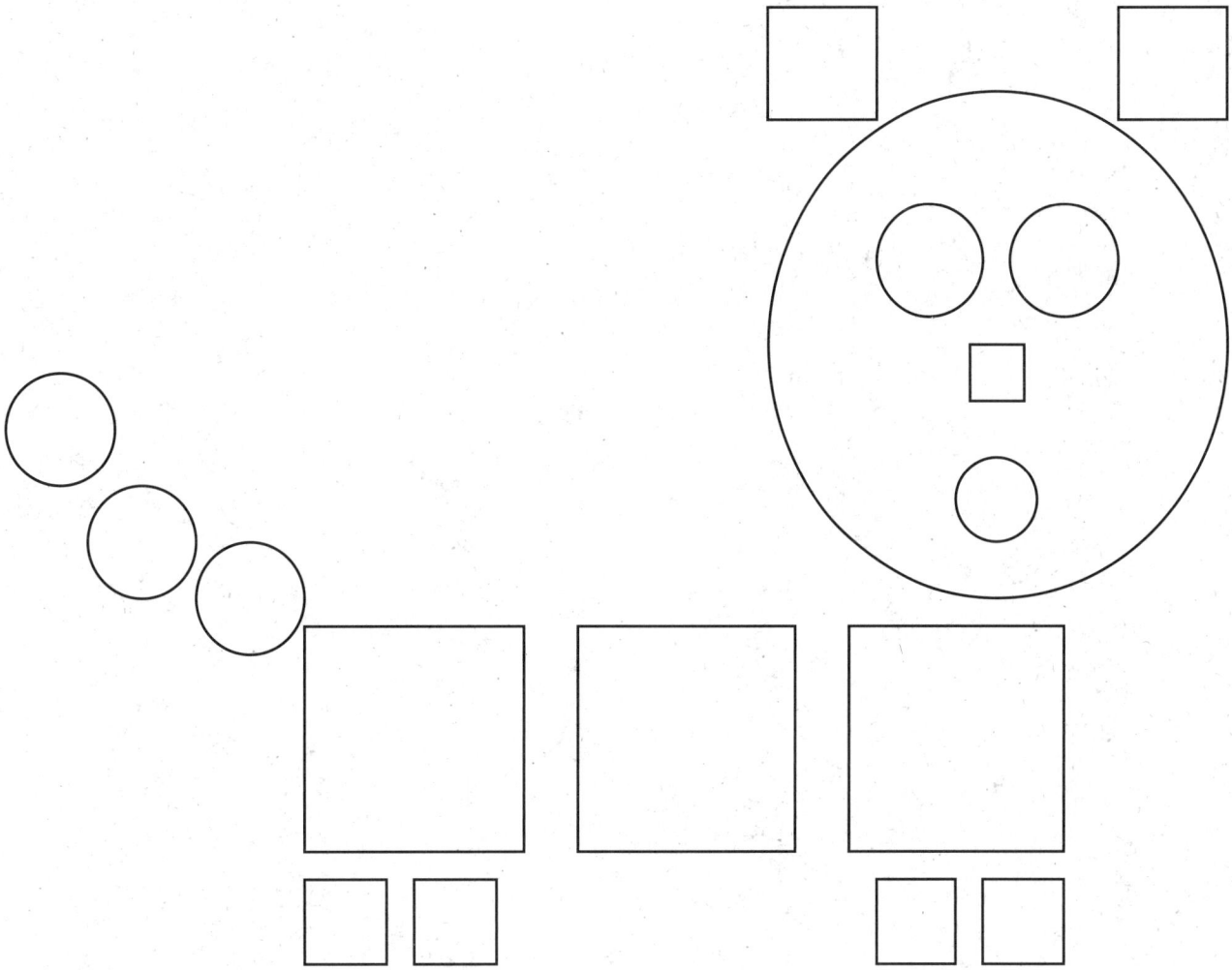

DIRECTIONS 1. Color the squares in the picture.

© Houghton Mifflin Harcourt Publishing Company

Lesson Check

1

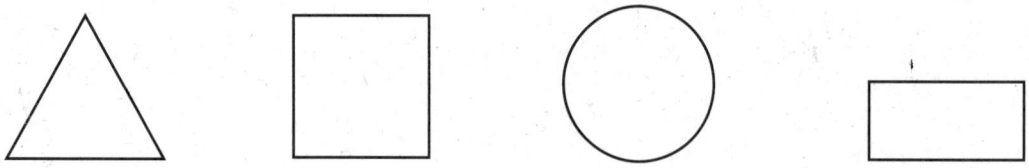

Spiral Review

2

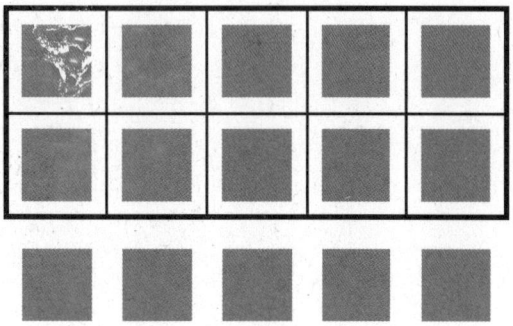

3

2 and 2

DIRECTIONS 1. Which shape is a square? Color the square. 2. How many tiles are there? Write the number. 3. Trace the number of puppies. Trace the number of puppies being added. Write the number that shows how many puppies there are now.

© Houghton Mifflin Harcourt Publishing Company

Name _____

Describe Squares

Essential Question How can you describe squares?

Learning Objective You will use informal language to describe the attributes of squares.

Listen and Draw

DIRECTIONS Use your finger to trace around the square. Talk about the number of sides and the number of vertices. Draw an arrow pointing to another vertex. Trace around the sides.

© Houghton Mifflin Harcourt Publishing Company

Share and Show

square

1 _____

_____

_____ vertices

2 _____

_____

_____ sides

DIRECTIONS 1. Place a counter on each corner, or vertex. Write how many corners, or vertices. 2. Trace around the sides. Write how many sides.

© Houghton Mifflin Harcourt Publishing Company

Name _____

3

DIRECTIONS 3. Draw and color a square.

© Houghton Mifflin Harcourt Publishing Company

Problem Solving • Applications

4

WRITE Math

DIRECTIONS 4. I have 4 sides of equal length and 4 vertices. What shape am I? Draw the shape. Tell a friend the name of the shape.

HOME ACTIVITY • Have your child describe a square.

© Houghton Mifflin Harcourt Publishing Company

Name _____

Describe Squares

Learning Objective You will use informal language to describe the attributes of squares.

1

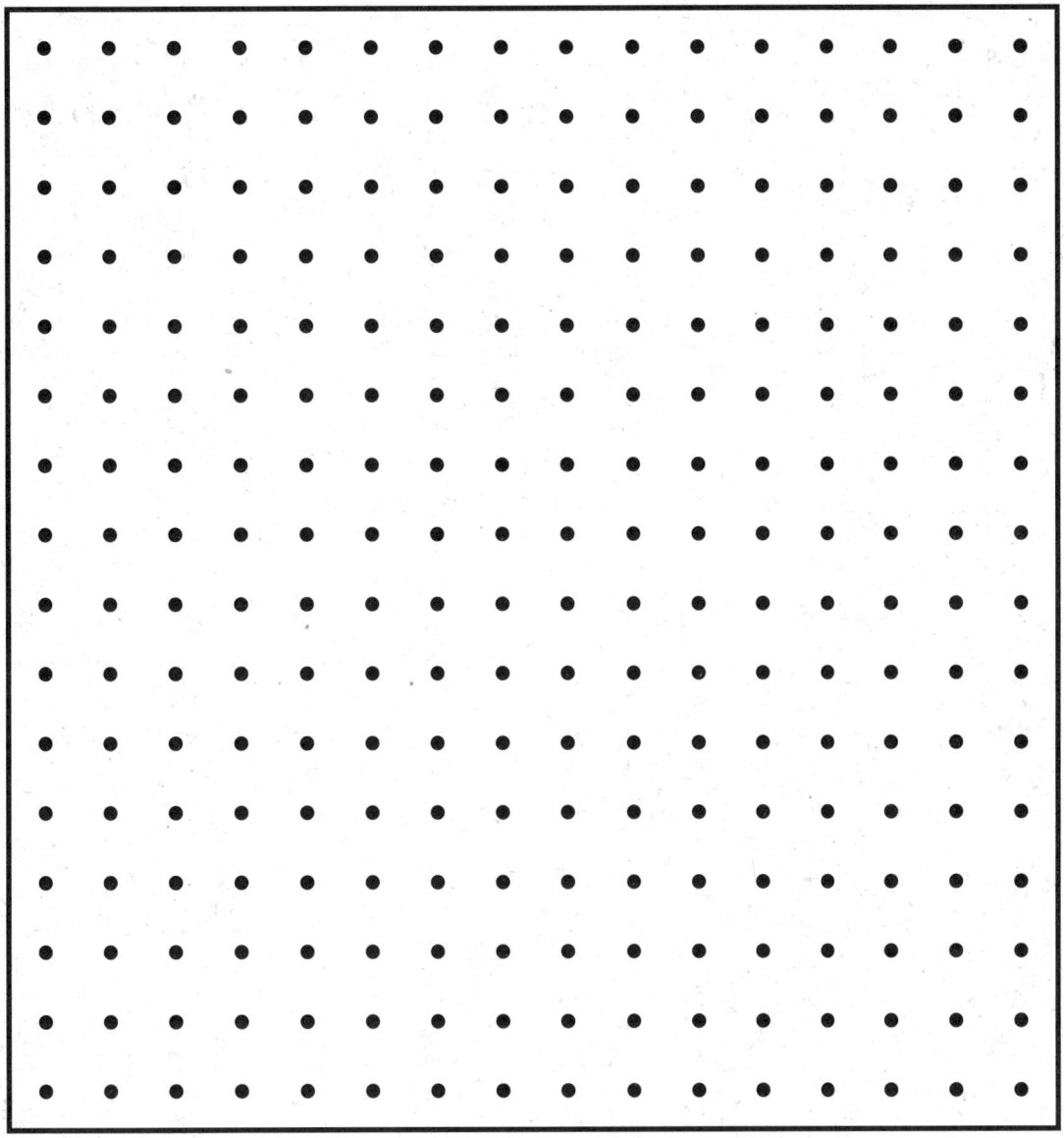

2 _____

_ _ _ _ _

_____ **vertices**

3 _____

_ _ _ _ _

_____ **sides**

DIRECTIONS **1.** Draw and color a square. **2.** Place a counter on each corner, or vertex, of the square that you drew. Write how many corners, or vertices. **3.** Trace around the sides of the square that you drew. Write how many sides.

© Houghton Mifflin Harcourt Publishing Company

Lesson Check

1

_____ vertices

Spiral Review

2

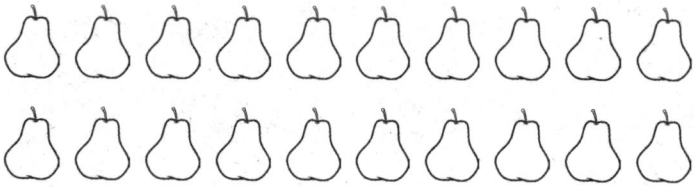

_____

3

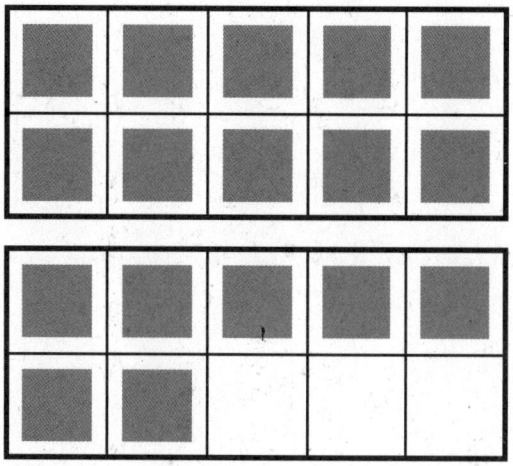

_____

DIRECTIONS 1. How many vertices does the square have? Write the number. 2. Count and tell how many pieces of fruit. Write the number. 3. How many tiles are there? Write the number.

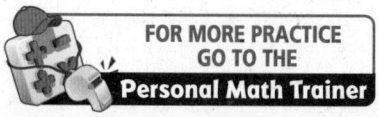

© Houghton Mifflin Harcourt Publishing Company

Name _____

Identify and Name Triangles

Essential Question How can you identify and name triangles?

Learning Objective You will identify and name triangles.

Listen and Draw

Real World

Hands On

triangles	not triangles

DIRECTIONS Place two-dimensional shapes on the page. Identify and name the triangles. Sort the shapes by triangles and not triangles. Trace and color the shapes on the sorting mat.

© Houghton Mifflin Harcourt Publishing Company

Share and Show

1

© Houghton Mifflin Harcourt Publishing Company

DIRECTIONS 1. Mark an X on all of the triangles.

Name _____

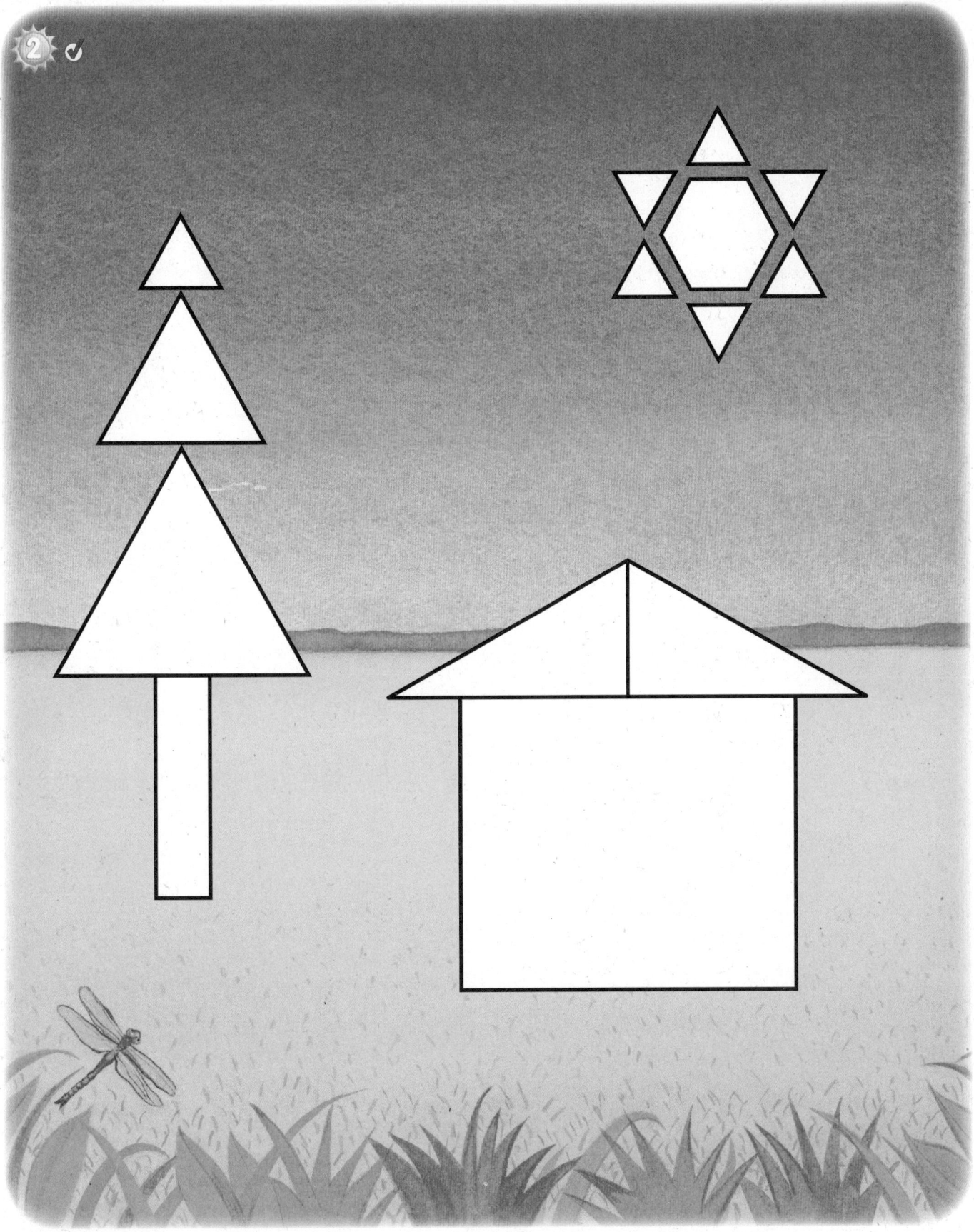

© Houghton Mifflin Harcourt Publishing Company

DIRECTIONS 2. Color the triangles in the picture.

Problem Solving • Applications Real World

WRITE Math

3

4

DIRECTIONS 3. Anita put her shapes in a row. Which shapes are triangles? Mark an X on those shapes. 4. Draw to show what you know about triangles. Tell a friend about your drawing.

HOME ACTIVITY • Have your child show you an object that is shaped like a triangle.

© Houghton Mifflin Harcourt Publishing Company

Name _____

Identify and Name Triangles

Learning Objective You will identify and name triangles.

1

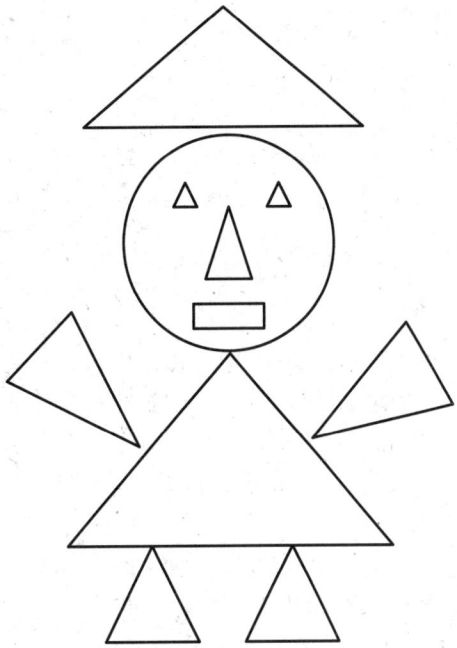

2

© Houghton Mifflin Harcourt Publishing Company

DIRECTIONS 1–2. Color the triangles in the picture.

Lesson Check

1

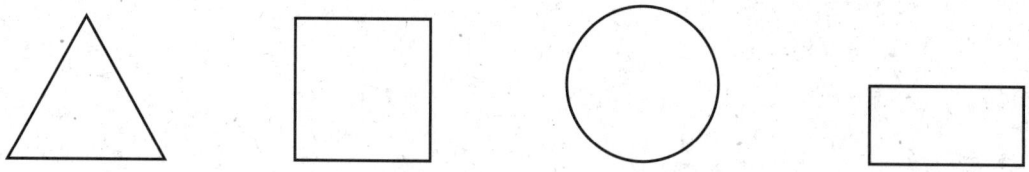

Spiral Review

2

1	2	3	4	5	6	7	8	9	10
11	12	13	14	15	16	17	18	19	20
21	22	23	24	25	26	27	28	29	30

3

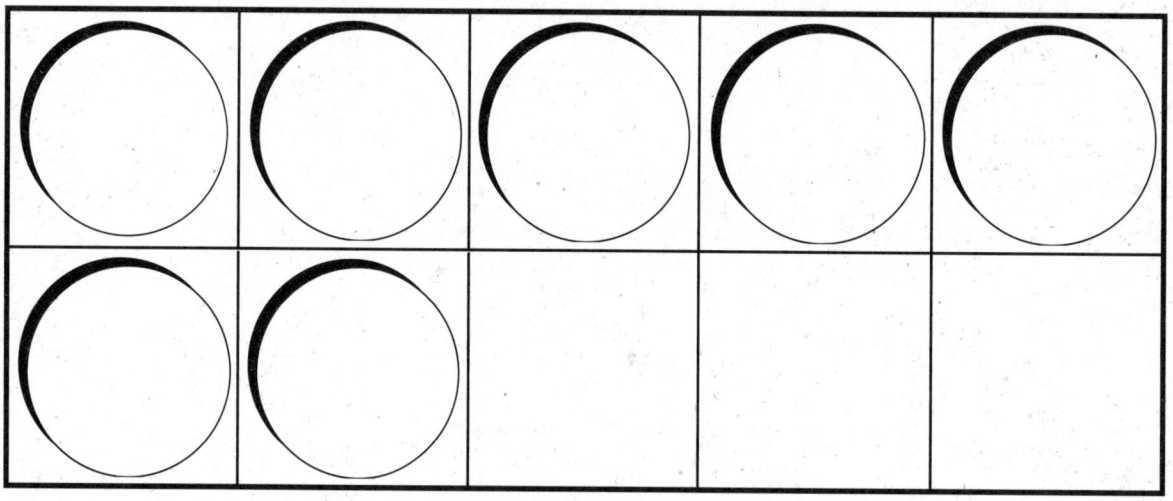

DIRECTIONS 1. Which shape is a triangle? Color the triangle. 2. Begin with 1 and count forward to 24. What is the next number? Draw a line under that number. 3. How many more counters would you place to model a way to make 10? Draw the counters.

FOR MORE PRACTICE GO TO THE Personal Math Trainer

© Houghton Mifflin Harcourt Publishing Company

Name _____

Describe Triangles

Essential Question How can you describe triangles?

Learning Objective You will use informal language to describe the attributes of triangles.

Listen and Draw

DIRECTIONS Use your finger to trace around the triangle. Talk about the number of sides and the number of vertices. Draw an arrow pointing to another vertex. Trace around the sides.

© Houghton Mifflin Harcourt Publishing Company

Share and Show

triangle

1 _____

_____ vertices

2 _____

_____ sides

DIRECTIONS 1. Place a counter on each corner, or vertex. Write how many corners, or vertices. 2. Trace around the sides. Write how many sides.

© Houghton Mifflin Harcourt Publishing Company

Name _____

3

DIRECTIONS 3. Draw and color a triangle.

HOME ACTIVITY • Have your child describe a triangle.

© Houghton Mifflin Harcourt Publishing Company

Mid-Chapter Checkpoint

Personal Math Trainer
Online Assessment and Intervention

Concepts and Skills

1

_____ sides

_____ vertices

2

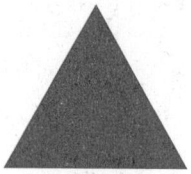

_____ sides

_____ vertices

3 THINK SMARTER

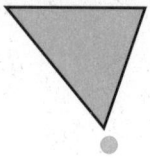

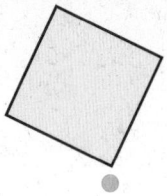

circle square triangle

DIRECTIONS 1–2. Trace around each side. Write how many sides. Place a counter on each corner or vertex. Write how many vertices. 3. Draw lines to match the shape to its name.

© Houghton Mifflin Harcourt Publishing Company

Name _____

Describe Triangles

Learning Objective You will use informal language to describe the attributes of triangles.

1

2 _____ _ _ _ _ _ _____ **vertices**

3 _____ _ _ _ _ _ _____ **sides**

DIRECTIONS 1. Draw and color a triangle. 2. Place a counter on each corner, or vertex, of the triangle that you drew. Write how many corners, or vertices. 3. Trace around the sides of the triangle that you drew. Write how many sides.

© Houghton Mifflin Harcourt Publishing Company

Lesson Check

1

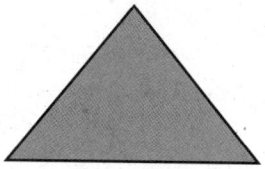

_____ sides

Spiral Review

2

$5 - 2 =$ _____

3

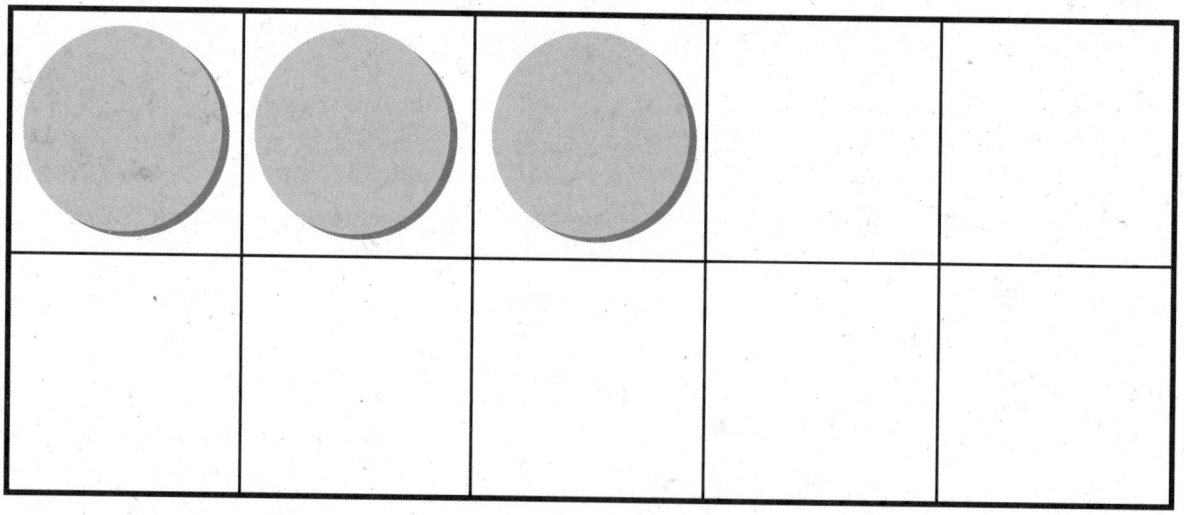

DIRECTIONS **1.** How many sides does the triangle have? Write the number. **2.** How many kittens are left? Write the number. **3.** How many more counters would you place to model a way to make 7? Draw the counters.

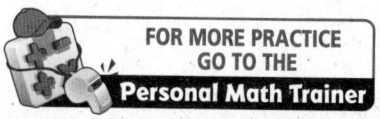

© Houghton Mifflin Harcourt Publishing Company

Name _____

Identify and Name Rectangles

Essential Question How can you identify and name rectangles?

Learning Objective You will identify and name rectangles.

Listen and Draw

Real World

Hands On

rectangles	not rectangles

DIRECTIONS Place two-dimensional shapes on the page. Identify and name the rectangles. Sort the shapes by rectangles and not rectangles. Trace and color the shapes on the sorting mat.

© Houghton Mifflin Harcourt Publishing Company

Share and Show

1

DIRECTIONS 1. Mark an X on all of the rectangles.

© Houghton Mifflin Harcourt Publishing Company

Name _____

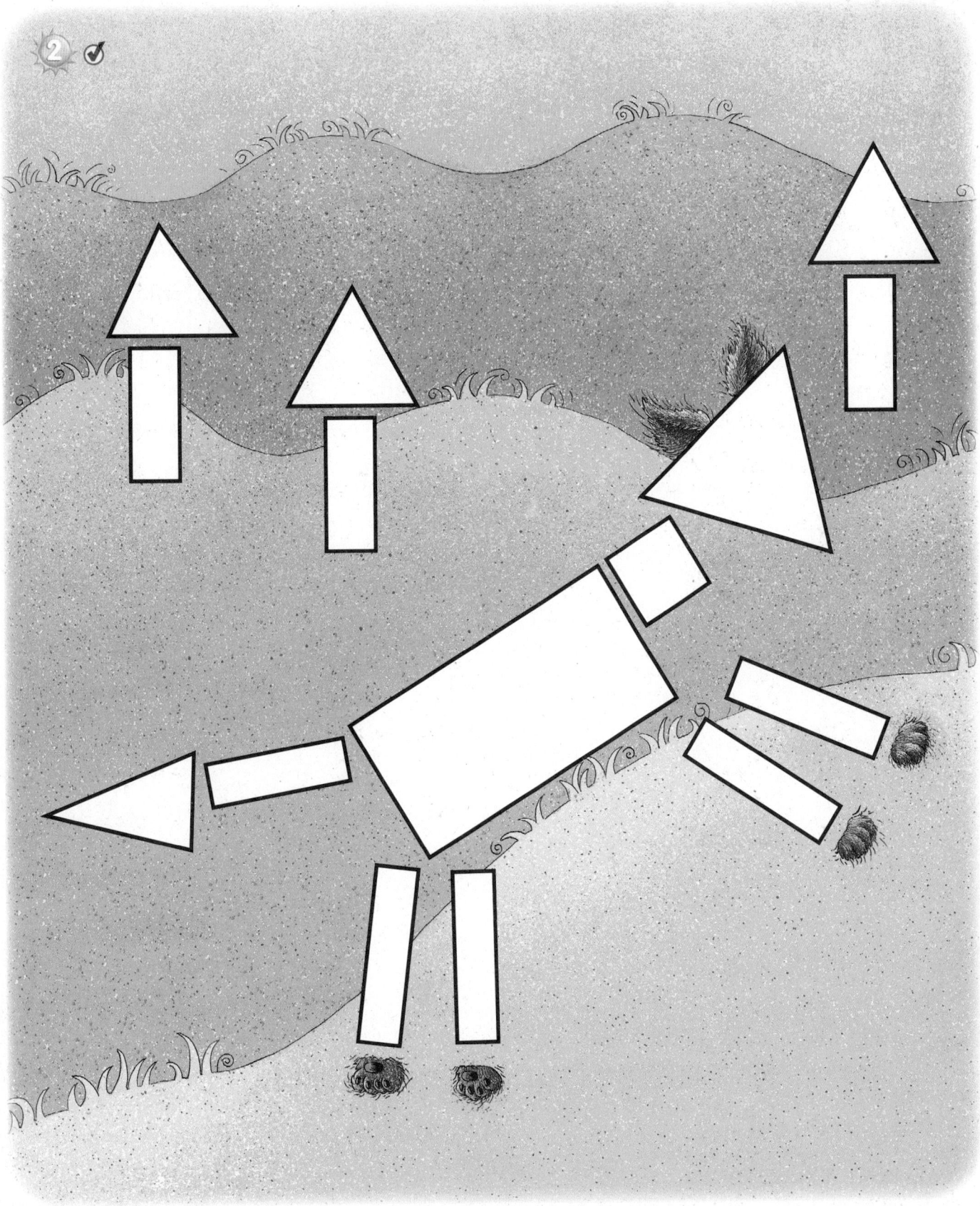

© Houghton Mifflin Harcourt Publishing Company

DIRECTIONS 2. Color the rectangles in the picture.

Problem Solving • Applications (Real World)

3

4

DIRECTIONS 3. Max looked at his shapes. Which of his shapes are rectangles? Mark an X on those shapes. 4. Draw to show what you know about rectangles. Tell a friend about your drawing.

HOME ACTIVITY • Have your child show you an object that is shaped like a rectangle.

© Houghton Mifflin Harcourt Publishing Company

Name _____

Identify and Name Rectangles

Learning Objective You will identify and name rectangles.

1

DIRECTIONS 1. Color the rectangles in the picture.

© Houghton Mifflin Harcourt Publishing Company

Lesson Check

1

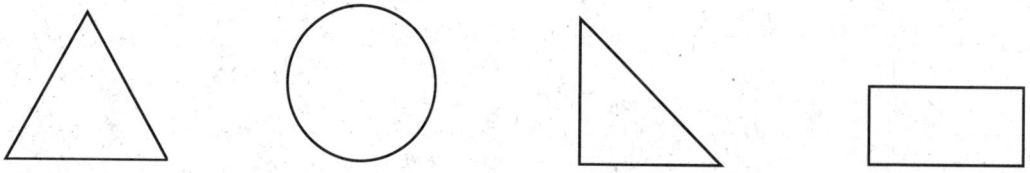

Spiral Review

2

1	2	3	4	5	6	7	8	9	10
11	12	13	14	15	16	17	18	19	20
21	22	23	24	25	26	27	28	29	30

3

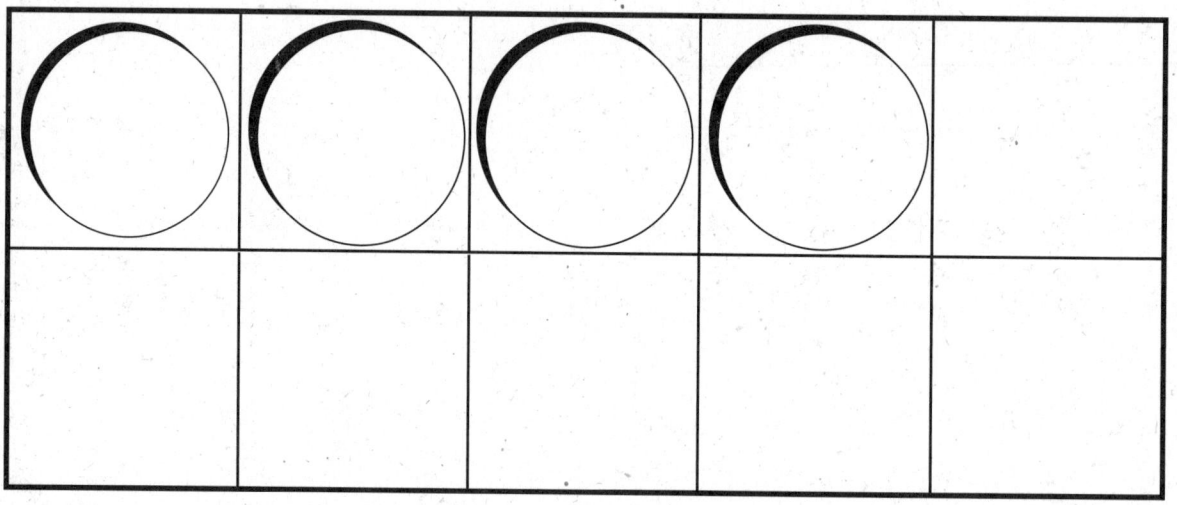

DIRECTIONS **1.** Which shape is a rectangle? Color the rectangle. **2.** Count by tens as you point to the numbers in the shaded boxes. Start with the number 10. What number do you end with? Draw a line under that number. **3.** How many more counters would you place to model a way to make 6? Draw the counters.

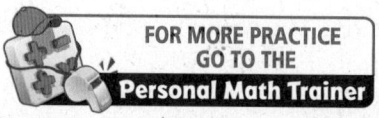

© Houghton Mifflin Harcourt Publishing Company

Name _____

Describe Rectangles

Essential Question How can you describe rectangles?

Learning Objective You will use informal language to describe the attributes of rectangles.

Listen and Draw

DIRECTIONS Use your finger to trace around the rectangle. Talk about the number of sides and the number of vertices. Draw an arrow pointing to another vertex. Trace around the sides.

© Houghton Mifflin Harcourt Publishing Company

Share and Show

rectangle

1 _____

_____ vertices

2 _____

_____ sides

DIRECTIONS 1. Place a counter on each corner, or vertex. Write how many corners, or vertices. 2. Trace around the sides. Write how many sides.

© Houghton Mifflin Harcourt Publishing Company

Name _____

3

DIRECTIONS 3. Draw and color a rectangle.

© Houghton Mifflin Harcourt Publishing Company

Problem Solving • Applications

WRITE Math

4

DIRECTIONS 4. I have 4 sides and 4 vertices. What shape am I? Draw the shape. Tell a friend the name of the shape.

HOME ACTIVITY • Have your child describe a rectangle.

© Houghton Mifflin Harcourt Publishing Company

Name _____

Describe Rectangles

Learning Objective You will use informal language to describe the attributes of rectangles.

1

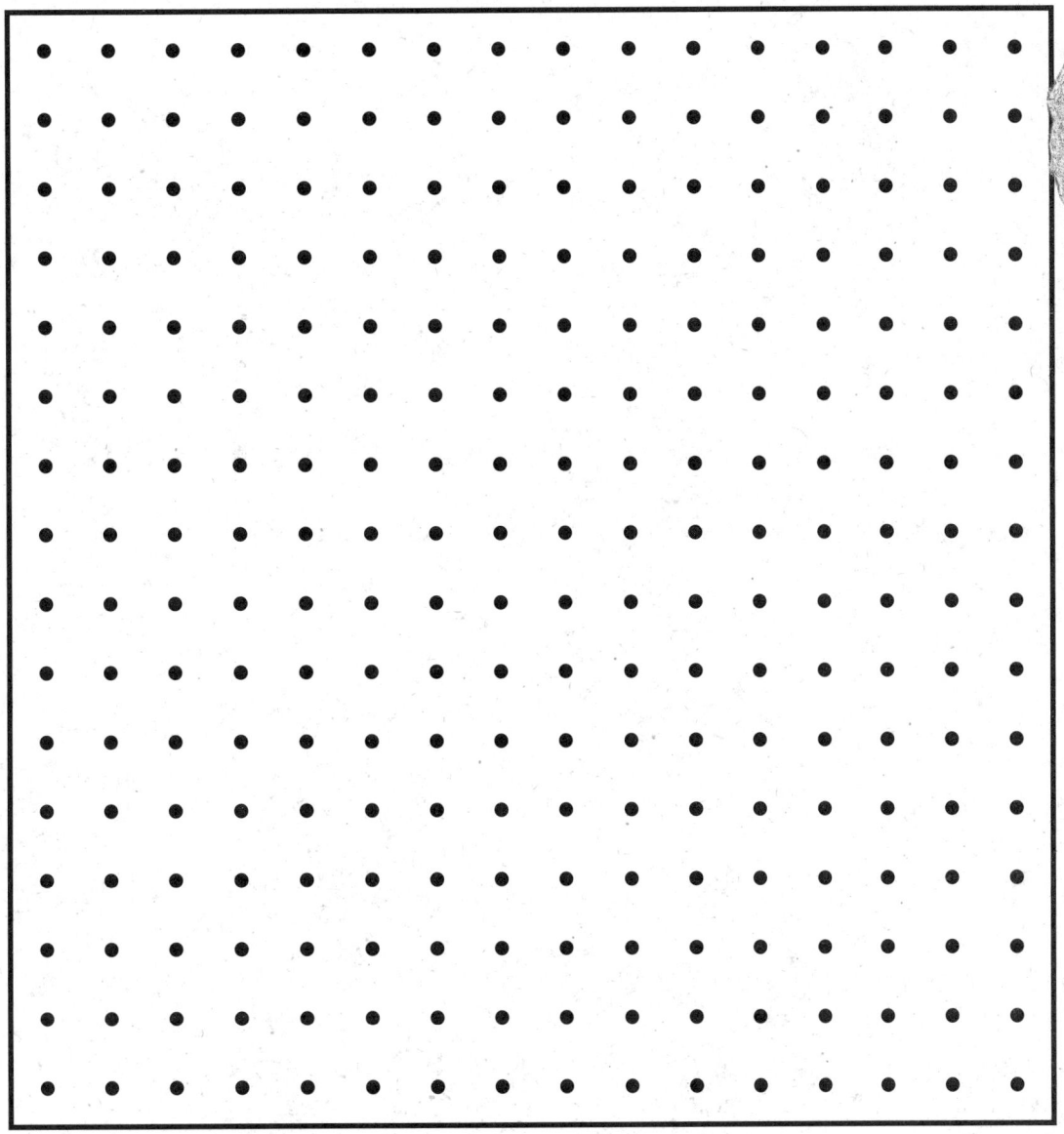

2 _____

_____ **vertices**

3 _____

_____ **sides**

DIRECTIONS **1.** Draw and color a rectangle. **2.** Place a counter on each corner, or vertex, of the rectangle that you drew. Write how many corners, or vertices. **3.** Trace around the sides of the rectangle that you drew. Write how many sides.

© Houghton Mifflin Harcourt Publishing Company

Lesson Check

1

_____ sides

Spiral Review

2

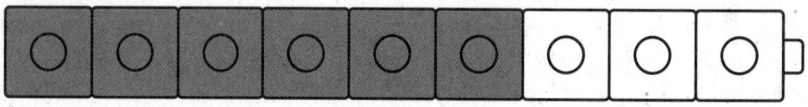

_____ + _____ = _____

3

_____

© Houghton Mifflin Harcourt Publishing Company

DIRECTIONS 1. How many sides does the rectangle have? Write the number. 2. Complete the addition sentence to show the numbers that match the cube train. 3. Draw a set that has 20 connecting cubes. Write the number.

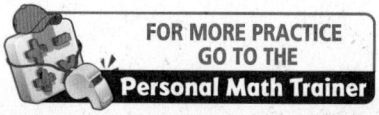

Name _____

Identify and Name Hexagons

Essential Question How can you identify and name hexagons?

Learning Objective You will identify and name hexagons.

Listen and Draw

Real World

Hands On

hexagons	not hexagons

DIRECTIONS Place two-dimensional shapes on the page. Identify and name the hexagons. Sort the shapes by hexagons and not hexagons. Trace and color the shapes on the sorting mat.

© Houghton Mifflin Harcourt Publishing Company

Share and Show

1

DIRECTIONS 1. Mark an X on all of the hexagons.

© Houghton Mifflin Harcourt Publishing Company

Name _____

© Houghton Mifflin Harcourt Publishing Company

DIRECTIONS **2.** Color the hexagons in the picture.

Problem Solving • Applications Real World

WRITE Math

3

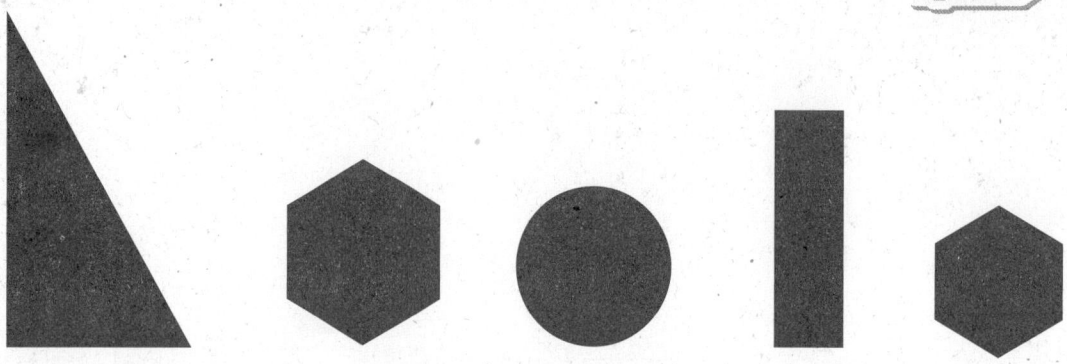

4

DIRECTIONS **3.** Ryan is looking at his shapes. Which of his shapes are hexagons? Mark an X on those shapes. **4.** Draw to show what you know about hexagons. Tell a friend about your drawing.

HOME ACTIVITY • Draw some shapes on a page. Include several hexagons. Have your child circle the hexagons.

© Houghton Mifflin Harcourt Publishing Company

Name _____

Identify and Name Hexagons

Learning Objective You will identify and name hexagons.

1

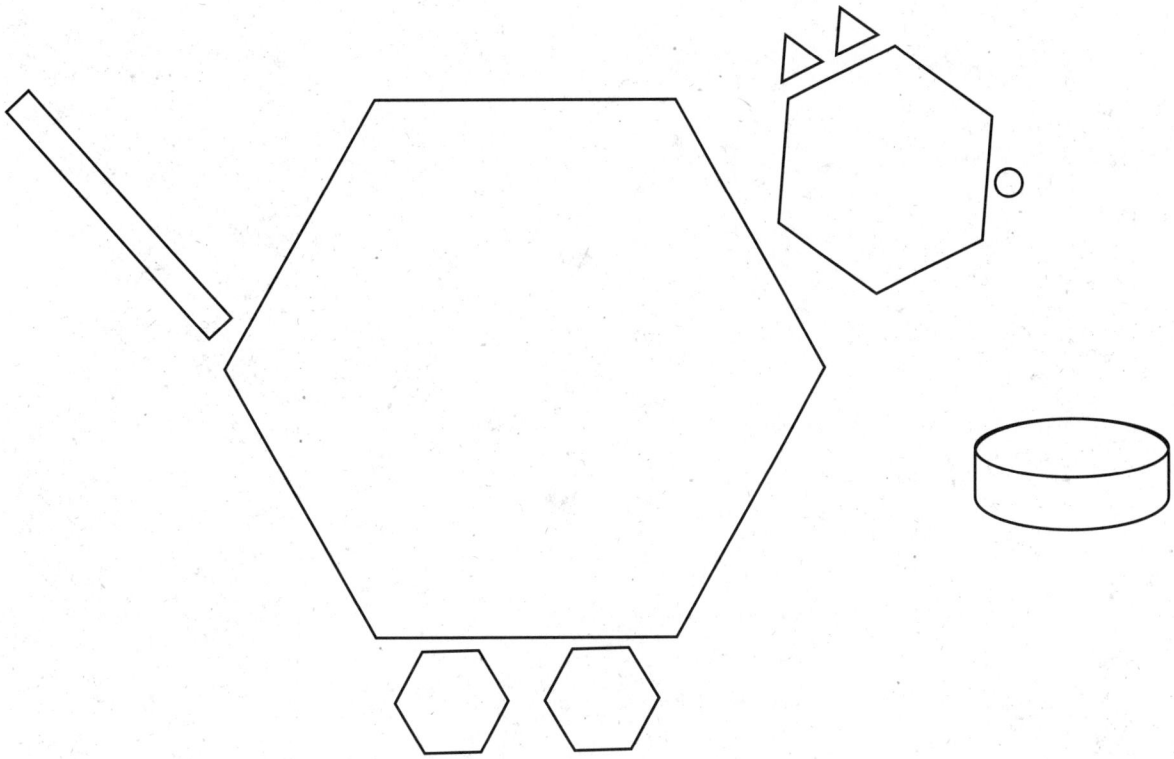

DIRECTIONS 1. Color the hexagons in the picture.

© Houghton Mifflin Harcourt Publishing Company

Lesson Check

1

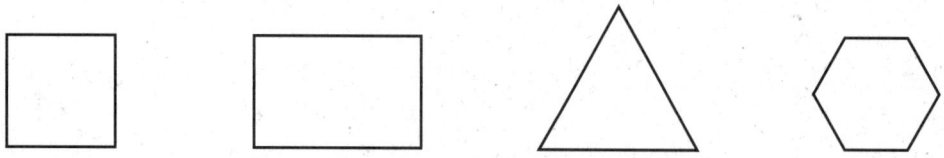

Spiral Review

2

71	72	73	74	75	76	77	78	79	80
81	82	83	84	85	86	87	88	89	90
91	92	93	94	95	96	97	98	99	100

3

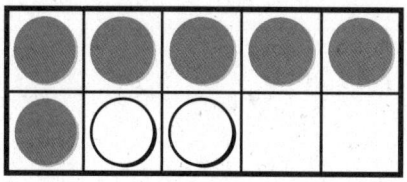

_____ _____

_____ + _____

_____ _____

DIRECTIONS **1.** Which shape is a hexagon? Color the hexagon. **2.** Begin with 81 and count forward to 90. What is the next number? Draw a line under that number. **3.** What numbers show the sets that are put together? Write the numbers and trace the symbol.

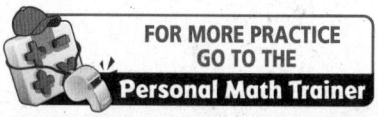

© Houghton Mifflin Harcourt Publishing Company

Name _____

Describe Hexagons

Essential Question How can you describe hexagons?

Learning Objective You will use informal language to describe the attributes of hexagons.

Listen and Draw

DIRECTIONS Use your finger to trace around the hexagon. Talk about the number of sides and the number of vertices. Draw an arrow pointing to another vertex. Trace around the sides.

© Houghton Mifflin Harcourt Publishing Company

Share and Show

hexagon

1 ✓

_____

_____

_____ vertices

2 ✓

_____

_____

_____ sides

DIRECTIONS 1. Place a counter on each corner, or vertex. Write how many corners, or vertices. 2. Trace around the sides. Write how many sides.

© Houghton Mifflin Harcourt Publishing Company

Name _____

3

DIRECTIONS 3. Draw and color a hexagon.

© Houghton Mifflin Harcourt Publishing Company

Problem Solving • Applications

WRITE Math

4

DIRECTIONS 4. I have 6 sides and 6 vertices. What shape am I? Draw the shape. Tell a friend the name of the shape.

HOME ACTIVITY • Have your child describe a hexagon.

© Houghton Mifflin Harcourt Publishing Company

Name _____

Describe Hexagons

Learning Objective You will use informal language to describe the attributes of hexagons.

1

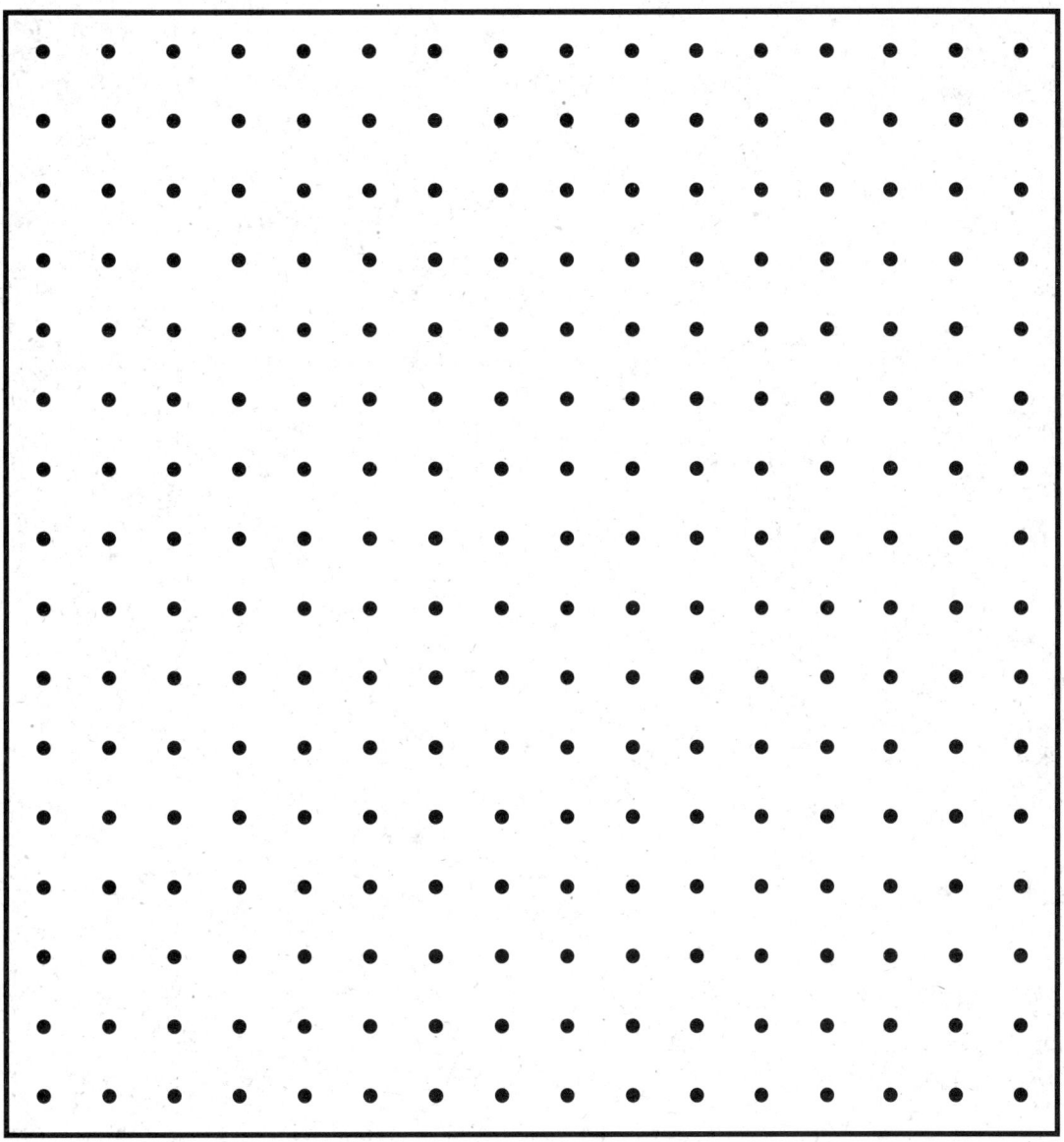

2

_____

_ _ _ _ _

_____ **vertices**

3

_____

_ _ _ _ _

_____ **sides**

DIRECTIONS **1.** Draw and color a hexagon. **2.** Place a counter on each corner, or vertex, of the hexagon that you drew. Write how many corners, or vertices. **3.** Trace around the sides of the hexagon that you drew. Write how many sides.

© Houghton Mifflin Harcourt Publishing Company

Lesson Check

1

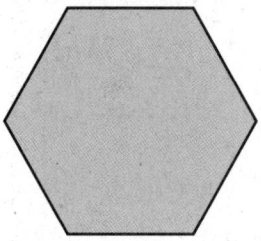

_____ sides

Spiral Review

2

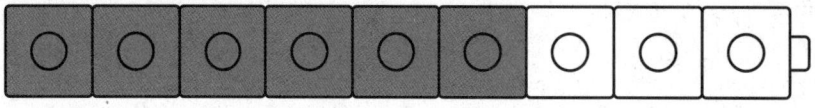

9 = _____ + _____

3

6 7

DIRECTIONS 1. How many sides does the hexagon have? Write the number. 2. Complete the addition sentence to show the numbers that match the cube train. 3. Compare the numbers. Circle the number that is greater.

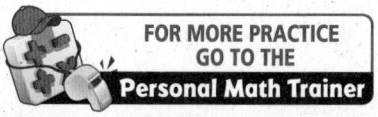

© Houghton Mifflin Harcourt Publishing Company

Name _____

Algebra • Compare Two-Dimensional Shapes

Essential Question How can you use the words ***alike*** and ***different*** to compare two-dimensional shapes?

Learning Objective You will use the words alike and different to compare two-dimensional shapes.

Listen and Draw

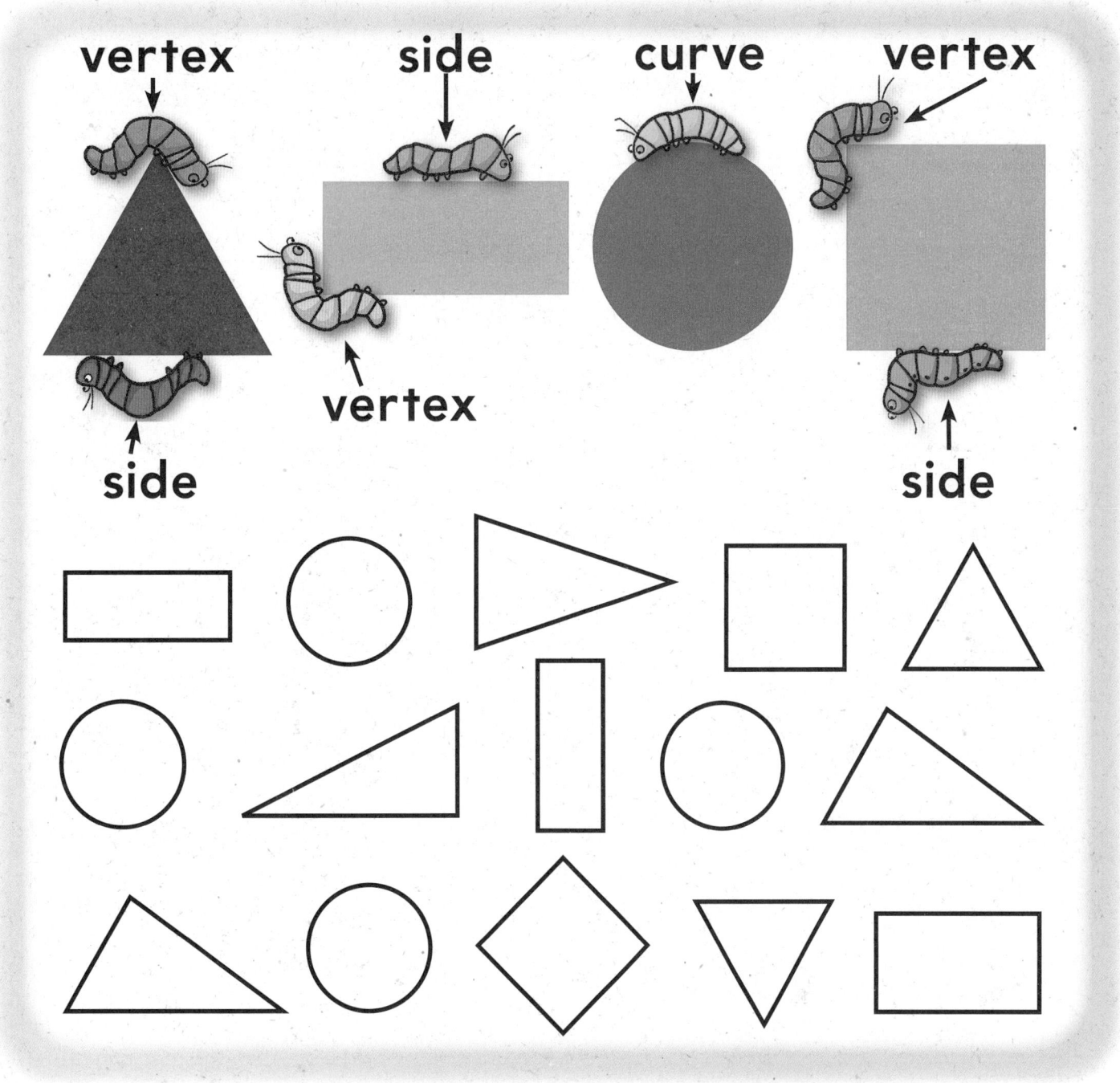

DIRECTIONS Look at the worms and the shapes. Use the words ***alike*** and ***different*** to compare the shapes. Use green to color the shapes with four vertices and four sides. Use blue to color the shapes with curves. Use red to color the shapes with three vertices and three sides.

© Houghton Mifflin Harcourt Publishing Company

Share and Show

1

alike	different

DIRECTIONS 1. Place two-dimensional shapes on the page. Sort the shapes by the number of vertices. Draw the shapes on the sorting mat. Use the words ***alike*** and ***different*** to tell how you sorted the shapes.

© Houghton Mifflin Harcourt Publishing Company

Name _____

alike	different

DIRECTIONS **2.** Place two-dimensional shapes on the page. Sort the shapes by the number of sides. Draw the shapes on the sorting mat. Use the words ***alike*** and ***different*** to tell how you sorted the shapes.

© Houghton Mifflin Harcourt Publishing Company

Problem Solving • Applications

3

WRITE Math

4

curve	no curve

DIRECTIONS **3.** I have a curve. What shape am I? Draw the shape. **4.** Draw to show shapes sorted by curves and no curves.

HOME ACTIVITY • Describe a shape and ask your child to name the shape that you are describing.

© Houghton Mifflin Harcourt Publishing Company

Name _____

Algebra • Compare Two-Dimensional Shapes

Learning Objective You will use the words alike and different to compare two-dimensional shapes.

alike	different

DIRECTIONS 1. Place two-dimensional shapes on the page. Sort the shapes by the number of sides. Draw the shapes on the sorting mat. Use the words *alike* and *different* to tell how you sorted the shapes.

© Houghton Mifflin Harcourt Publishing Company

Lesson Check

1

Spiral Review

2

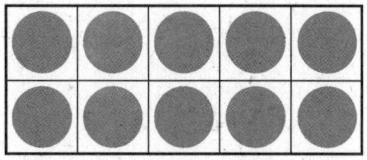

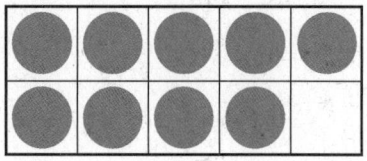

_____

_____

3

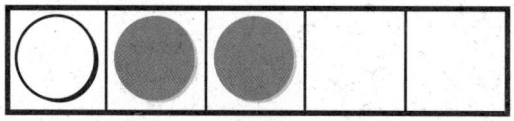

_____ _____

_____ _____

_____ **and** _____

DIRECTIONS **1.** Look at the shape. Draw a shape that is alike in some way. Tell how the two shapes are alike. **2.** Count and tell how many. Write the number. **3.** How many of each color counter? Write the numbers.

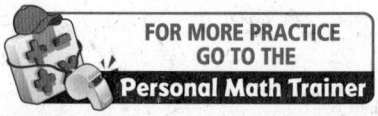

© Houghton Mifflin Harcourt Publishing Company

Name _____

Problem Solving • Draw to Join Shapes

Essential Question How can you solve problems using the strategy ***draw a picture***?

Learning Objective You will use the strategy *draw a picture* by joining shapes to make new shapes to solve problems.

Unlock the Problem

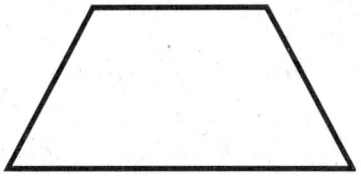

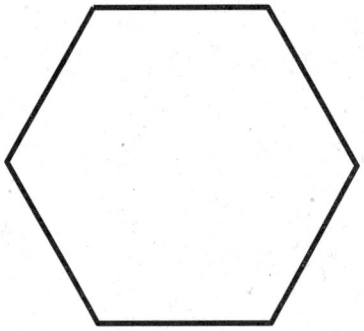

DIRECTIONS How can you join triangles to make the shapes? Draw and color the triangles.

© Houghton Mifflin Harcourt Publishing Company

Try Another Problem

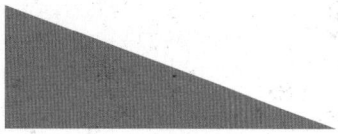

1

2

DIRECTIONS 1. How can you join the two triangles to make a rectangle? Trace around the triangles to draw the rectangle. 2. How can you join the two triangles to make a larger triangle? Use the triangle shapes to draw a larger triangle.

© Houghton Mifflin Harcourt Publishing Company

Name _____

Share and Show

3

4

DIRECTIONS **3.** How can you join some of the squares to make a larger square? Use the square shapes to draw a larger square. **4.** How can you join some or all of the squares to make a rectangle? Use the square shapes to draw a rectangle.

© Houghton Mifflin Harcourt Publishing Company

On Your Own

WRITE Math

5

6

DIRECTIONS **5.** Can you join these shapes to make a hexagon? Use the shapes to draw a hexagon. **6.** Which shapes could you join to make a larger shape that looks like a flower? Draw and color to show the shapes you used.

HOME ACTIVITY • Have your child join shapes to form a larger shape, and then tell you about the shape.

© Houghton Mifflin Harcourt Publishing Company

Name _____

Problem Solving • Draw to Join Shapes

Learning Objective You will use the strategy *draw a picture* by joining shapes to make new shapes to solve problems.

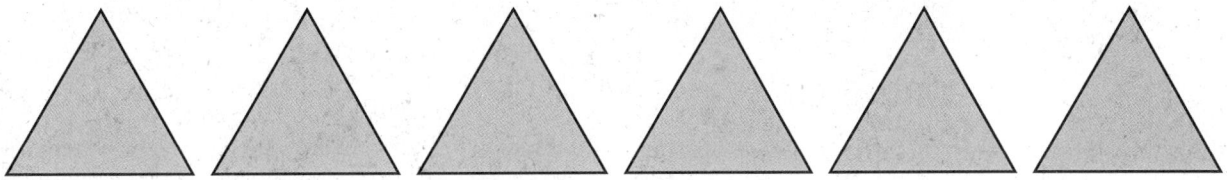

1

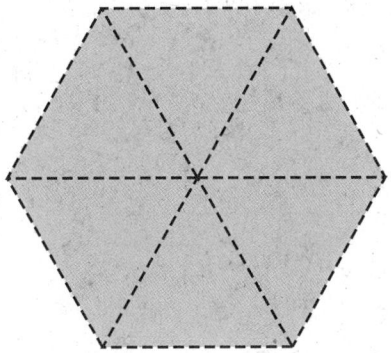

2

DIRECTIONS **1.** Place triangles on the page as shown. How can you join all of the triangles to make a hexagon? Trace around the triangles to draw the hexagon. **2.** How can you join some of the triangles to make a larger triangle? Trace around the triangles to draw the larger triangle.

© Houghton Mifflin Harcourt Publishing Company

Lesson Check

1

Spiral Review

2

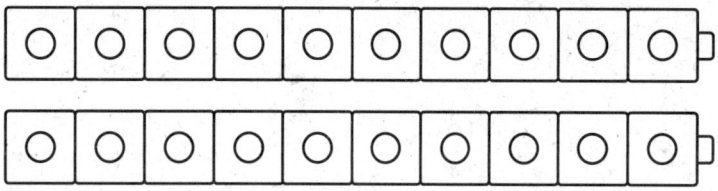

3

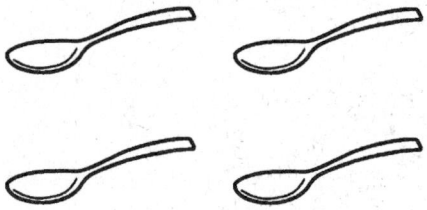

DIRECTIONS **1.** Join two triangles to make a shape. Draw and color the triangles you used. **2.** Count and tell how many. Write the number. **3.** Count and tell how many in each set. Write the numbers. Compare the numbers. Circle the number that is less.

© Houghton Mifflin Harcourt Publishing Company

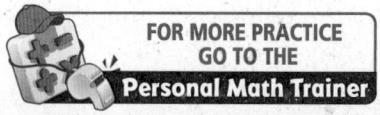

Name _____

Chapter 9 Review/Test

1

○ Yes ○ No

○ Yes ○ No

○ Yes ○ No

2

○ ○ ○ ○

3

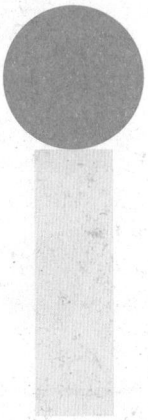

_____

_____

_____ squares

DIRECTIONS 1. Is the shape a circle? Choose Yes or No. 2. Mark under all the shapes that have curves. 3. How many squares are in the picture? Write the number.

© Houghton Mifflin Harcourt Publishing Company

4

_____ sides

5

○ ○ ○ ○

6 THINK SMARTER+

Personal Math Trainer

DIRECTIONS **4.** Look at the square. Write the number of sides on a square. **5.** Mark under all of the shapes that are triangles. **6.** Mark an X on each shape that has 3 sides and 3 vertices.

© Houghton Mifflin Harcourt Publishing Company

Name _____

7

Personal Math Trainer

8 THINK SMARTER +

9

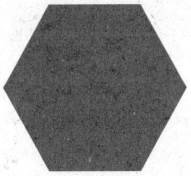

© Houghton Mifflin Harcourt Publishing Company

DIRECTIONS **7.** Mark an X on the shape that is not a rectangle. **8.** Draw a shape that is the same as the boxcars on the train. **9.** Mark an X on all of the hexagons.

10

4 sides

3 sides

6 sides

11

12 THINK SMARTER+

Personal Math Trainer

DIRECTIONS **10.** Match the shape to the number with that many sides. **11.** Look at the shapes. Compare them to see how they are alike and how they are different. Use red to color the shapes with four sides. Use green to color the shapes with curves. Use blue to color the shapes with three vertices. **12.** Join shapes to make an arrow. Draw the arrow.

© Houghton Mifflin Harcourt Publishing Company

Chapter 10

Identify and Describe Three-Dimensional Shapes

Curious About Math with Curious George

Many of the shapes in our environment are three-dimensional shapes.

Name some of the shapes you see in this picture.

© Houghton Mifflin Harcourt Publishing Company
Curious George by Margret and H.A. Rey. Copyright © 2010 by Houghton Mifflin Harcourt Publishing Company.
All rights reserved. The character Curious George®, including without limitation the character's name and the character's likenesses, are registered trademarks of Houghton Mifflin Harcourt Publishing Company.

Name _____

Show What You Know

Personal Math Trainer
Online Assessment and Intervention

Identify Shapes

1

Describe Shapes

2

_____ sides

_____ vertices

3

_____ sides

_____ vertices

Sort Shapes

4

This page checks understanding of important skills needed for success in Chapter 10.

DIRECTIONS **1.** Use red to color the squares. Use blue to color the triangles. **2–3.** Look at the shape. Write how many sides. Write how many vertices. **4.** Mark an X on the shapes with three sides.

© Houghton Mifflin Harcourt Publishing Company

Name _____

Vocabulary Builder

DIRECTIONS Mark an X on the food shaped like a circle. Draw a line under the food shaped like a square. Circle the food shaped like a triangle.

GO DIGITAL
- Interactive Student Edition
- Multimedia eGlossary

© Houghton Mifflin Harcourt Publishing Company

Game Follow the Shapes

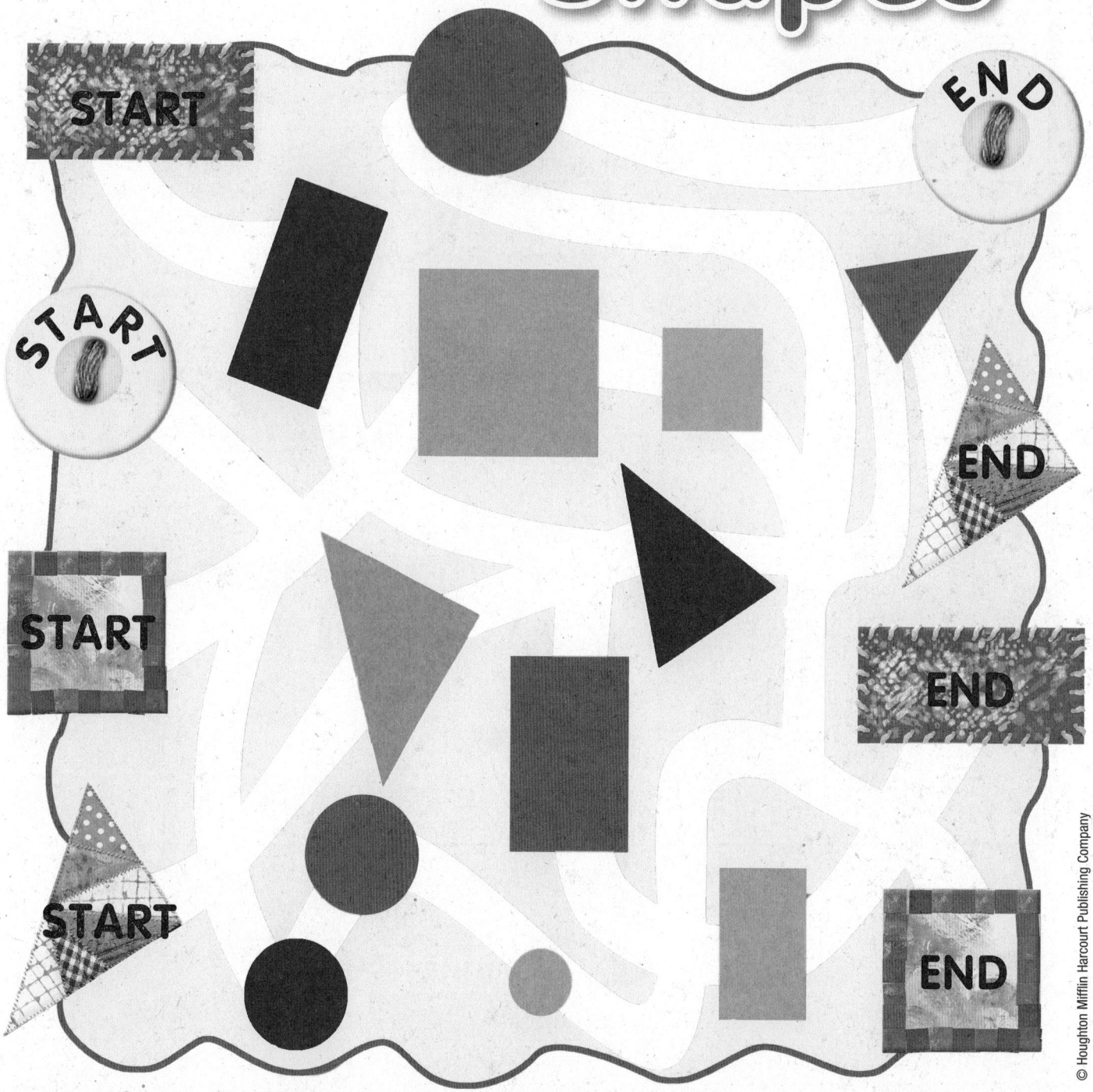

© Houghton Mifflin Harcourt Publishing Company

DIRECTIONS Choose a shape from START. Follow the path that has the same shapes. Draw a line to show the path to the END with the same shape.

Chapter 10 Vocabulary

above

arriba, encima

1

behind

detrás

5

below

debajo

6

beside

al lado

7

cone

cono

14

cube

cubo

15

curved surface

superficie curva

17

cylinder

cilindro

18

© Houghton Mifflin Harcourt Publishing Company

← **behind**

© Houghton Mifflin Harcourt Publishing Company

← **above**

© Houghton Mifflin Harcourt Publishing Company

The flowers are **beside** the tree.

© Houghton Mifflin Harcourt Publishing Company

below →

© Houghton Mifflin Harcourt Publishing Company

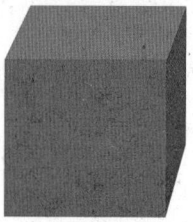

cube

© Houghton Mifflin Harcourt Publishing Company

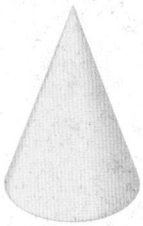

cone

© Houghton Mifflin Harcourt Publishing Company

cylinder

© Houghton Mifflin Harcourt Publishing Company

curved surface

flat surface

superficie plana

27

in front of

delante de

35

next to

al lado de

44

roll

rodar

54

slide

deslizar

67

sphere

esfera

69

stack

apilar

71

three-dimensional shapes

figuras tridimensionales

78

© Houghton Mifflin Harcourt Publishing Company

in front of →

© Houghton Mifflin Harcourt Publishing Company

flat surface

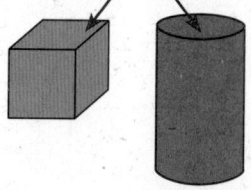

© Houghton Mifflin Harcourt Publishing Company

roll

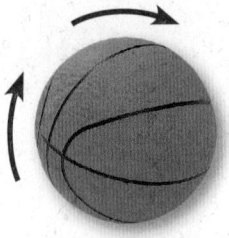

© Houghton Mifflin Harcourt Publishing Company

The flowers are **next to** the tree.

© Houghton Mifflin Harcourt Publishing Company

sphere

© Houghton Mifflin Harcourt Publishing Company
Credit: ©Eyewire/Getty Images

slide →

© Houghton Mifflin Harcourt Publishing Company

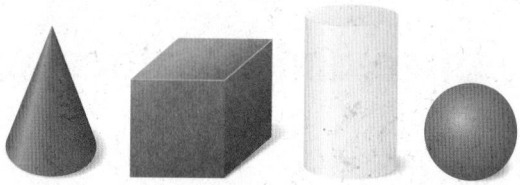

three-dimensional shapes

© Houghton Mifflin Harcourt Publishing Company

The cubes **stack** on top of one another.

Game

Picture It

Word Box
above
behind
below
beside
next to
in front of
cone
cube

Word Box
curved surface
cylinder
flat surface
roll
slide
sphere
stack
three-dimensional shape

Secret Words

Player 1				
Player 2				

DIRECTIONS Players take turns. A player chooses a secret word from the Word Box and then sets the timer. The player draws pictures to give hints about the secret word. If the other player guesses the secret word before time runs out, he or she puts a counter in the chart. The first player who has counters in all his or her boxes is the winner.

MATERIALS timer, drawing paper, two-color counters for each player

© Houghton Mifflin Harcourt Publishing Company • Image Credits: (bg) ©Studio-Pro/Getty Images; (bl) ©Grzegorz Petrykowski/Alamy; (br) ©Comstock/Getty Images

Journal

The Write Way

DIRECTIONS Choose one idea. • Choose 2 three-dimensional shapes. Draw to show what you know about the shapes. • Draw to show *above*, *below*, and *next to*.
Reflect Be ready to tell about your drawing.

© Houghton Mifflin Harcourt Publishing Company • Image Credits: (bg) ©Studio-Pro/Getty Images; (r) ©Radoman Durkovic/Shutterstock

Name _____

Three-Dimensional Shapes

Essential Question How can you show which shapes stack, roll, or slide?

Learning Objective You will show which shapes stack, roll, or slide and describe them using informal language.

Listen and Draw

Real World

Hands On

does stack	does not stack

DIRECTIONS Place three-dimensional shapes on the page. Sort the shapes by whether they stack or do not stack. Describe the shapes. Match a picture of each shape to the shapes on the sorting mat. Glue the shape pictures on the sorting mat.

© Houghton Mifflin Harcourt Publishing Company

Share and Show

1

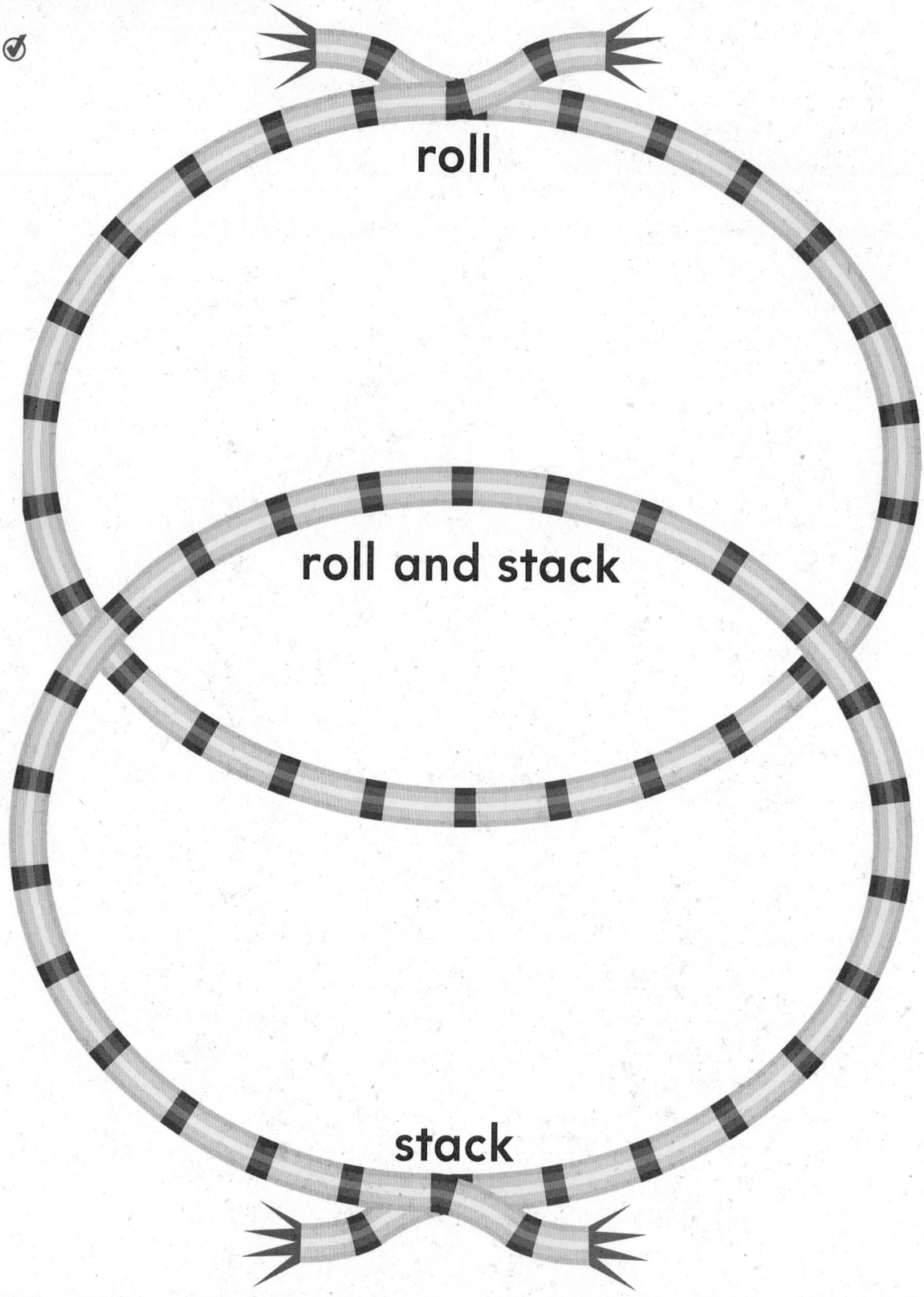

DIRECTIONS 1. Place three-dimensional shapes on the page. Sort the shapes by whether they roll, roll and stack, or stack. Describe the shapes. Match a picture of each shape to the shapes. Glue the shape pictures on the page.

© Houghton Mifflin Harcourt Publishing Company

Name _____

2

roll

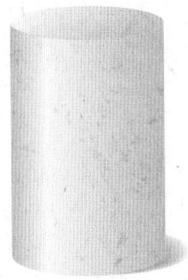

3

stack

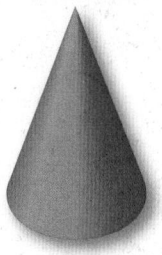

4

slide

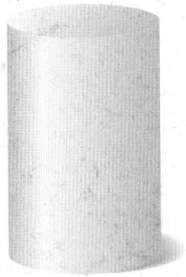

5

stack and slide

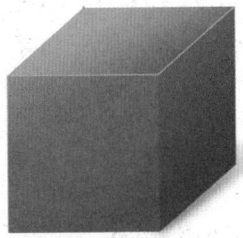

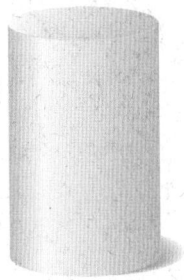

DIRECTIONS **2.** Which shape does not roll? Mark an X on that shape. **3.** Which shapes do not stack? Mark an X on those shapes. **4.** Which shape does not slide? Mark an X on that shape. **5.** Which shape does not stack and slide? Mark an X on that shape.

© Houghton Mifflin Harcourt Publishing Company • Images Credits (bcl) ©Getty Images

Problem Solving • Applications Real World

WRITE Math

6

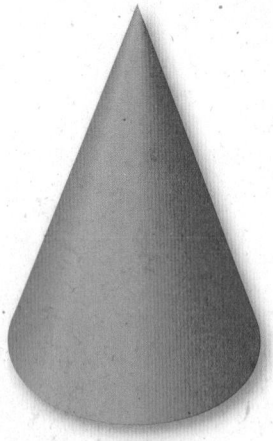

7

DIRECTIONS **6.** I roll and do not stack. Describe the shape. Mark an X on that shape. **7.** Draw to show what you know about a real object that rolls and does not stack.

HOME ACTIVITY • Have your child identify and describe an object in the house that rolls and does not stack.

© Houghton Mifflin Harcourt Publishing Company

Name _____

Three-Dimensional Shapes

Learning Objective You will show which shapes stack, roll, or slide and describe them using informal language.

1

roll

2

stack

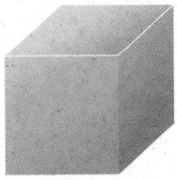

3

slide

4

stack and slide

DIRECTIONS 1. Which shape does not roll? Mark an X on that shape. 2. Which shapes do not stack? Mark an X on those shapes. 3. Which shape does not slide? Mark an X on that shape. 4. Which shape does not stack and slide? Mark an X on that shape.

© Houghton Mifflin Harcourt Publishing Company

Lesson Check

1

Spiral Review

2

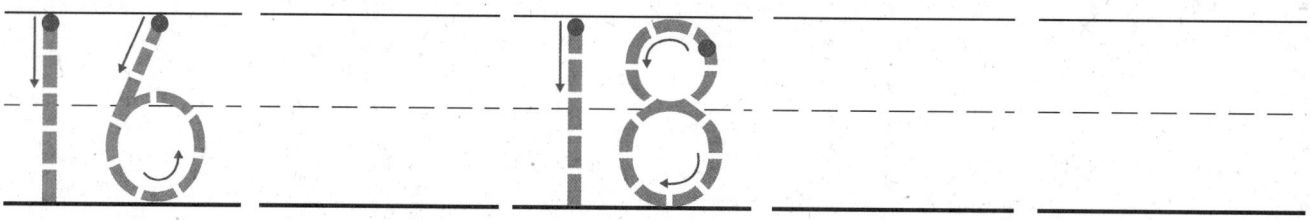

3

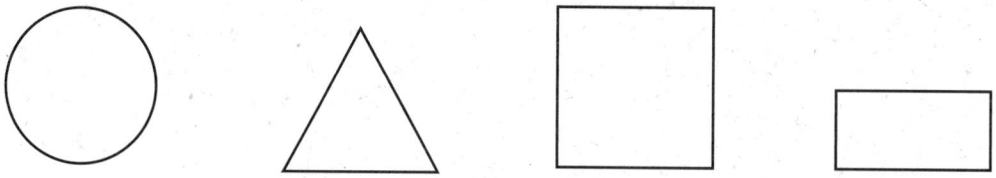

DIRECTIONS **1.** Which shape does not roll? Mark an X on the shape. **2.** Count forward. Trace and write the numbers in order. **3.** Which shape has a curve? Color the shape.

© Houghton Mifflin Harcourt Publishing Company

FOR MORE PRACTICE GO TO THE Personal Math Trainer

Name _____

Identify, Name, and Describe Spheres

Essential Question How can you identify, name, and describe spheres?

Learning Objective You will identify, name, and describe spheres using informal language.

Listen and Draw

Real World

Hands On

sphere	not a sphere

DIRECTIONS Place three-dimensional shapes on the page. Identify and name the sphere. Sort the shapes on the sorting mat. Describe the sphere. Match a picture of each shape to the shapes on the sorting mat. Glue the shape pictures on the sorting mat.

© Houghton Mifflin Harcourt Publishing Company

Share and Show

1

sphere

flat surface

curved surface

2

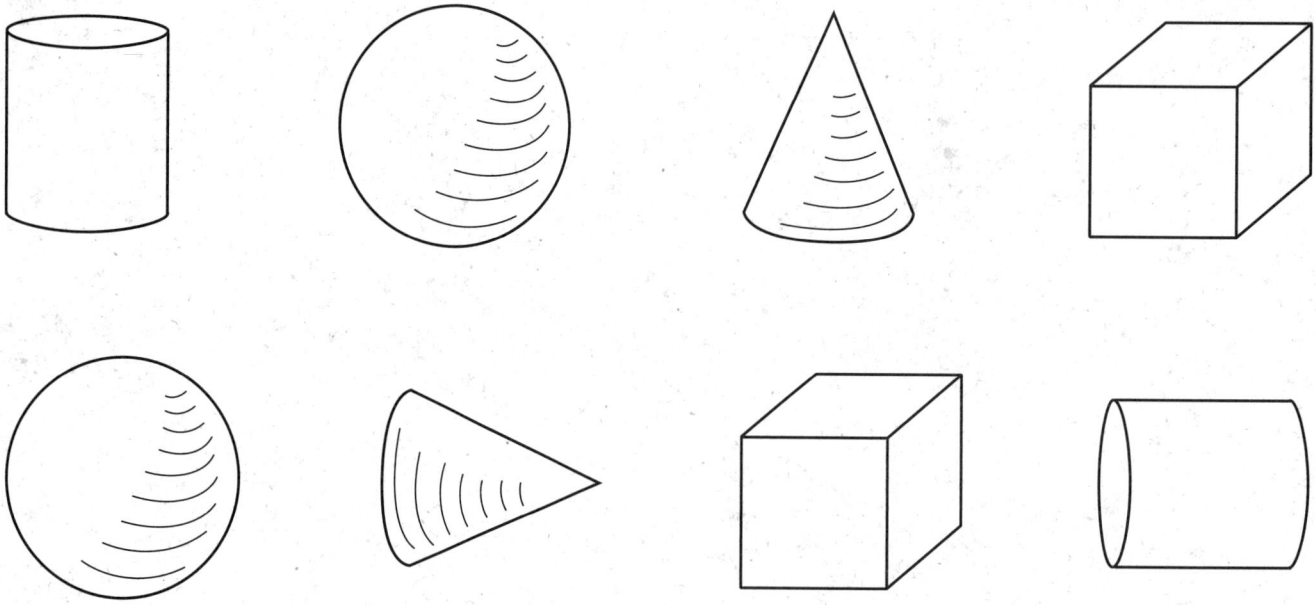

DIRECTIONS **1.** Look at the sphere. Circle the words that describe a sphere. **2.** Color the spheres.

© Houghton Mifflin Harcourt Publishing Company

Name _____

3

DIRECTIONS 3. Identify the objects that are shaped like a sphere. Mark an X on those objects.

© Houghton Mifflin Harcourt Publishing Company

Problem Solving • Applications Real World

WRITE Math

4

5

DIRECTIONS **4.** I have a curved surface. Which shape am I? Mark an X on that shape. **5.** Draw to show what you know about a real object that is shaped like a sphere.

HOME ACTIVITY • Have your child identify and describe an object in the house that is shaped like a sphere.

© Houghton Mifflin Harcourt Publishing Company

Name _____

Identify, Name, and Describe Spheres

Learning Objective You will identify, name, and describe spheres using informal language.

1

DIRECTIONS 1. Identify the objects that are shaped like a sphere. Mark an X on those objects.

© Houghton Mifflin Harcourt Publishing Company

Lesson Check

1

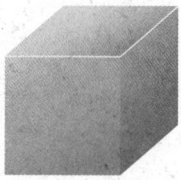

Spiral Review

2

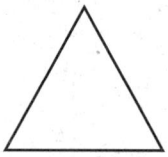

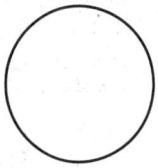

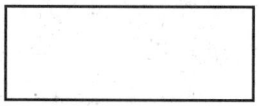

3

_____

_ _ _ _ _

_____

DIRECTIONS **1.** Which shape is a sphere? Mark an X on the shape. **2.** Which shape is a square? Color the square. **3.** How many school buses are there? Write the number.

© Houghton Mifflin Harcourt Publishing Company

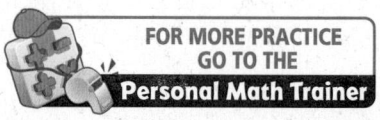

Name _____

HANDS ON
Lesson 10.3

Identify, Name, and Describe Cubes

Essential Question How can you identify, name, and describe cubes?

Learning Objective You will identify, name, and describe cubes using informal language.

Listen and Draw

Real World

Hands On

cube	not a cube

DIRECTIONS Place three-dimensional shapes on the page. Identify and name the cube. Sort the shapes on the sorting mat. Describe the cube. Match a picture of each shape to the shapes on the sorting mat. Glue the shape pictures on the sorting mat.

© Houghton Mifflin Harcourt Publishing Company

Share and Show

1

cube

flat surface

curved surface

2

_____ flat surfaces

DIRECTIONS **1.** Look at the cube. Circle the words that describe a cube. **2.** Use a cube to count how many flat surfaces. Write the number.

© Houghton Mifflin Harcourt Publishing Company

Name _____

3

DIRECTIONS 3. Identify the objects that are shaped like a cube. Mark an X on those objects.

© Houghton Mifflin Harcourt Publishing Company

Problem Solving • Applications (Real World)

4

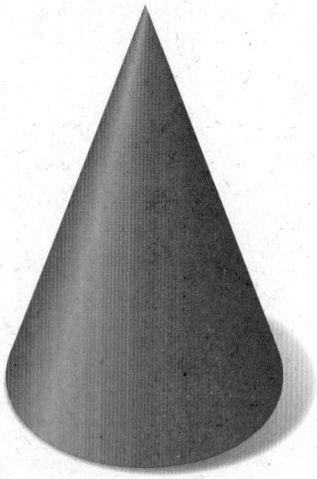

5

DIRECTIONS **4.** I have 6 flat surfaces. Which shape am I? Mark an X on that shape. **5.** Draw to show what you know about a real object that is shaped like a cube.

HOME ACTIVITY • Have your child identify and describe an object in the house that is shaped like a cube.

© Houghton Mifflin Harcourt Publishing Company

Name _____

Identify, Name, and Describe Cubes

Learning Objective You will identify, name, and describe cubes using informal language.

DIRECTIONS 1. Identify the objects that are shaped like a cube. Mark an X on those objects.

© Houghton Mifflin Harcourt Publishing Company

Lesson Check

1

Spiral Review

2

_____

_____ **sides**

3

71	72	73	74	75	76	77	78	79	80
81	82	83	84	85	86	87	88	89	90
91	92	93	94	95	96	97	98	99	100

DIRECTIONS 1. Which shape is a cube? Mark an X on the shape. 2. How many sides does the square have? Write the number. 3. Begin with 81 and count forward to 90. What is the next number? Draw a line under that number.

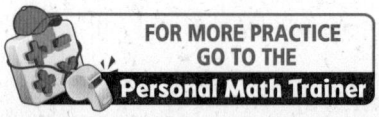

© Houghton Mifflin Harcourt Publishing Company

Name _____

Identify, Name, and Describe Cylinders

Essential Question How can you identify, name, and describe cylinders?

Learning Objective You will identify, name, and describe cylinders using informal language.

Listen and Draw

Real World

Hands On

cylinder	not a cylinder

DIRECTIONS Place three-dimensional shapes on the page. Identify and name the cylinder. Sort the shapes on the sorting mat. Describe the cylinder. Match a picture of each shape to the shapes on the sorting mat. Glue the shape pictures on the sorting mat.

© Houghton Mifflin Harcourt Publishing Company

Share and Show

1 cylinder

flat surface

curved surface

2

_____ flat surfaces

DIRECTIONS 1. Look at the cylinder. Circle the words that describe a cylinder.
2. Use a cylinder to count how many flat surfaces. Write the number.

© Houghton Mifflin Harcourt Publishing Company

Name _____

3

DIRECTIONS 3. Identify the objects that are shaped like a cylinder. Mark an X on those objects.

© Houghton Mifflin Harcourt Publishing Company

Problem Solving • Applications Real World

WRITE Math

4

5

DIRECTIONS **4.** I have 2 flat surfaces. Which shape am I? Mark an X on that shape. **5.** Draw to show what you know about a real object that is shaped like a cylinder.

HOME ACTIVITY • Have your child identify and describe an object in the house that is shaped like a cylinder.

© Houghton Mifflin Harcourt Publishing Company

Name _____

Identify, Name, and Describe Cylinders

Learning Objective You will identify, name, and describe cylinders using informal language.

1

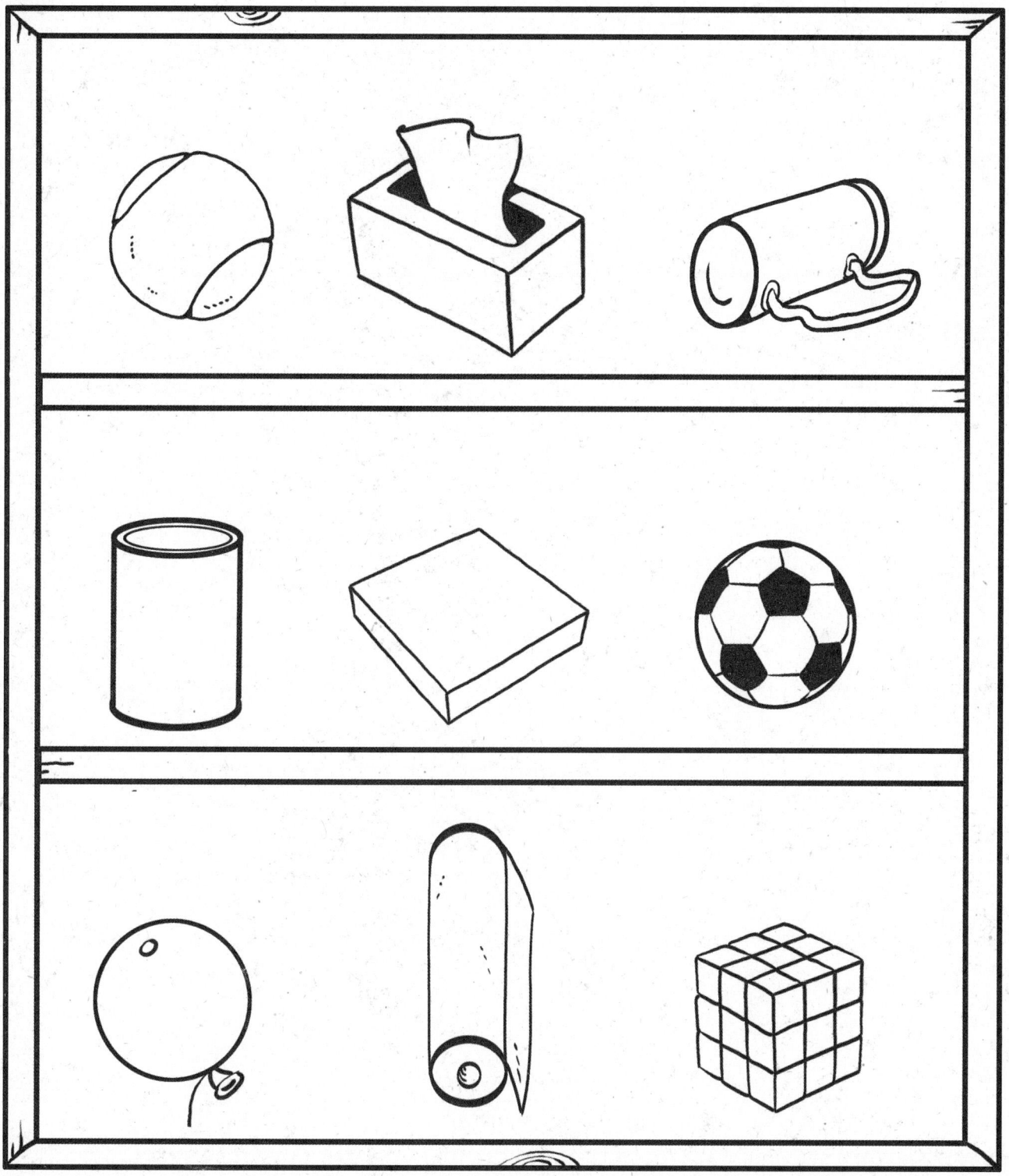

DIRECTIONS 1. Identify the objects that are shaped like a cylinder. Mark an X on those objects.

© Houghton Mifflin Harcourt Publishing Company

Lesson Check

1

Spiral Review

2

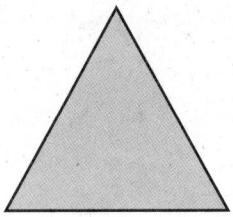

_____ vertices

3

5 — _____ = 2

DIRECTIONS 1. Which shape is a cylinder? Mark an X on the shape. 2. How many vertices does the triangle have? Write the number. 3. Write the number to show how many are being taken from the set.

© Houghton Mifflin Harcourt Publishing Company

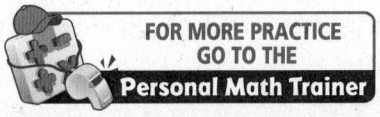

Name _____

HANDS ON
Lesson 10.5

Identify, Name, and Describe Cones

Essential Question How can you identify, name, and describe cones?

Learning Objective You will identify, name, and describe cones using informal language.

Listen and Draw

Real World

Hands On

cone	not a cone

DIRECTIONS Place three-dimensional shapes on the page. Identify and name the cone. Sort the shapes on the sorting mat. Describe the cone. Match a picture of each shape to the shapes on the sorting mat. Glue the shape pictures on the sorting mat.

© Houghton Mifflin Harcourt Publishing Company

Share and Show

1

cone

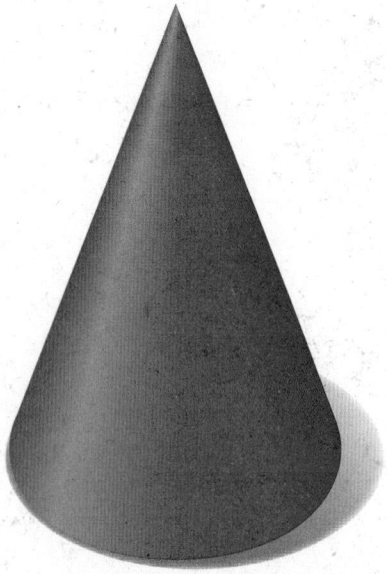

flat surface

curved surface

2

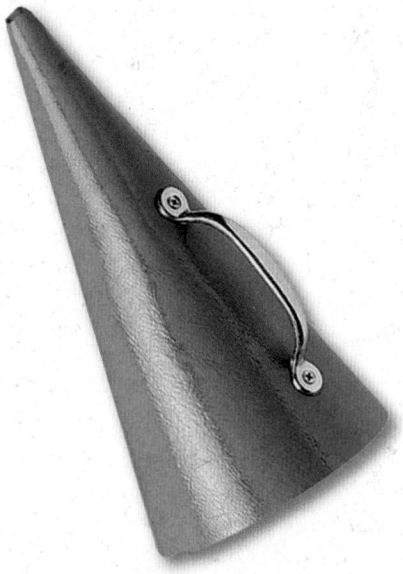

_____

_____ flat surface

DIRECTIONS 1. Look at the cone. Circle the words that describe a cone. 2. Use a cone to count how many flat surfaces. Write the number.

© Houghton Mifflin Harcourt Publishing Company

Name _____

3

DIRECTIONS 3. Identify the objects that are shaped like a cone. Mark an X on those objects.

HOME ACTIVITY • Have your child identify and describe an object in the house that is shaped like a cone.

© Houghton Mifflin Harcourt Publishing Company

Mid-Chapter Checkpoint

Personal Math Trainer
Online Assessment and Intervention

Concepts and Skills

1

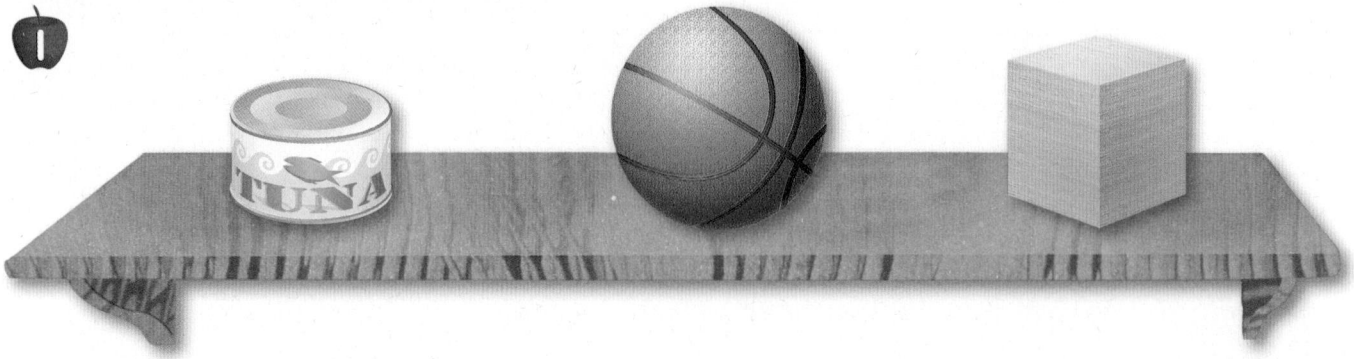

2

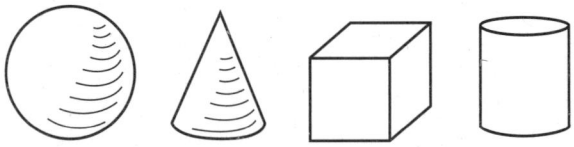

3

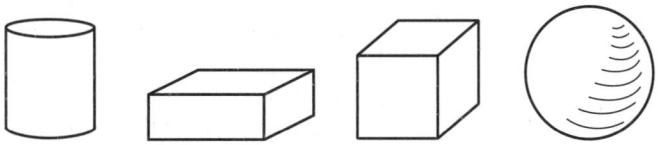

4 THINK SMARTER

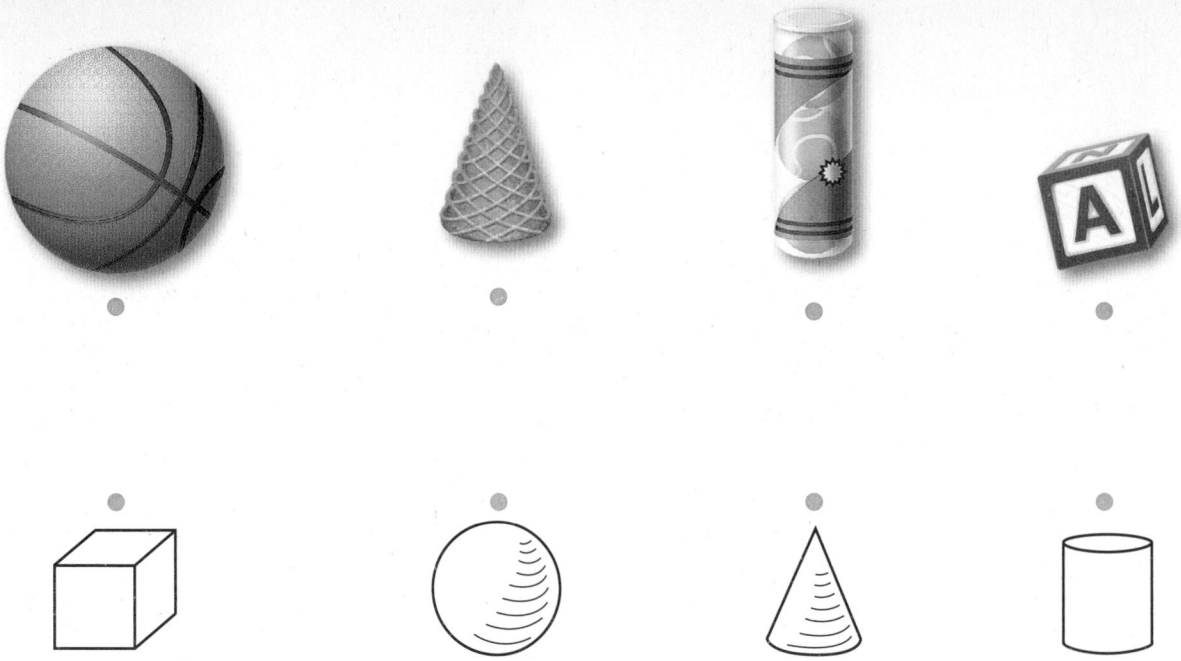

DIRECTIONS 1. Mark an X on the object that is shaped like a cylinder. **2.** Color the sphere. **3.** Color the cube. **4.** Draw lines to match the objects to their shapes.

© Houghton Mifflin Harcourt Publishing Company

Name _____

Identify, Name, and Describe Cones

Learning Objective You will identify, name, and describe cones using informal language.

1

DIRECTIONS 1. Identify the objects that are shaped like a cone. Mark an X on those objects.

© Houghton Mifflin Harcourt Publishing Company

Lesson Check

1

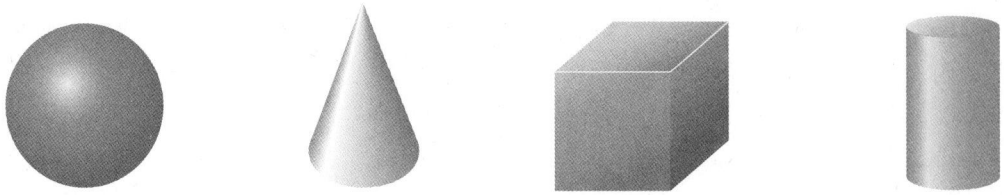

Spiral Review

2

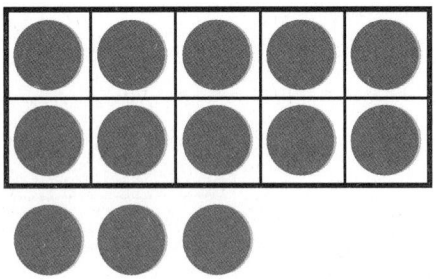

3

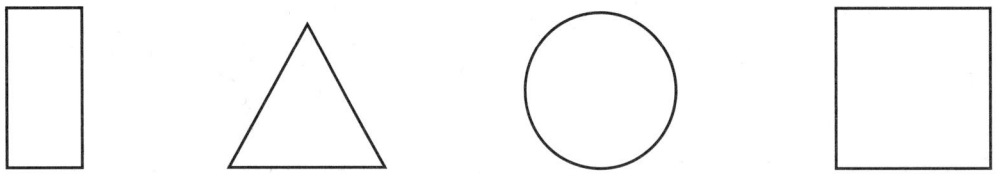

DIRECTIONS **1.** Which shape is a cone? Mark an X on the shape. **2.** Count and tell how many. Write the number. **3.** Which shape is a circle? Color the circle.

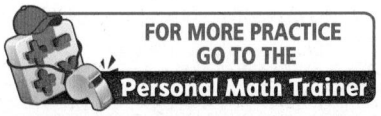

© Houghton Mifflin Harcourt Publishing Company

Name _____

Problem Solving • Two- and Three-Dimensional Shapes

Essential Question How can you solve problems using the strategy ***use logical reasoning***?

Learning Objective You will use the strategy *use logical reasoning* by sorting two- and three-dimensional shapes to solve problems.

Unlock the Problem Real World

two-dimensional shapes	three-dimensional shapes

DIRECTIONS Place shapes on the page. Sort the shapes on the sorting mat into sets of two-dimensional and three-dimensional shapes. Match a picture of each shape to a shape on the sorting mat. Glue the shape pictures on the sorting mat.

© Houghton Mifflin Harcourt Publishing Company

Try Another Problem

1

DIRECTIONS 1. Identify the two-dimensional or flat shapes. Trace the circle around the square. Circle the other flat shapes. Identify the three-dimensional or solid shapes. Trace the X on the sphere. Mark an X on the other solid shapes.

© Houghton Mifflin Harcourt Publishing Company

Name _____

Share and Show

2

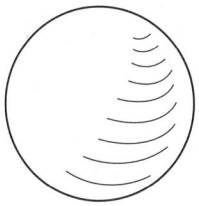

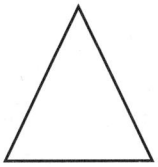

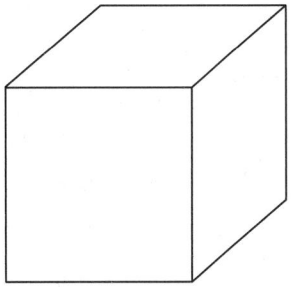

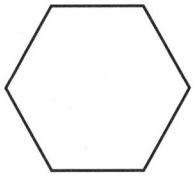

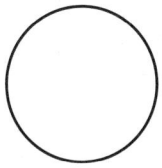

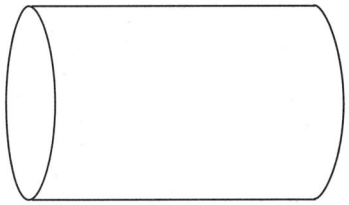

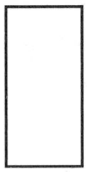

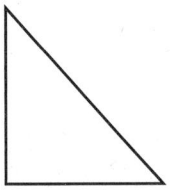

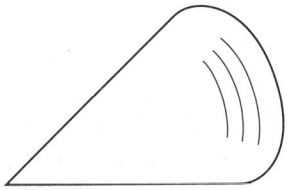

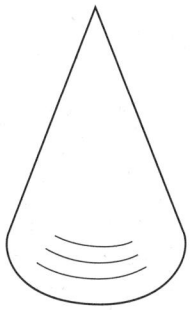

DIRECTIONS 2. Identify the two-dimensional or flat shapes. Use red to color the flat shapes. Identify the three-dimensional or solid shapes. Use blue to color the solid shapes.

© Houghton Mifflin Harcourt Publishing Company

On Your Own Real World

WRITE Math

3

4

DIRECTIONS **3.** Draw to show what you know about a flat shape. Name the shape. **4.** Draw to show what you know about a real object that has a solid shape. Name the object and the shape.

HOME ACTIVITY • Have your child identify a household object that is shaped like a three-dimensional shape. Have him or her name the three-dimensional shape.

© Houghton Mifflin Harcourt Publishing Company

Name _____

Problem Solving • Two- and Three-Dimensional Shapes

Learning Objective You will use the strategy *use logical reasoning* by sorting two- and three-dimensional shapes to solve problems.

1

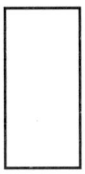
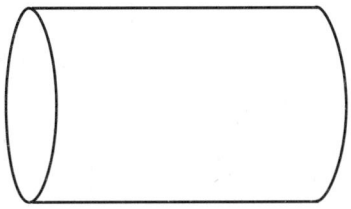
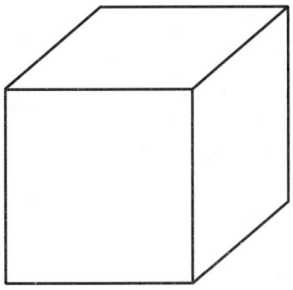

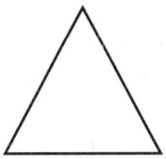
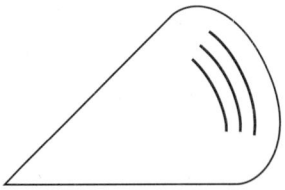

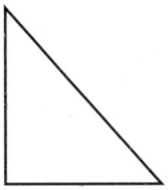
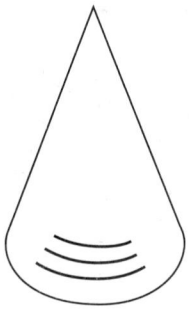
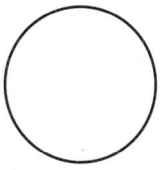

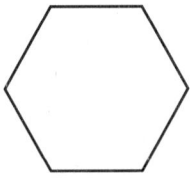

DIRECTIONS 1. Identify the two-dimensional or flat shapes. Use red to color the flat shapes. Identify the three-dimensional or solid shapes. Use blue to color the solid shapes.

© Houghton Mifflin Harcourt Publishing Company

Lesson Check

1

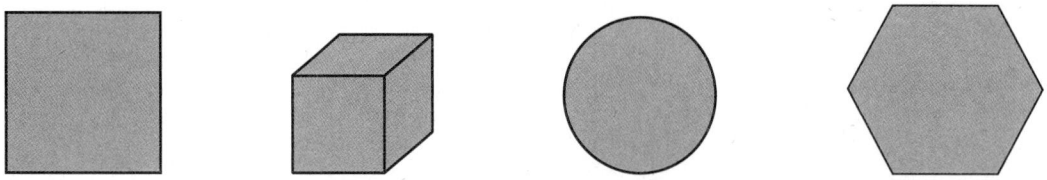

Spiral Review

2

3

1	2	3	4	5	6	7	8	9	10
11	12	13	14	15	16	17	18	19	20
21	22	23	24	25	26	27	28	29	30

DIRECTIONS **1.** Which is a three-dimensional or solid shape? Mark an X on the shape. **2.** Join two triangles to make a shape. Draw and color the shape you created. **3.** Begin with 1 and count forward to 19. What is the next number? Draw a line under that number.

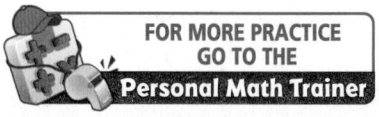

© Houghton Mifflin Harcourt Publishing Company

Name _____

Model Shapes

Essential Question How can you model shapes in the real world?

HANDS ON Lesson 10.7

Learning Objective You will model shapes in the world by composing flat and solid shapes using straws and clay.

Listen and Draw

DIRECTIONS Use your finger to trace around the shape. Name the shape. Tell a friend whether this shape is flat or solid. Talk about the number of sides and the number of vertices.

© Houghton Mifflin Harcourt Publishing Company

Share and Show

1

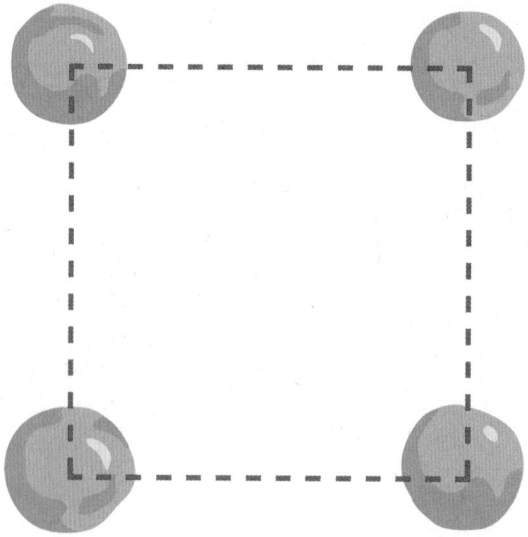

2

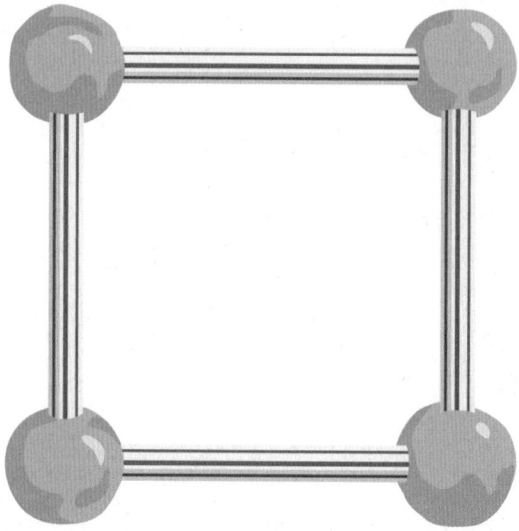

DIRECTIONS 1. Use clay to model 4 spheres as shown. Trace the square. The clay spheres will model the corners of the squares. 2. Place straws into the spheres as shown.

© Houghton Mifflin Harcourt Publishing Company

Name _____

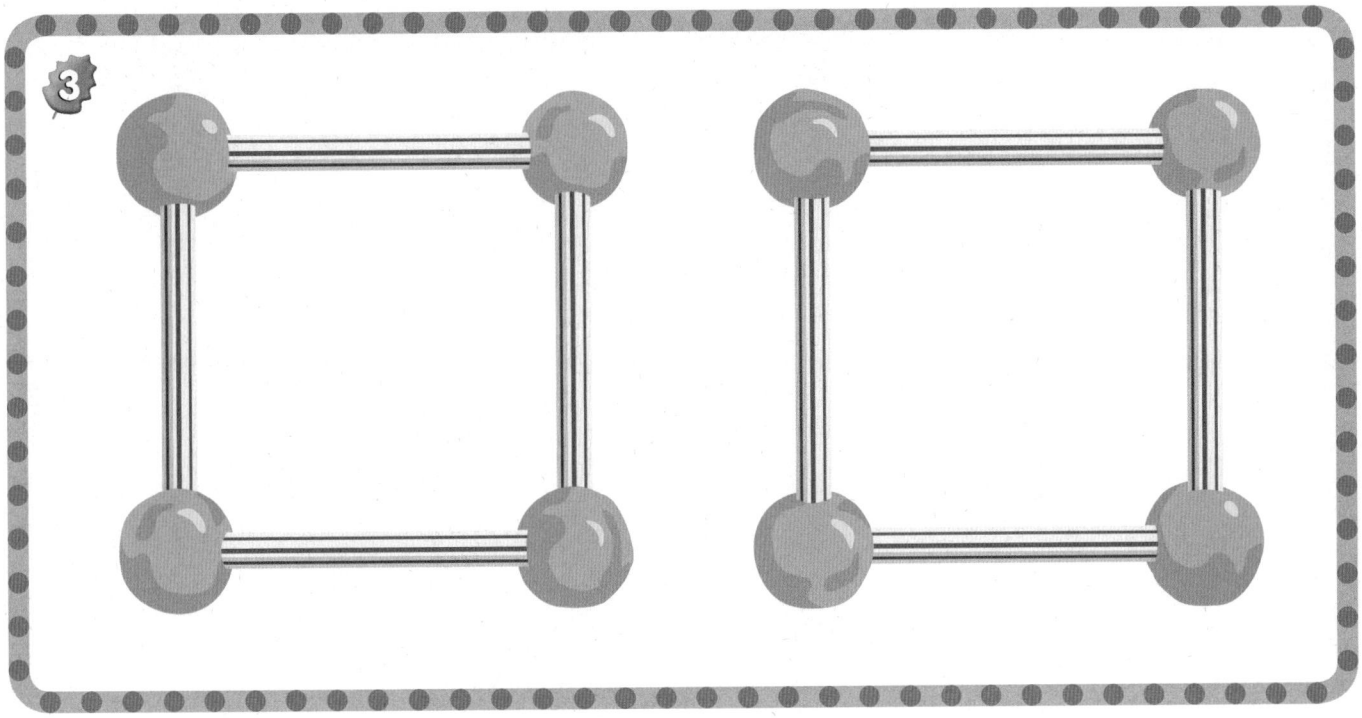

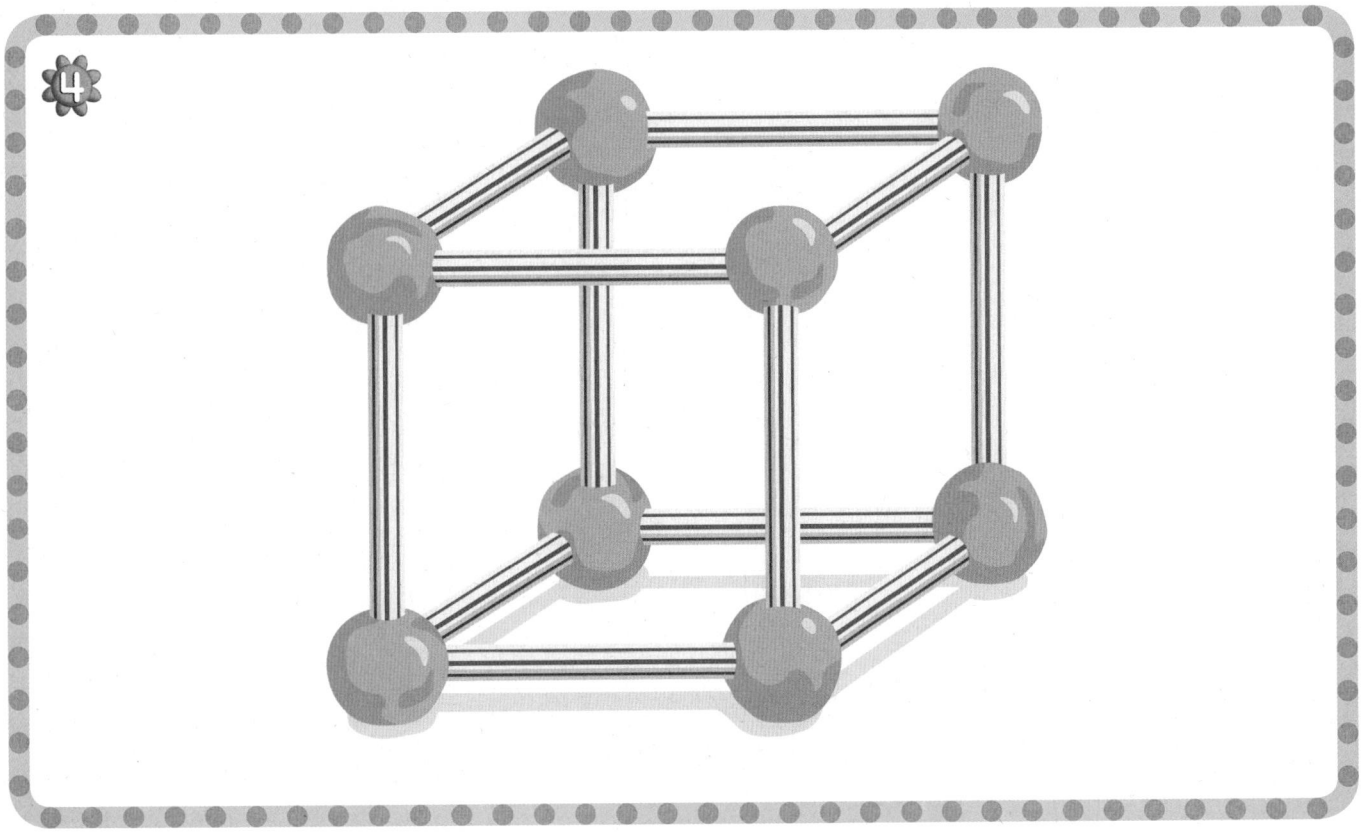

DIRECTIONS **3.** Use clay and straws to model another shape. Match the shape that you modeled in Exercise 2. **4.** Stand a straw into each corner of one of the shapes. Carefully lift the other shape and place it onto the straws as shown. Name the solid shape you modeled.

© Houghton Mifflin Harcourt Publishing Company

Problem Solving • Applications Real World

WRITE Math

5

6

DIRECTIONS 5. Maria's window has the shape of a square. Draw a picture of the shape. Tell a friend whether this shape is flat or solid. Talk about the number of sides and the number of vertices. 6. Use objects such as clay and straws to model a solid shape. Draw a picture of the solid shape. Tell a friend about the shape.

HOME ACTIVITY • Have your child identify a household object that has a flat shape. Have your child model the shape with a drawing. Repeat the activity with a solid object, and have your child model the shape with materials such as clay and toothpicks.

© Houghton Mifflin Harcourt Publishing Company

Name _____

Model Shapes

Learning Objective You will model shapes in the world by composing flat and solid shapes using straws and clay.

1

_____

_____ **sides**

2

_____

_____ **flat surfaces**

DIRECTIONS 1. Draw to show what you know about a square. Write how many sides. 2. Declan's can of corn has the shape of a cylinder. Use clay to model a cylinder. Draw the cylinder. How many flat surfaces are there? Write the number.

© Houghton Mifflin Harcourt Publishing Company

Lesson Check

1

_____ flat surface

Spiral Review

2

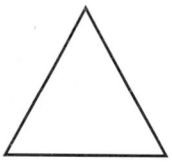

3

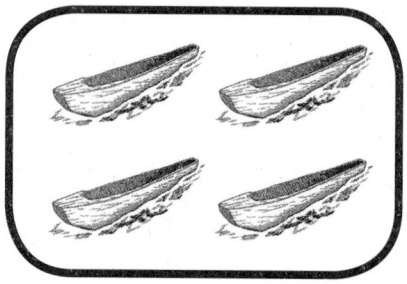

4 + _____ = 5

DIRECTIONS 1. How many flat surfaces does this shape have? Write the number. 2. Which shape is flat? Color the flat shape. 3. Tell an addition word problem about the boats. Write the number to complete the addition sentence.

© Houghton Mifflin Harcourt Publishing Company

Name _____

Above and Below

Essential Question How can you use the terms *above* and *below* to describe shapes in the environment?

Learning Objective You will use the terms *above* and *below* to describe the positions of objects in space.

Listen and Draw Real World

DIRECTIONS Trace the circle around the object shaped like a cylinder that is below the shelf. Trace the X on the object shaped like a sphere that is above the cabinet.

© Houghton Mifflin Harcourt Publishing Company

Share and Show

1

DIRECTIONS 1. Circle the object that is shaped like a cone below the play set. Mark an X on the object that is shaped like a cube above the play set. Color the object that is shaped like a cylinder above the play set.

© Houghton Mifflin Harcourt Publishing Company

Name _____

DIRECTIONS **2.** Circle the object shaped like a sphere above the net. Mark an X on the object shaped like a cube directly below the net.

© Houghton Mifflin Harcourt Publishing Company

Problem Solving • Applications Real World

3

WRITE Math

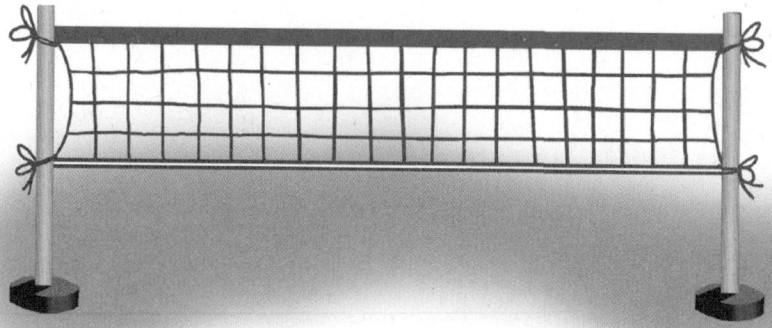

DIRECTIONS 3. Draw to show what you know about real world three-dimensional objects that might be above or below the net. Tell a friend about your drawing as you name the shape of the objects.

HOME ACTIVITY • Tell your child you are thinking of something in the room that is above or below another object. Have your child tell you what the object might be.

© Houghton Mifflin Harcourt Publishing Company

Name _____

Above and Below

Learning Objective You will use the terms *above* and *below* to describe the positions of objects in space.

1

DIRECTIONS 1. Mark an X on the object that is shaped like a sphere below the table. Circle the object that is shaped like a cube above the table.

© Houghton Mifflin Harcourt Publishing Company

Lesson Check

1

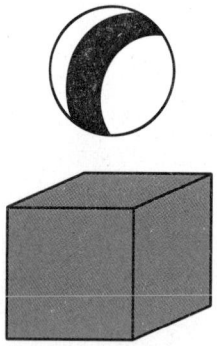

Spiral Review

2

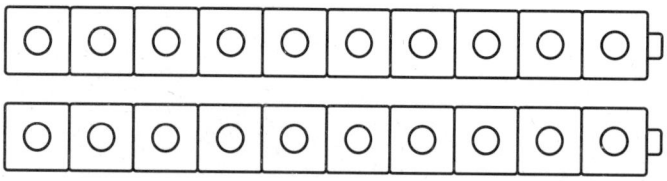

_____

_____

_____

3

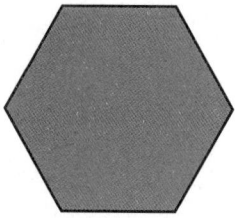

_____

_____

_____ **vertices**

DIRECTIONS **1.** Circle the set that shows an object shaped like a sphere above the object shaped like a cube. **2.** Count and tell how many. Write the number. **3.** How many vertices does the hexagon have? Write the number.

© Houghton Mifflin Harcourt Publishing Company

Name _____

Beside and Next To

Essential Question How can you use the terms *beside* and *next to* to describe shapes in the environment?

Learning Objective You will use the terms *beside* and *next to* to describe the positions of objects in space.

Listen and Draw

Real World

DIRECTIONS Trace the X on the object shaped like a cone that is beside the object shaped like a sphere. Trace the circle around the object shaped like a sphere that is next to the object shaped like a cube.

© Houghton Mifflin Harcourt Publishing Company

Share and Show

1

DIRECTIONS 1. Mark an X on the bead shaped like a cube that is beside the bead shaped like a cone. Draw a circle around the bead shaped like a cone that is next to the bead shaped like a cylinder. Use the words *next to* and *beside* to name the position of other bead shapes.

© Houghton Mifflin Harcourt Publishing Company

Name _____

DIRECTIONS **2.** Mark an X on the object shaped like a cylinder that is next to the object shaped like a sphere. Draw a circle around the object shaped like a cone that is beside the object shaped like a cube. Use the words *next to* and *beside* to describe the position of other package shapes.

© Houghton Mifflin Harcourt Publishing Company

Problem Solving • Applications Real World

3

DIRECTIONS 3. Draw or use pictures to show what you know about real world three-dimensional objects beside and next to other objects.

HOME ACTIVITY • Tell your child you are thinking of something in the room that is beside or next to another object. Have your child tell you the shape of the object.

© Houghton Mifflin Harcourt Publishing Company

Name _____

Beside and Next To

Learning Objective You will use the terms *beside* and *next to* to describe the positions of objects in space.

1

DIRECTIONS 1. Mark an X on the object shaped like a cylinder that is next to the object shaped like a sphere. Circle the object shaped like a cone that is beside the object shaped like a cube. Use the words *next to* and *beside* to name the position of other shapes.

© Houghton Mifflin Harcourt Publishing Company

Lesson Check

1

Spiral Review

2

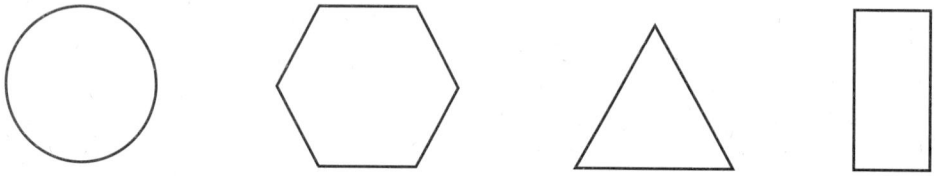

3

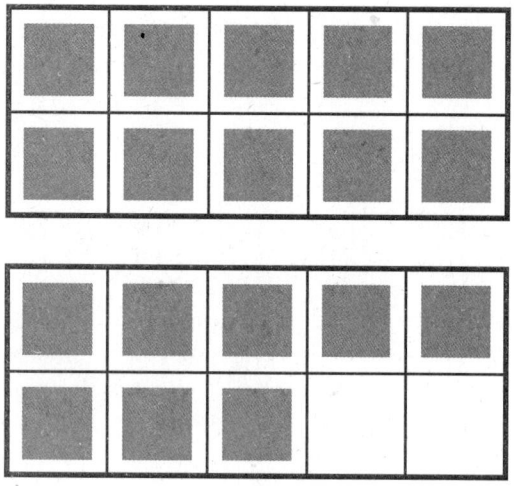

_____

_____

DIRECTIONS **1.** Circle the set that shows an object shaped like a cube beside the object shaped like a cone. **2.** Which shape is a hexagon? Color the hexagon. **3.** How many tiles are there? Write the number.

© Houghton Mifflin Harcourt Publishing Company

Name _____

In Front Of and Behind

Essential Question How can you use the terms *in front of* and *behind* to describe shapes in the environment?

Learning Objective You will use the terms *in front of* and *behind* to describe the positions of objects in space.

Listen and Draw Real World

DIRECTIONS Trace the X on the object shaped like a sphere that is in front of the object shaped like a cube. Trace the circle around the object shaped like a cylinder that is behind the object shaped like a cube.

© Houghton Mifflin Harcourt Publishing Company

Share and Show

1

DIRECTIONS 1. Mark an X on the object shaped like a cylinder that is behind the object shaped like a cube. Draw a circle around the object shaped like a sphere that is directly in front of the object shaped like a cone. Use the words *in front of* and *behind* to name the position of other shapes.

© Houghton Mifflin Harcourt Publishing Company

Name _____

DIRECTIONS **2.** Mark an X on the object shaped like a cube that is in front of the object shaped like a cylinder. Draw a circle around the object shaped like a cylinder that is behind the object shaped like a sphere. Use the words *in front of* and *behind* to name the position of other shaped objects.

© Houghton Mifflin Harcourt Publishing Company

Problem Solving • Applications Real World

WRITE Math

3

DIRECTIONS 3. Draw or use pictures to show what you know about real world three-dimensional objects in front of and behind other objects.

HOME ACTIVITY • Tell your child you are thinking of something in the room that is in front of or behind another object. Have your child tell you the shape of the object.

© Houghton Mifflin Harcourt Publishing Company

Name _____

In Front Of and Behind

Learning Objective You will use the terms *in front of* and *behind* to describe the positions of objects in space.

1

DIRECTIONS 1. Mark an X on the object shaped like a cylinder that is behind the object shaped like a cone. Draw a circle around the object shaped like a cylinder that is in front of the object shaped like a cube. Use the words *in front of* and *behind* to name the position of other shapes.

© Houghton Mifflin Harcourt Publishing Company

Lesson Check

1

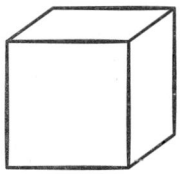

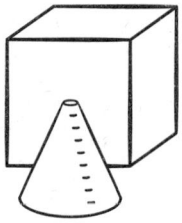

Spiral Review

2

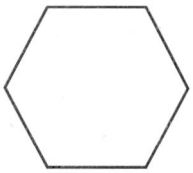

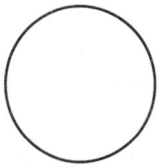

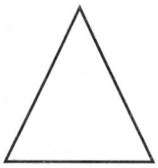

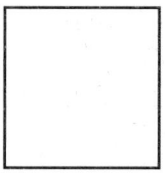

3

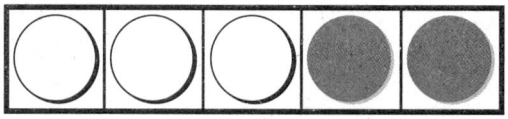

_____ _____

_____ _____

_____ **and** _____

DIRECTIONS 1. Circle the set that shows an object shaped like a cone in front of the object shaped like a cube. 2. Which shape is a triangle? Color the triangle. 3. How many of each color counter? Write the numbers.

© Houghton Mifflin Harcourt Publishing Company

Name _____

Chapter 10 Review/Test

Personal Math Trainer
Online Assessment and Intervention

1

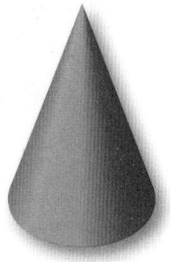
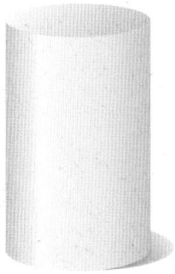

2

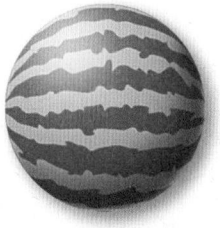

Personal Math Trainer

3 THINK SMARTER+

6 sides	Yes	No
curved surface	Yes	No

DIRECTIONS **1.** Mark under all the shapes that stack. **2.** Which objects are shaped like a sphere? Mark an X on each of those objects. **3.** Do the words describe a cube? Circle Yes or No.

© Houghton Mifflin Harcourt Publishing Company

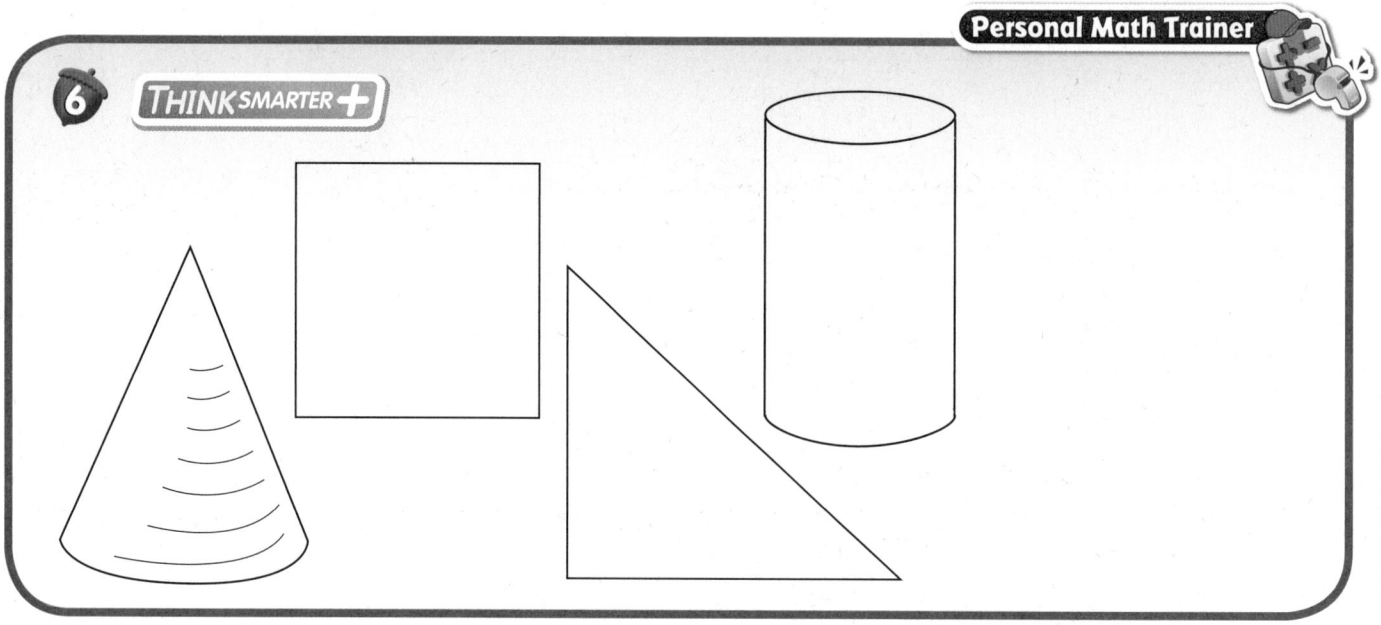

DIRECTIONS **4.** Draw lines to match the objects to their shapes. **5.** Which objects are shaped like a cone? Mark an X on each of those objects. **6.** Color the solid shapes blue. Color the flat shapes red. Draw another flat shape that is different.

© Houghton Mifflin Harcourt Publishing Company

Name _____

7

8

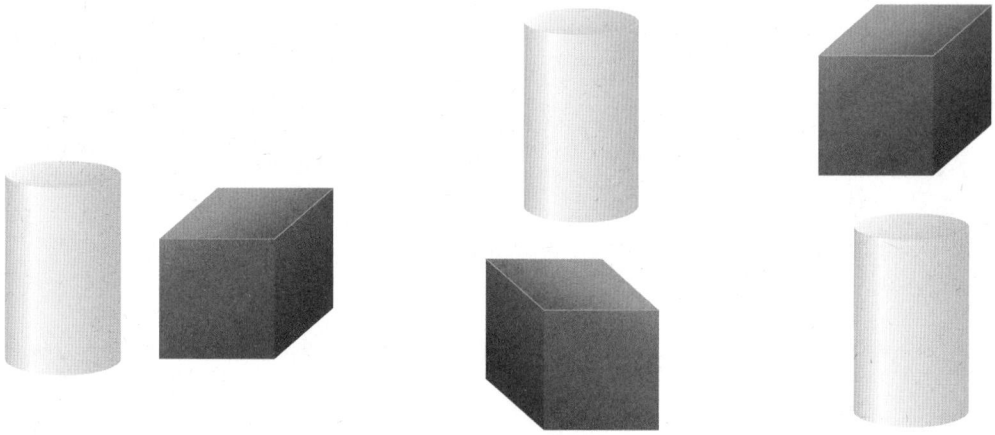

9

© Houghton Mifflin Harcourt Publishing Company

DIRECTIONS **7.** Draw an object that has the shape of a cylinder. **8.** Circle the shapes that show the cylinder above the cube. **9.** Mark an X on the object shaped like a cylinder next to the object shaped like a cone.

10

11

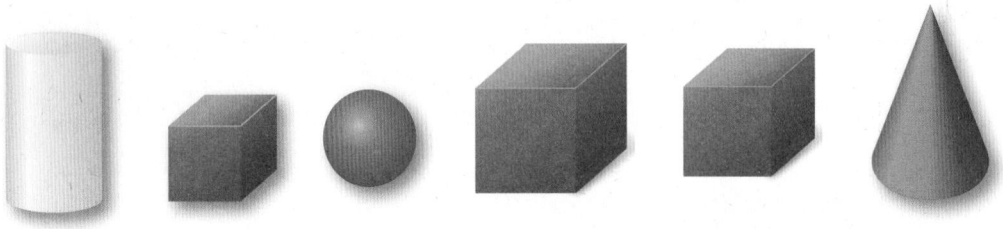

12

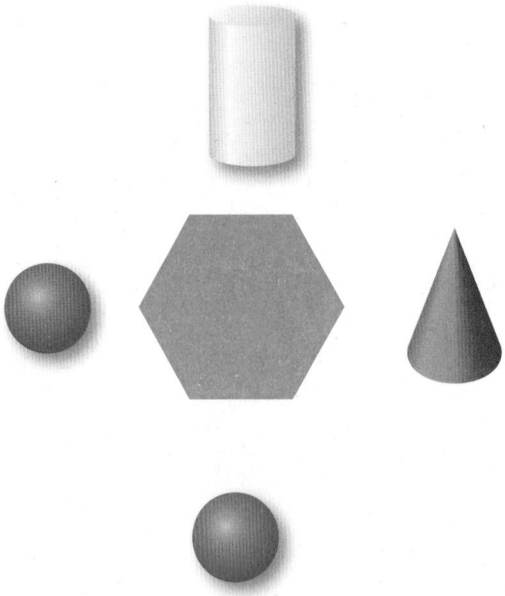

DIRECTIONS **10.** Mark an X on the cone in front of the cube. **11.** Mark an X on the cube that is beside the cone. **12.** Mark an X on the sphere that is below the hexagon.

© Houghton Mifflin Harcourt Publishing Company

© Houghton Mifflin Harcourt Publishing Company

BIG IDEA Develop a conceptual understanding of measurement and data. Classify and count by color, shape, and size.

Two leaves fall from a tree.

Circle the leaf that is longer.

Science

Why do plants have leaves?

© Houghton Mifflin Harcourt Publishing Company • Image Credits: (bkgd) ©Purestock/Alamy

Two flowers grow near a wall.

Circle the flower that is shorter.

Science

Why do plants have flowers?

© Houghton Mifflin Harcourt Publishing Company • Image credits: (bg) ©PHOTO 24/Getty Images

These carrots grow under the ground.

Circle the carrot that is longer.

Science

Why do plants have roots?

© Houghton Mifflin Harcourt Publishing Company • Image Credits: ©(t) Pierro Smits/Alamy

Cattails can be short or tall.

Circle the two cattails that are about the same height.

© Houghton Mifflin Harcourt Publishing Company • Image Credits: ©Juliens Sélarchiv/Alamy

Science

Why do plants have stems?

One leaf is shorter than the other leaf.

Draw a leaf that is about the same length as the shorter leaf.

Science

How are all these plants the same?

© Houghton Mifflin Harcourt Publishing Company • Image credits: (bg) ©Stephen Simon/All Canada Photos/Corbis

Name _____

Write About the Story

WRITE Math

Draw a purple flower. Make it shorter than the orange flower and taller than the yellow flower.

Vocabulary Review

longer	taller
shorter	same

© Houghton Mifflin Harcourt Publishing Company

Name _____

Longer and Shorter

1. Look at the carrot. Draw a shorter carrot on the left. Draw a longer carrot on the right.

2. Look at the leaf. Draw a longer leaf above it. Draw a shorter leaf below it.

© Houghton Mifflin Harcourt Publishing Company

Chapter 11

Measurement

Curious About Math with Curious George

A playground is an area designed for children to play.

- Which person on the park bench is bigger?

© Houghton Mifflin Harcourt Publishing Company • Image Credits: ©Andre Jenny Photography/Corbis
Curious George, by Margret and H.A. Rey, copyright © 2010 by Houghton Mifflin Harcourt Publishing Company.
All rights reserved. The character Curious George®, including without limitation the character's name and the character's likenesses, are registered trademarks of Houghton Mifflin Harcourt Publishing Company.

Name _____

Show What You Know

Personal Math Trainer
Online Assessment and Intervention

More and Fewer

1

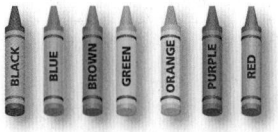

_____

_____

2

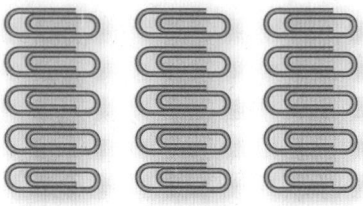

_____

_____

Compare Numbers

3

_____

_____

_____

_____

This page checks understanding of important skills needed for success in Chapter 11.

DIRECTIONS 1. Write how many in each set. Circle the set with fewer objects. 2. Write how many in each set. Circle the set with more objects. 3. Write how many cubes in each set. Circle the greater number.

© Houghton Mifflin Harcourt Publishing Company

Name _____

Vocabulary Builder

DIRECTIONS Are there more flowers in the bigger pot or the smaller pot? Circle to show the pot with more flowers.

GO DIGITAL
- Interactive Student Edition
- Multimedia *e*Glossary

© Houghton Mifflin Harcourt Publishing Company

Chapter 11 Game

Connecting Cube Challenge

© Houghton Mifflin Harcourt Publishing Company

DIRECTIONS Take turns with a partner tossing the number cube. Move your marker that number of spaces. If a player lands on a cube, he or she takes a cube for making a cube train. At the end of the game, players compare cube trains. Each player identifies the number of cubes in his or her cube train. If one player has a greater number of cubes, partners should identify that as the larger quantity of cubes.

MATERIALS game markers, number cube (1–6), connecting cubes

Chapter 11 Vocabulary

heavier

más pesado

33

lighter

más liviano

39

longer

más largo

40

same height

de la misma altura

55

same length

del mismo largo

56

same weight

del mismo peso

58

shorter

más corto

62

taller

más alto

73

© Houghton Mifflin Harcourt Publishing Company

lighter

© Houghton Mifflin Harcourt Publishing Company

heavier

© Houghton Mifflin Harcourt Publishing Company

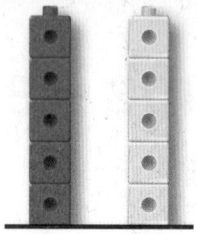

same height

© Houghton Mifflin Harcourt Publishing Company

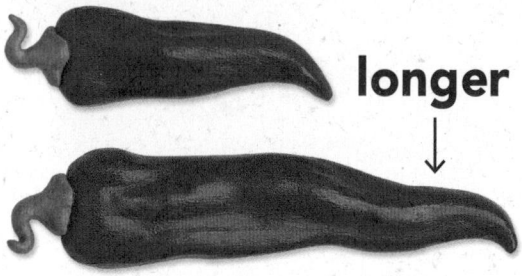

longer

© Houghton Mifflin Harcourt Publishing Company

same weight

© Houghton Mifflin Harcourt Publishing Company

same length

© Houghton Mifflin Harcourt Publishing Company

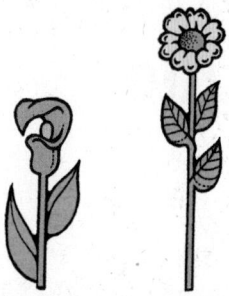

taller

© Houghton Mifflin Harcourt Publishing Company

shorter

Game

Measurement

heavier

lighter

longer

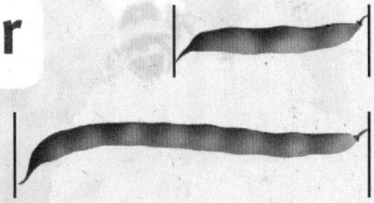

shorter

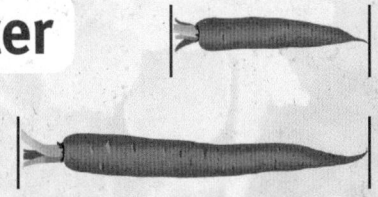

taller

same height

same length

same weight

© Houghton Mifflin Harcourt Publishing Company • Image Credits: (bg) ©Olena Mykhaylova/Shutterstock; ©Olena Mykhaylova/Shutterstock

DIRECTIONS Say each word. Tell something you know about the word.

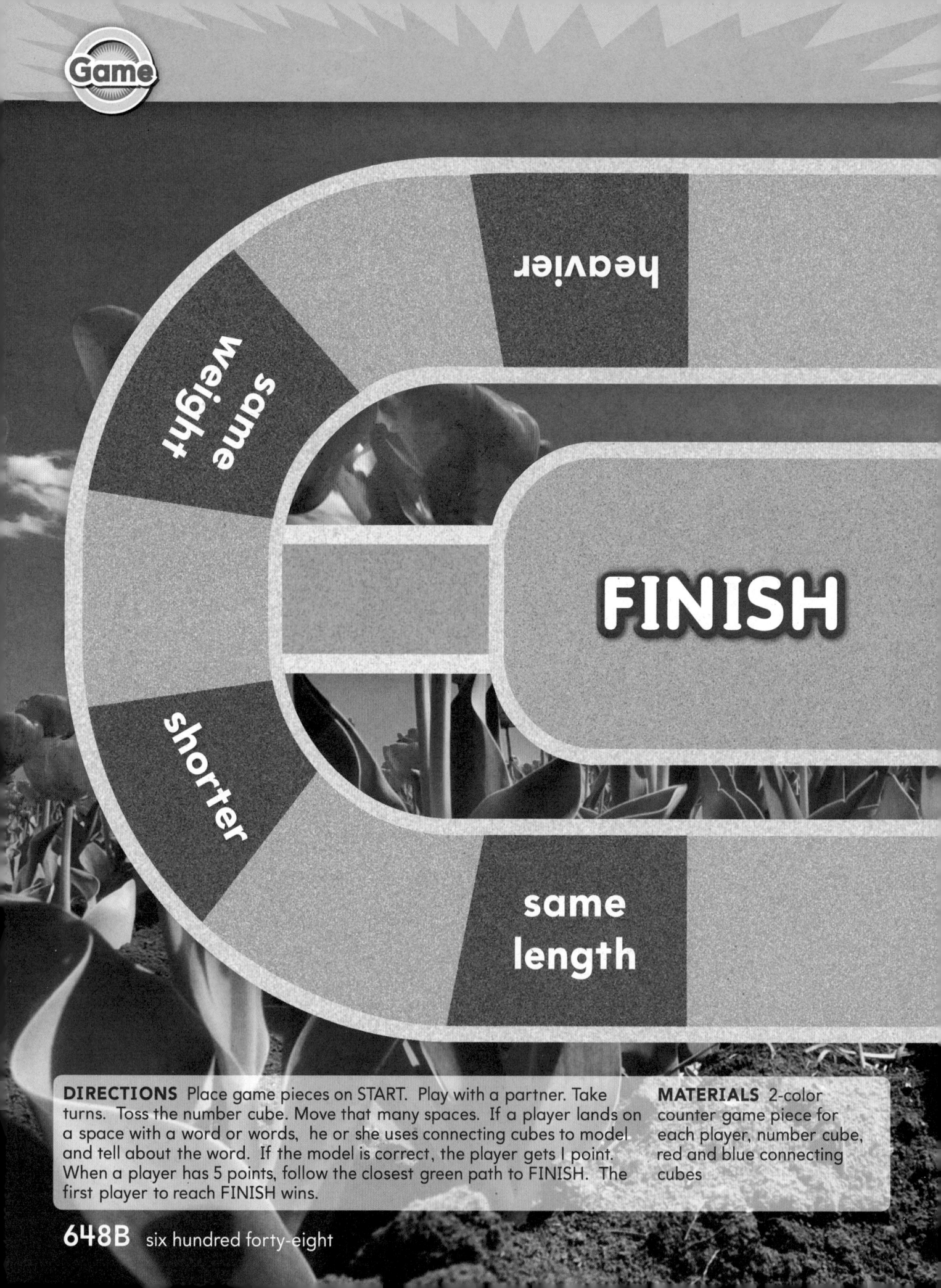

DIRECTIONS Place game pieces on START. Play with a partner. Take turns. Toss the number cube. Move that many spaces. If a player lands on a space with a word or words, he or she uses connecting cubes to model and tell about the word. If the model is correct, the player gets 1 point. When a player has 5 points, follow the closest green path to FINISH. The first player to reach FINISH wins.

MATERIALS 2-color counter game piece for each player, number cube, red and blue connecting cubes

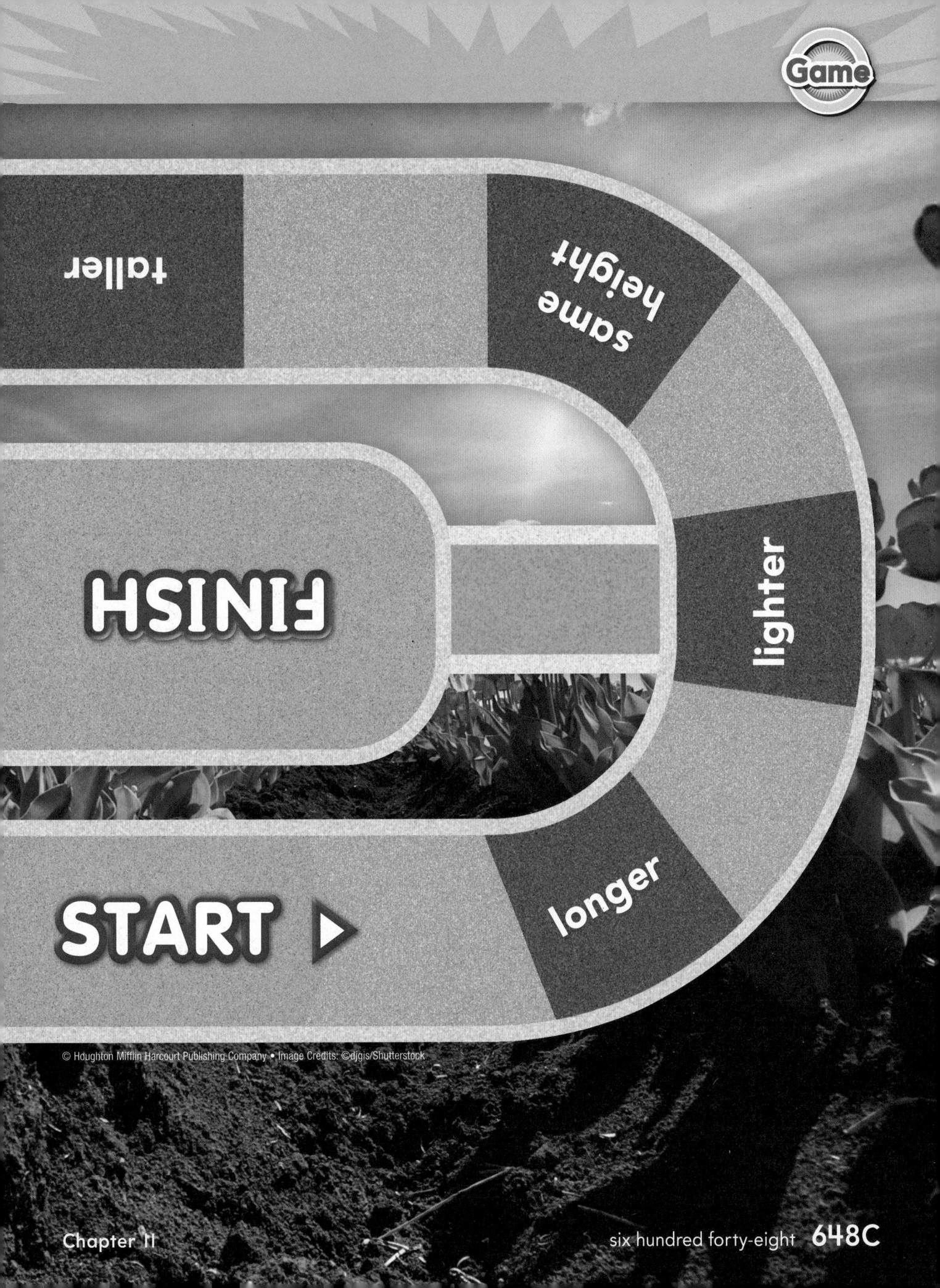

© Houghton Mifflin Harcourt Publishing Company • Image Credits: ©djgis/Shutterstock

The Write Way

DIRECTIONS Draw to show how to compare the length of two objects.
Reflect Be ready to tell about your drawing.

© Houghton Mifflin Harcourt Publishing Company • Image Credits: ©Olena Mykhaylova/Shutterstock

Name _____

Compare Lengths

Essential Question How can you compare the lengths of two objects?

Learning Objective You will make a direct comparison of the lengths of two objects.

Listen and Draw

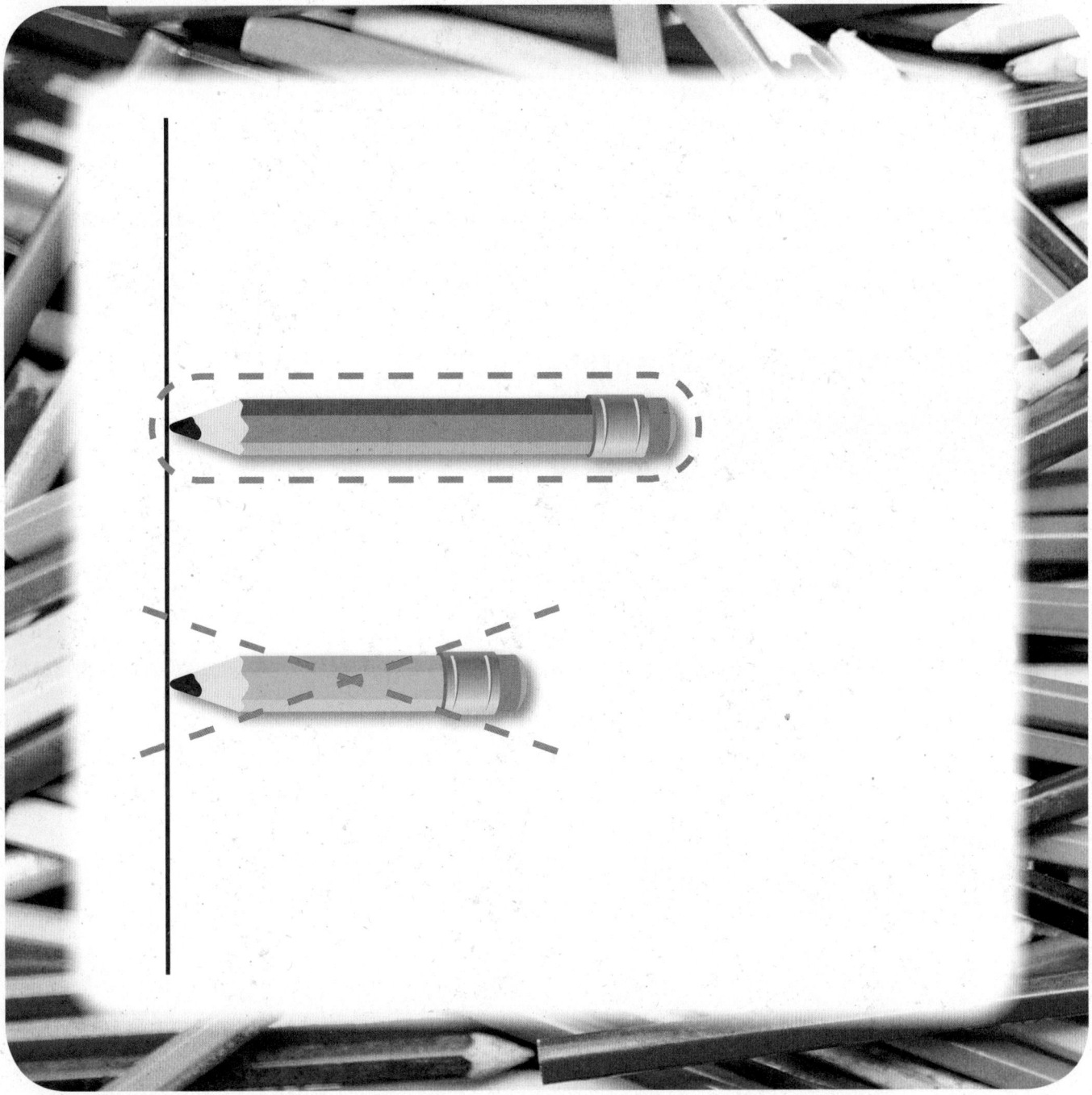

DIRECTIONS Look at the pencils. Compare the lengths of the two pencils. Use the words *longer than*, *shorter than*, or *about the same length* to describe the lengths. Trace the circle around the longer pencil. Trace the X on the shorter pencil.

© Houghton Mifflin Harcourt Publishing Company • Image Credits: (bg) ©Corbis Premium RF/Alamy

Share and Show

1

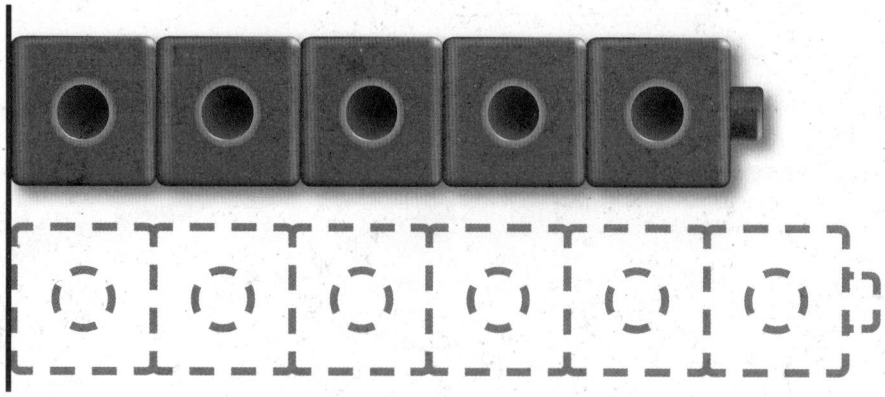

2

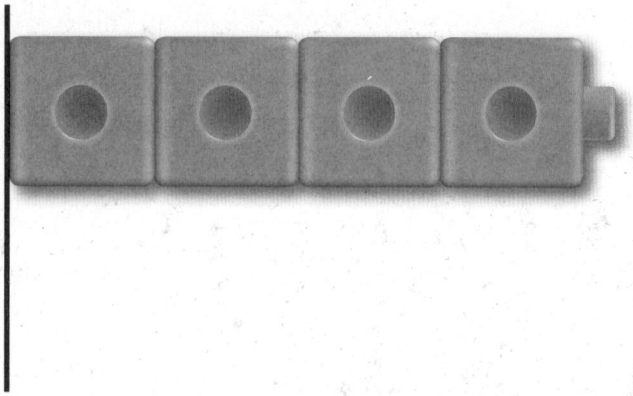

3 ✓

DIRECTIONS **1.** Place cubes on the longer cube train. Trace and color the cube train. **2–3.** Make a cube train that is longer than the cube train shown. Draw and color the cube train.

© Houghton Mifflin Harcourt Publishing Company

Name _____

4

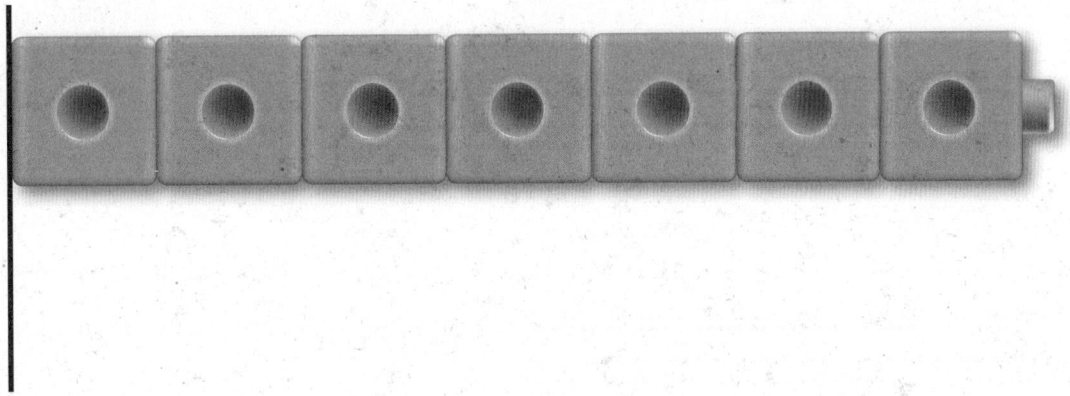

5

6

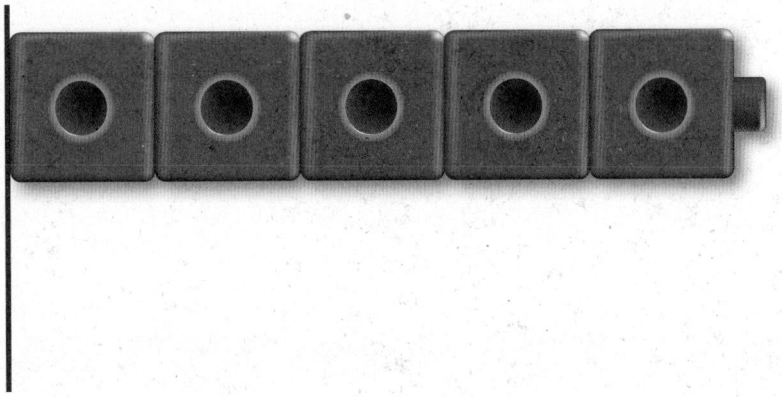

DIRECTIONS 4–6. Make a cube train that is shorter than the cube train shown. Draw and color the cube train.

© Houghton Mifflin Harcourt Publishing Company

Problem Solving • Applications Real World

WRITE Math

7

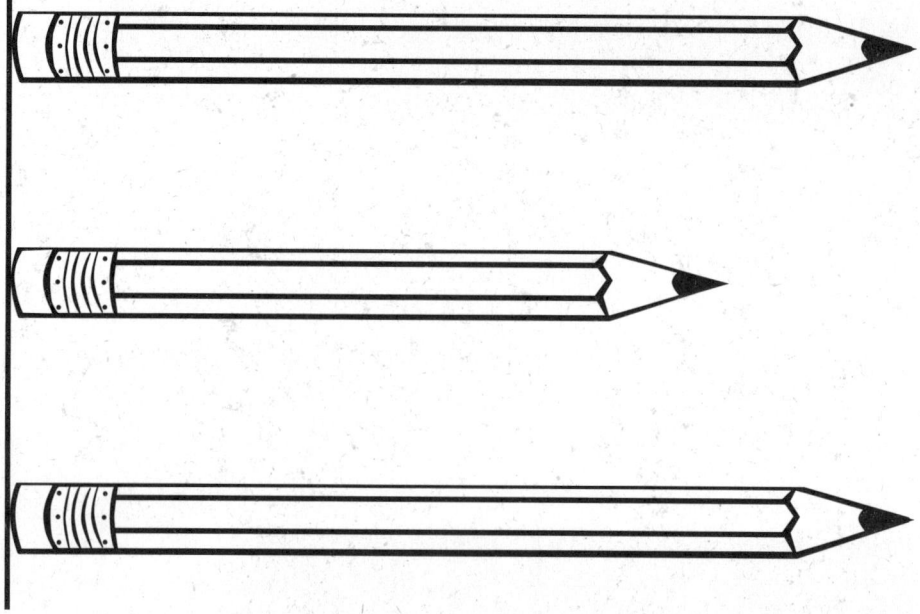

8

DIRECTIONS 7. Two of these pencils are about the same length. Color those pencils. 8. Draw to show what you know about two objects that are about the same length. Tell a friend about your drawing.

HOME ACTIVITY • Show your child a pencil and ask him or her to find an object that is longer than the pencil. Repeat with an object that is shorter than the pencil.

© Houghton Mifflin Harcourt Publishing Company

Name _____

Compare Lengths

Learning Objective You will make a direct comparison of the lengths of two objects.

1

2

3

DIRECTIONS **1.** Make a cube train that is longer than the cube train shown. Draw and color the cube train. **2.** Make a cube train that is shorter than the cube train shown. Draw and color the cube train. **3.** Make a cube train that is about the same length as the cube train shown. Draw and color the cube train.

© Houghton Mifflin Harcourt Publishing Company

Lesson Check

1

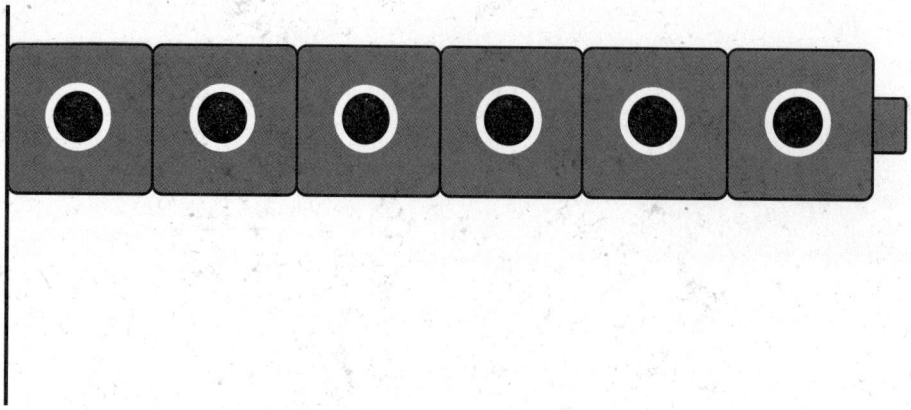

Spiral Review

2

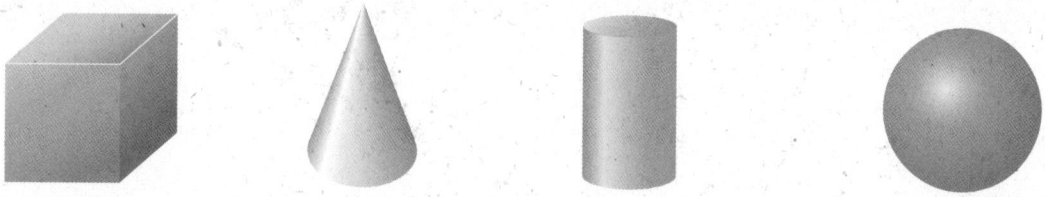

3

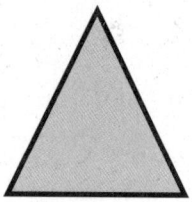

DIRECTIONS 1. Make a cube train that is shorter than the cube train shown. Draw and color the cube train. 2. Which shape is a sphere? Mark an X on the shape. 3. Look at the shape. Draw a shape that is alike in some way. Tell how the two shapes are alike.

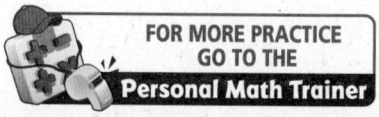

© Houghton Mifflin Harcourt Publishing Company

Name _____

Compare Heights

Essential Question How can you compare the heights of two objects?

Learning Objective You will make a direct comparison of the heights of two objects.

Listen and Draw Real World

DIRECTIONS Look at the chairs. Compare the heights of the two chairs. Use the words *taller than*, *shorter than*, or *about the same height* to describe the heights. Trace the circle around the taller chair. Trace the X on the shorter chair.

© Houghton Mifflin Harcourt Publishing Company • Image Credits: (bg) ©Gerry Gay / ...ny

Share and Show

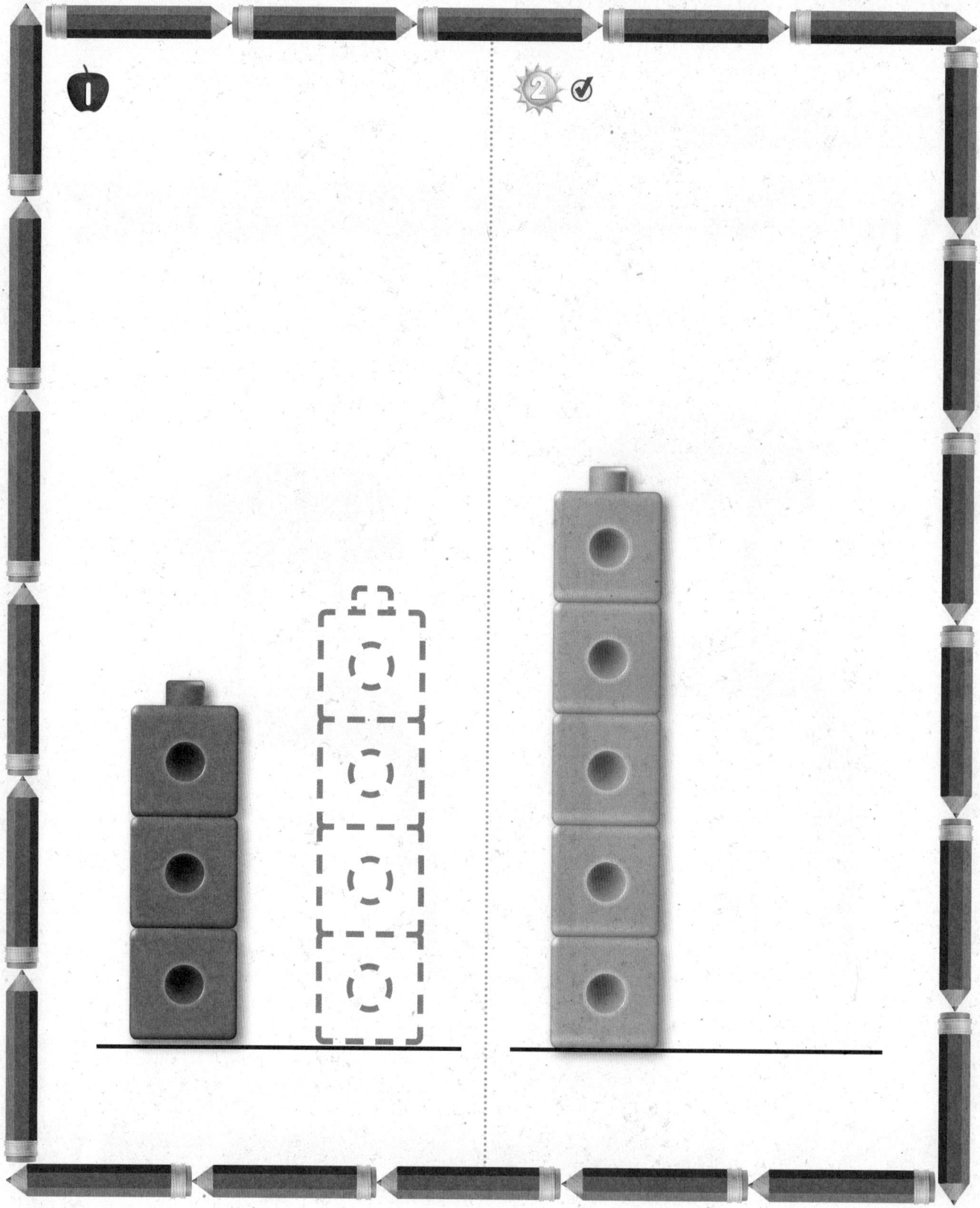

DIRECTIONS **1.** Place cubes on the taller cube tower. Trace and color the cube tower. **2.** Make a cube tower that is taller than the cube tower shown. Draw and color the cube tower.

© Houghton Mifflin Harcourt Publishing Company

Name _____

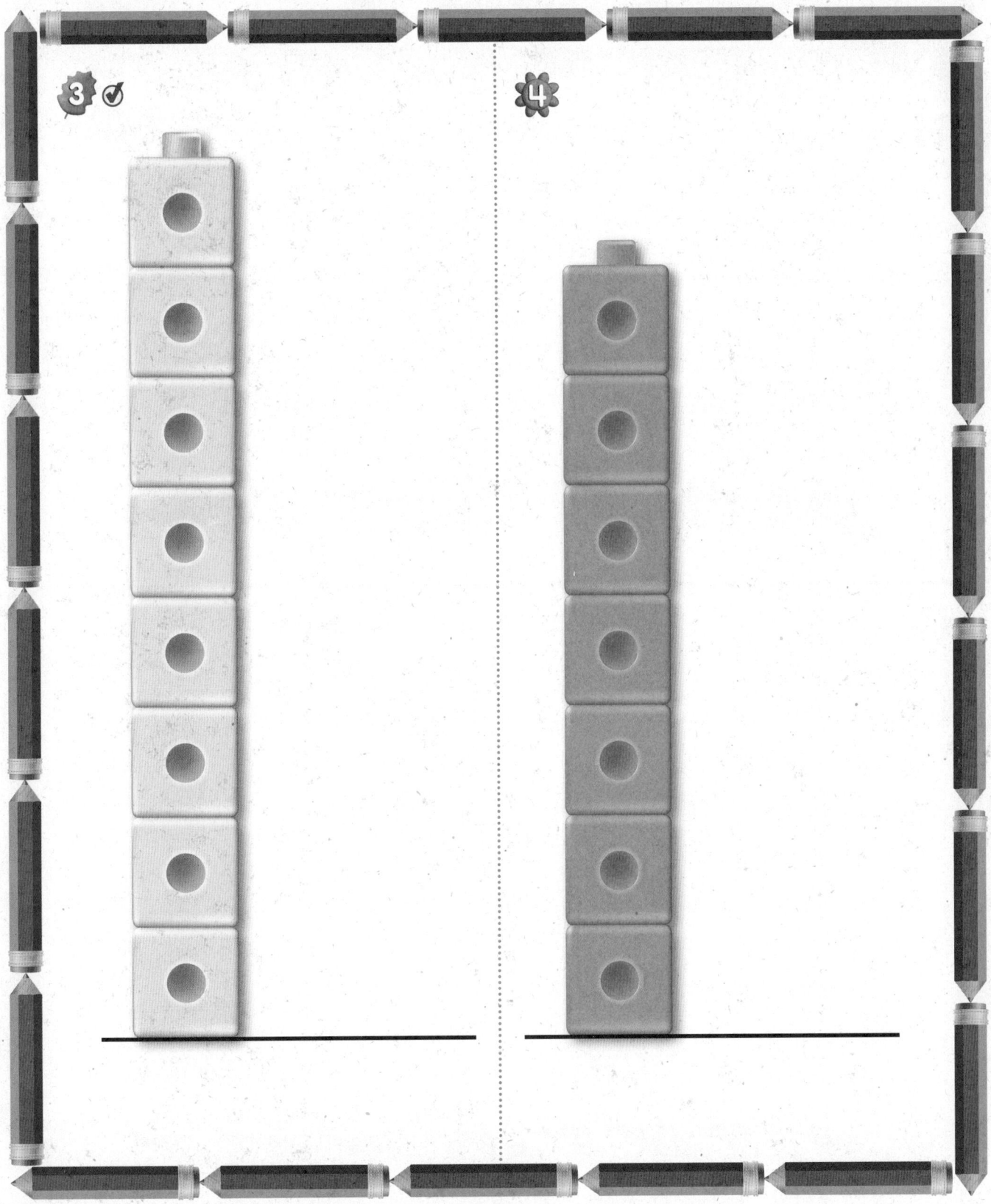

DIRECTIONS **3–4.** Make a cube tower that is shorter than the cube tower shown. Draw and color the cube tower.

© Houghton Mifflin Harcourt Publishing Company

Problem Solving • Applications Real World

WRITE Math

5

6

DIRECTIONS **5.** Color the trees that are about the same height. **6.** Draw to show what you know about two cube towers that are about the same height. Tell a friend about your drawing.

HOME ACTIVITY • Have your child find two objects, such as plastic toys or stuffed animals. Have him or her place the objects side by side to compare the heights. Ask your child which object is taller and which object is shorter.

© Houghton Mifflin Harcourt Publishing Company

Name _____

Compare Heights

Learning Objective You will make a direct comparison of the heights of two objects.

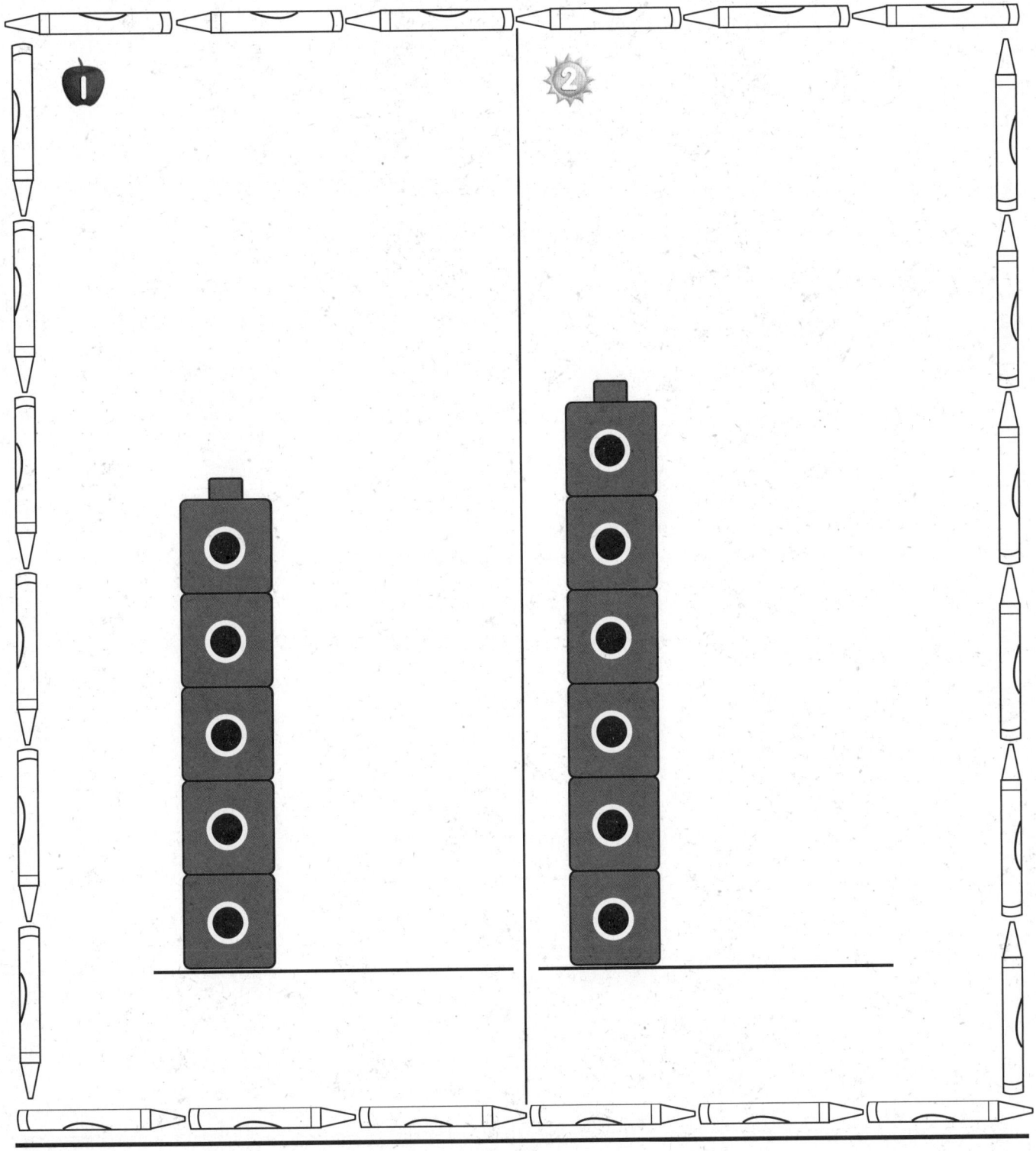

DIRECTIONS **1.** Make a cube tower that is taller than the cube tower shown. Draw and color the cube tower. **2.** Make a cube tower that is shorter than the cube tower shown. Draw and color the cube tower.

© Houghton Mifflin Harcourt Publishing Company

Lesson Check

1

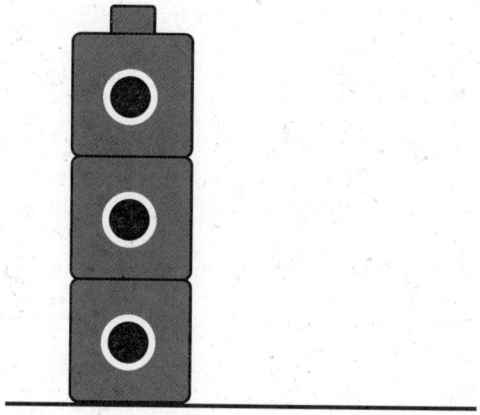

Spiral Review

2

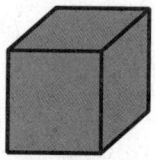

3

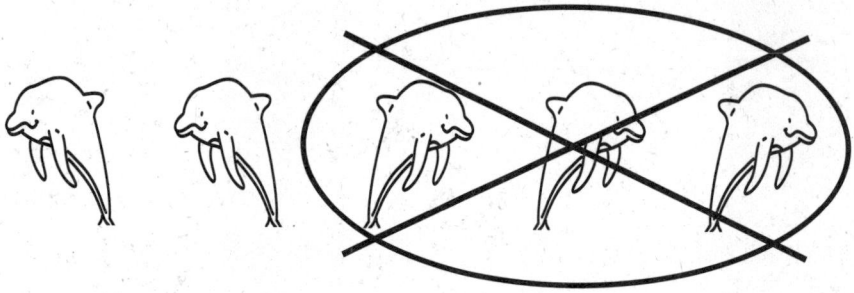

5 − ____ = 2

DIRECTIONS 1. Make a cube tower that is shorter than the cube tower shown. Draw and color the cube tower. 2. Circle the set that shows an object shaped like a sphere below the object shaped like a cube. 3. How many are being taken from the set? Write the number.

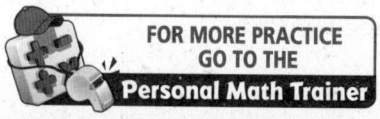

© Houghton Mifflin Harcourt Publishing Company

Name _____

Problem Solving • Direct Comparison

Essential Question How can you solve problems using the strategy ***draw a picture?***

Learning Objective You will use the strategy *draw a picture* by comparing the lengths or heights of objects to solve problems.

Unlock the Problem

Real World

Hands On

DIRECTIONS Compare the lengths or heights of two classroom objects. Draw the objects. Tell a friend about your drawing.

© Houghton Mifflin Harcourt Publishing Company • Image Credits: ©Bryan Mullennix/Getty Images

Try Another Problem

1

DIRECTIONS 1. Find two small classroom objects. Place one end of each object on the line. Compare the lengths. Draw the objects. Say *longer than*, *shorter than*, or *about the same length* to describe the lengths. Circle both objects if they are about the same length. Circle the longer object if one object is longer than the other.

© Houghton Mifflin Harcourt Publishing Company

Name _____

Share and Show

2 ✓

DIRECTIONS **2.** Find two small classroom objects. Place one end of each object on the line. Compare the heights. Draw the objects. Say *taller than*, *shorter than*, or *about the same height* to describe the heights. Circle both objects if they are about the same height. Circle the shorter object if one object is shorter than the other.

HOME ACTIVITY • Show your child two objects of different lengths. Have him or her put the ends of the objects on a straight line to compare the lengths and tell which object is shorter and which object is longer.

© Houghton Mifflin Harcourt Publishing Company

Mid-Chapter Checkpoint

Personal Math Trainer
Online Assessment and Intervention

Concepts and Skills

1

2

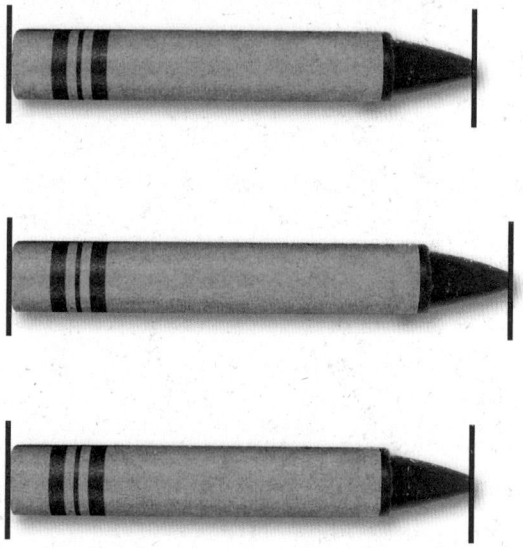

3

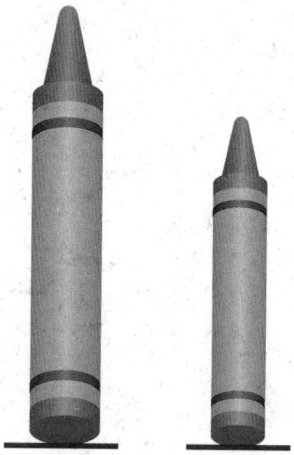

4 THINK SMARTER

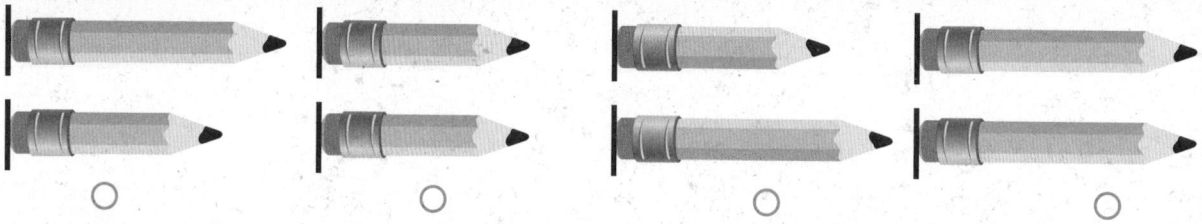

DIRECTIONS 1. Make a cube train that is shorter than the one shown. Draw the cube train. 2. Circle the crayons that are about the same length. 3. Circle the crayon that is shorter. 4. Choose all the sets with two pencils that are about the same length.

© Houghton Mifflin Harcourt Publishing Company

Name _____

Problem Solving • Direct Comparison

Learning Objective You will use the strategy *draw a picture* by comparing the lengths or heights of objects to solve problems.

1

2

DIRECTIONS **1.** Find two small classroom objects. Place one end of each object on the line. Compare the lengths. Draw the objects. Say *longer than*, *shorter than*, or *about the same length* to describe the lengths. Circle both objects if they are about the same length. Circle the longer object if one object is longer than the other. **2.** Find two small classroom objects. Place one end of each object on the line. Compare the heights. Draw the objects. Say *taller than*, *shorter than*, or *about the same height* to describe the heights. Circle both objects if they are about the same height. Circle the shorter object if one object is shorter than the other.

© Houghton Mifflin Harcourt Publishing Company

Lesson Check

1

Spiral Review

2

_____ vertices

3

DIRECTIONS 1. Find two pencils. Place one end of each pencil on the line. Compare the lengths. Draw the pencils. Say *longer than*, *shorter than*, or *about the same length* to describe the lengths. Circle both pencils if they are about the same length. Circle the shorter pencil if one pencil is shorter than the other. 2. How many vertices does the rectangle have? Write the number. 3. Use the cubes to complete the subtraction sentence.

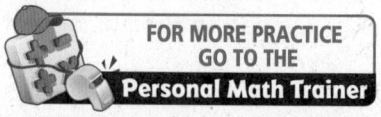

© Houghton Mifflin Harcourt Publishing Company

Name _____

HANDS ON
Lesson 11.4

Compare Weights

Essential Question How can you compare the weights of two objects?

Learning Objective You will make a direct comparison of the weights of two objects.

Listen and Draw Real World

DIRECTIONS Look at the picture. Compare the weights of the two objects. Use the words *heavier than*, *lighter than*, or *about the same weight* to describe the weights. Trace the circle around the lighter object. Trace the X on the heavier object.

© Houghton Mifflin Harcourt Publishing Company

Share and Show

left

right

1

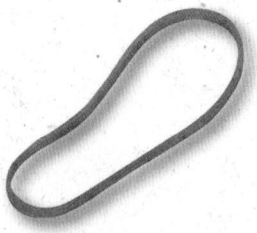

2

3

4

DIRECTIONS Find the first object in the row, and hold it in your left hand. Find the rest of the objects in the row, and take turns holding each of the objects in your right hand. **1.** Trace to show the object that is heavier than the object in your left hand. **2.** Circle the object that is heavier than the object in your left hand. **3–4.** Circle the object that is lighter than the object in your left hand.

© Houghton Mifflin Harcourt Publishing Company • Image Credits: (backpack) ©Siede Preis/PhotoDisc/Getty Images; (eraser) ©Artville/Getty Images

Name _____

5

6

DIRECTIONS Find a book in the classroom. **5.** Find a classroom object that is lighter than the book. Draw it in the work space. **6.** Find a classroom object that is heavier than the book. Draw it in the work space.

© Houghton Mifflin Harcourt Publishing Company

Problem Solving • Applications Real World

7

WRITE Math

DIRECTIONS **7.** Draw to show what you know about comparing the weights of two objects. Tell a friend about your drawing.

HOME ACTIVITY • Have your child compare the weights of two objects in a house. Then have him or her use the terms *heavier* and *lighter* to describe the weights.

© Houghton Mifflin Harcourt Publishing Company

Name _____

Compare Weights

Learning Objective You will make a direct comparison of the weights of two objects.

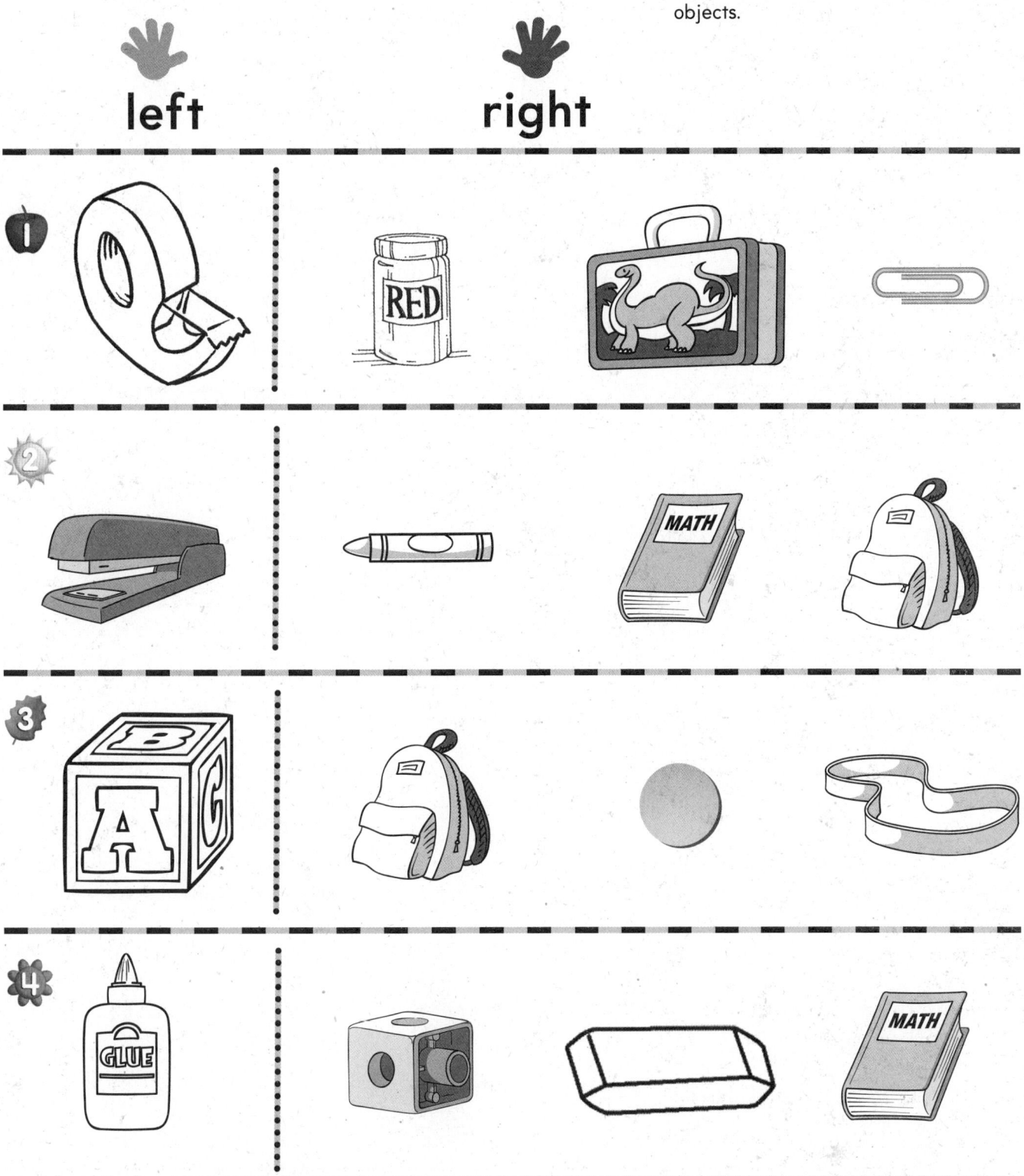

DIRECTIONS Find the first object in the row, and hold it in your left hand. Find the rest of the objects in the row, and hold each object in your right hand. **1–2.** Circle the object that is lighter than the object in your left hand. **3–4.** Circle the object that is heavier than the object in your left hand.

© Houghton Mifflin Harcourt Publishing Company

Lesson Check

1

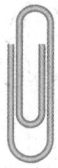

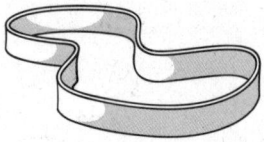

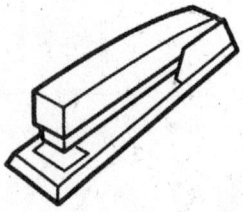

Spiral Review

2

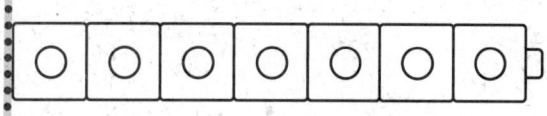

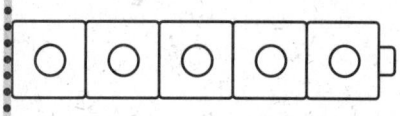

_____

_____

_____

_____

_____

_____

3

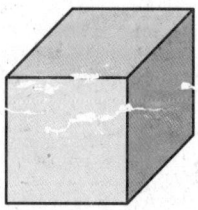

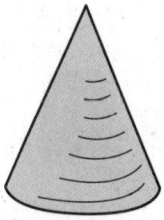

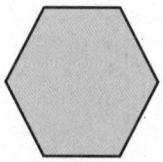

DIRECTIONS **1.** Find a paintbrush. Hold it in your left hand. Find the rest of the objects in the row, and hold each object in your right hand. Circle the object that is heavier than the paintbrush. **2.** Count the cubes. Write how many. Circle the number that is less. **3.** Which is a two-dimensional or flat shape? Mark an X on the shape.

© Houghton Mifflin Harcourt Publishing Company

FOR MORE PRACTICE GO TO THE Personal Math Trainer

Name _____

Length, Height, and Weight

Essential Question How can you describe several ways to measure one object?

Learning Objective You will describe several ways to measure one object.

Listen and Draw

DIRECTIONS Look at the book. Trace your finger over the line that shows how to measure the height of the book. Trace your finger over the line that shows how to measure the length of the book. Talk about another way to measure the book.

© Houghton Mifflin Harcourt Publishing Company • Image Credits: (bg) ©Corbis Premium RF/Alamy

Share and Show

1

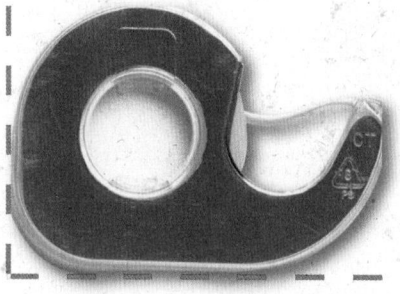

2

DIRECTIONS 1–2. Use red to trace the line that shows how to measure the length. Use blue to trace the line that shows how to measure the height. Talk about another way to measure the object.

© Houghton Mifflin Harcourt Publishing Company

Name _____

3

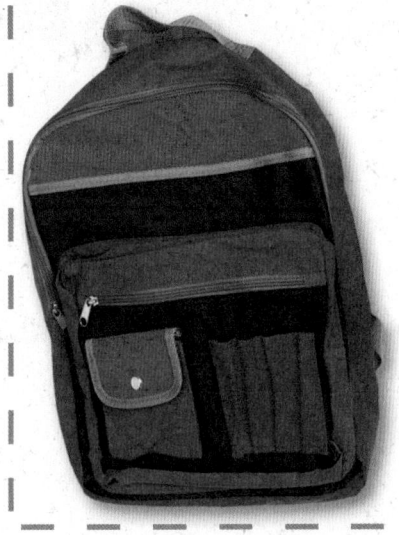

4

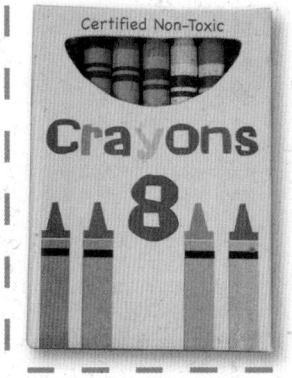

5

6

DIRECTIONS 3–6. Use red to trace the line that shows how to measure the length. Use blue to trace the line that shows how to measure the height. Talk about another way to measure the object.

© Houghton Mifflin Harcourt Publishing Company • Image Credits: (br) ©Stockbyte/Getty Images

Problem Solving • Applications Real World

7

DIRECTIONS **7.** Draw to show what you know about measuring an object in more than one way.

HOME ACTIVITY • Show your child an object in the house that can be easily measured by length, height, and weight. Ask him or her to describe the different ways to measure the object.

© Houghton Mifflin Harcourt Publishing Company

Name _____

Length, Height, and Weight

Learning Objective You will describe several ways to measure one object.

1

2

3

4

DIRECTIONS 1–4. Use red to trace the line that shows how to measure the length. Use blue to trace the line that shows how to measure the height. Talk about another way to measure the object.

© Houghton Mifflin Harcourt Publishing Company

Lesson Check

1

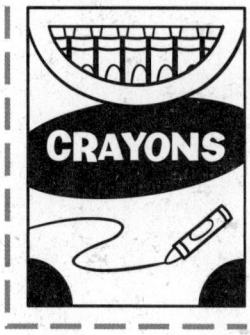

Spiral Review

2

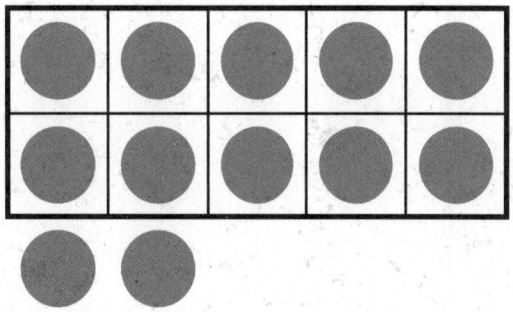

3

DIRECTIONS **1.** Use red to trace the line that shows how to measure the length. Use blue to trace the line that shows how to measure the height. **2.** Count and tell how many. Write the number. **3.** Which shape is a rectangle? Color the rectangle.

© Houghton Mifflin Harcourt Publishing Company

FOR MORE PRACTICE GO TO THE Personal Math Trainer

Name _____

Chapter 11 Review/Test

Personal Math Trainer
Online Assessment and Intervention

1

2

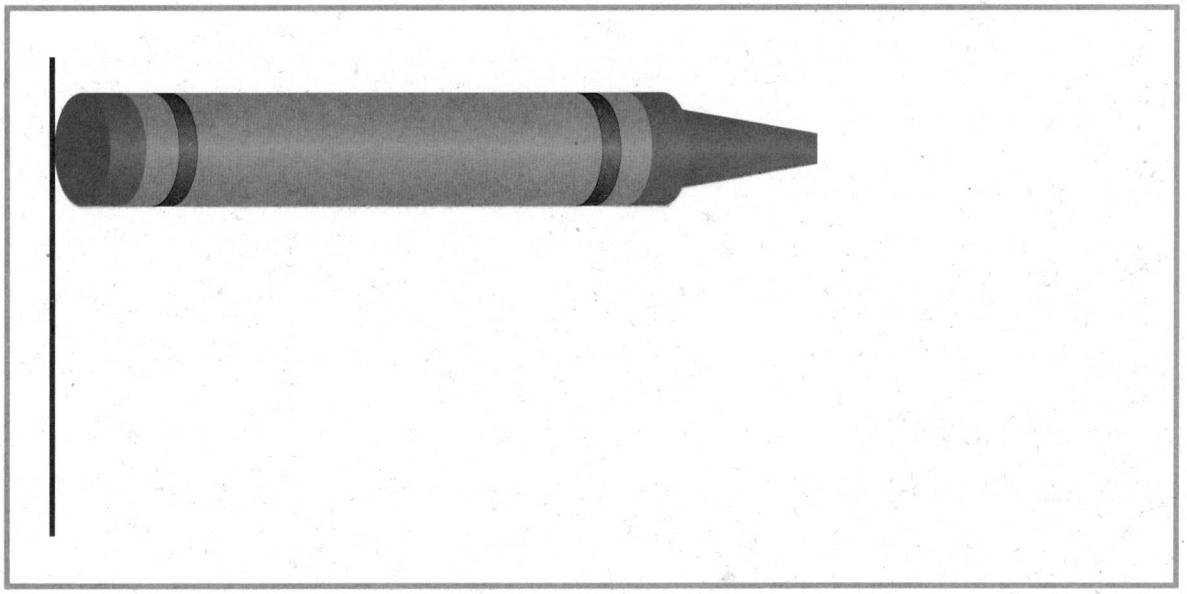

3

DIRECTIONS 1. Choose all the sets that have a green pencil that is longer than the orange pencil. 2. Draw a crayon that is shorter. 3. Circle the tree that is taller.

© Houghton Mifflin Harcourt Publishing Company

4

5

Personal Math Trainer

6 THINK SMARTER+

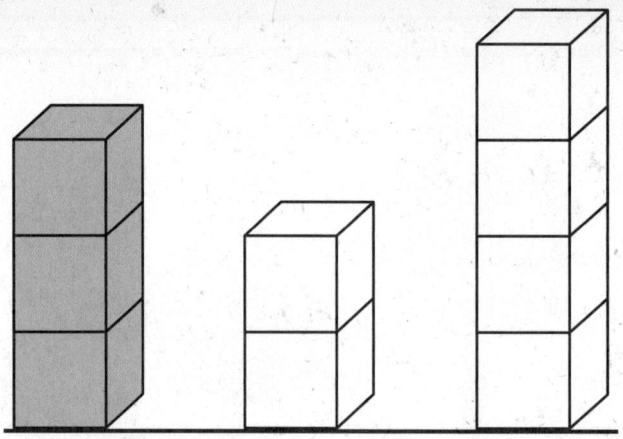

DIRECTIONS **4.** This tree is taller than another tree. Draw to show the other tree. **5.** Draw two pieces of yarn of different lengths. Draw a circle around the yarn that is longer. **6.** Which cube tower is shorter than the green cube tower? Color it blue. Which cube tower is taller than the green cube tower? Color it red.

© Houghton Mifflin Harcourt Publishing Company

Name _____

7

8

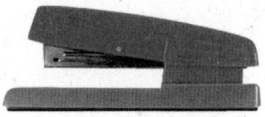

○ Yes ○ No

○ Yes ○ No

○ Yes ○ No

9 THINK SMARTER+

Personal Math Trainer

DIRECTIONS **7.** Circle all the objects that are lighter than the book. **8.** Is the object heavier than the tape dispenser? Choose Yes or No. **9.** Draw a line to show the height of the juice box. Draw a line to show the length of the lunchbox.

© Houghton Mifflin Harcourt Publishing Company • Image Credits: (tcr) ©Artville/Getty Images; (br) ©Stockbyte/Getty Images; (tc) ©Siede Preis/PhotoDisc/Getty Images

10

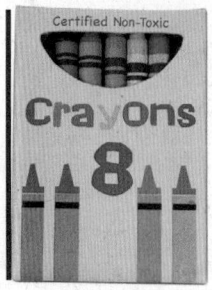

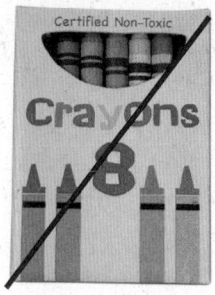

11

12

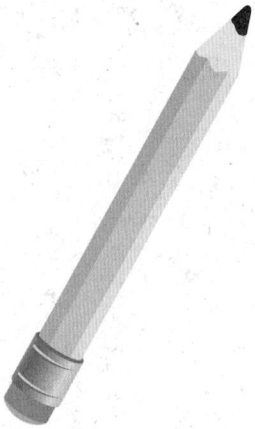

DIRECTIONS **10.** Choose all of the pictures that have lines that show how to measure height. **11.** Look at the objects. Mark an X on the lighter object. Circle the heavier object. **12.** Draw an object that is heavier than the pencil.

© Houghton Mifflin Harcourt Publishing Company • Image Credits: (cl) ©Siede Preis/PhotoDisc/Getty Images; (cr) ©Stockbyte/Getty Images

Chapter 12

Classify and Sort Data

Curious About Math with Curious George

Primary colors are blue, red, and yellow.

- How many primary colors is the girl sorting?

© Houghton Mifflin Harcourt Publishing Company • Image Credits: ©PhotoAlto/Laurence Mouton/Getty Images
Curious George by Margret and H.A. Rey. Copyright © 2010 by Houghton Mifflin Harcourt Publishing Company.
All rights reserved. The character Curious George®, including without limitation the character's name and the character's likenesses, are registered trademarks of Houghton Mifflin Harcourt Publishing Company.

Name _____

Show What You Know

Personal Math Trainer
Online Assessment and Intervention

Color and Shape

1

2

Compare Sets

3

_____

_____

_____

_____

_____

_____

4

_____

_____

_____

_____

_____

_____

This page checks understanding of important skills needed for success in Chapter 12.

DIRECTIONS 1. Circle the fruits that are red. 2. Circle the triangles. 3. Count and write how many in each set. Circle the set with more objects. 4. Count and write how many in each set. Circle the set with fewer objects.

© Houghton Mifflin Harcourt Publishing Company

Name _____

DIRECTIONS Tell what you know about the ladybugs. Some of the ladybugs are different. Circle those ladybugs and tell why they are different. Tell what you know about the butterflies.

GO DIGITAL
- Interactive Student Edition
- Multimedia *e*Glossary

© Houghton Mifflin Harcourt Publishing Company

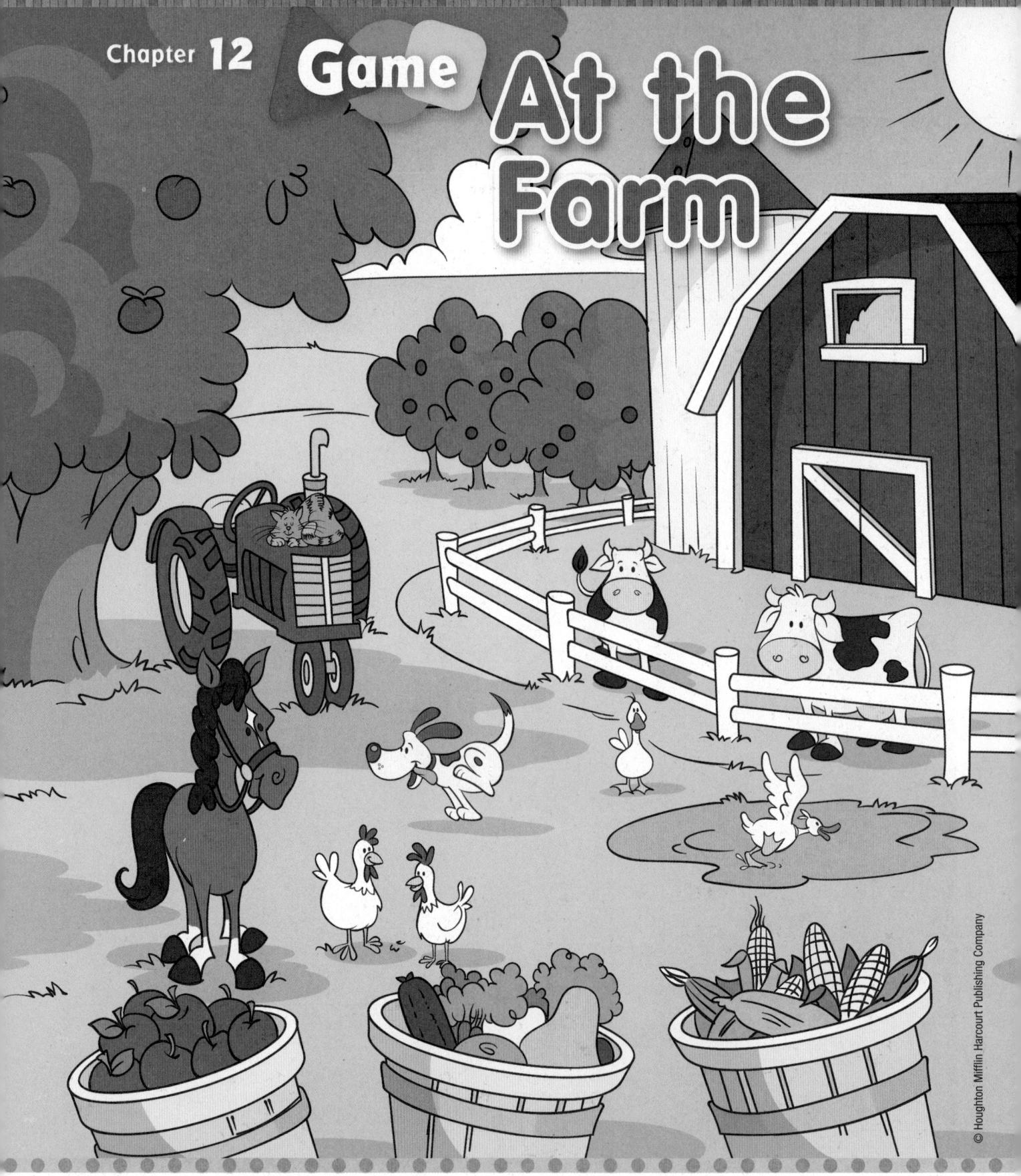

DIRECTIONS Use the picture to play with a partner. Decide who will go first. Player 1 looks at the picture, selects an object, and tells Player 2 the color of the object. Player 2 must guess what Player 1 sees. Once Player 2 guesses correctly, it is his or her turn to choose an object and have Player 1 guess.

Chapter 12 Vocabulary

big

grande

8

color (blue)

color (azul)

9

category

categoría

10

classify

clasificar

12

graph

gráfica

30

color (green)

color (verde)

32

color (red)

color (rojo)

53

shape

forma

61

© Houghton Mifflin Harcourt Publishing Company

blue

© Houghton Mifflin Harcourt Publishing Company

big

© Houghton Mifflin Harcourt Publishing Company
Credit: (red apple) ©Artville/Getty Images

apples

not apples

classify

© Houghton Mifflin Harcourt Publishing Company
Credit: (red apple) ©Artville/Getty Images; (toy boat) ©D. Hurst/Alamy; (toy truck) ©C Squared Studios/PhotoDisc/Getty Images

fruits

toys

category

© Houghton Mifflin Harcourt Publishing Company

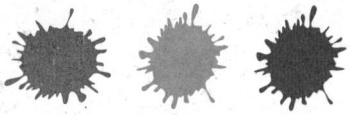

green

© Houghton Mifflin Harcourt Publishing Company

graph

© Houghton Mifflin Harcourt Publishing Company

shape

© Houghton Mifflin Harcourt Publishing Company

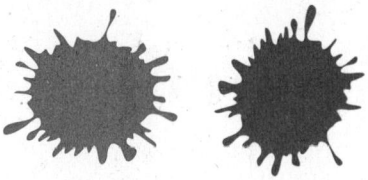

red

size tamaño 66	**small** pequeño 68
color (yellow) color (amarillo) 85	**zero** cero, ninguno 86

small

© Houghton Mifflin Harcourt Publishing Company

big

small

size

© Houghton Mifflin Harcourt Publishing Company

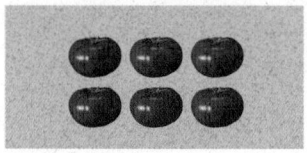

six tomatoes

zero tomatoes

© Houghton Mifflin Harcourt Publishing Company
Credit: ©Artville/Getty Images

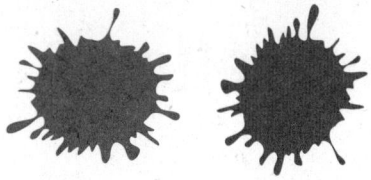

yellow

© Houghton Mifflin Harcourt Publishing Company

Game

Guess the Word

Word Box
red
blue
green
yellow
classify
category
shape
size
small
big
graph

Secret Words

Player 1					
Player 2					

DIRECTIONS Players take turns. A player chooses a secret word from the Word Box and then sets the timer. The player gives hints about the secret word. If the other player guesses the secret word before time runs out, he or she puts a connecting cube in the chart. The first player who has connecting cubes in all his or her boxes is the winner.

MATERIALS timer, connecting cubes for each player

© Houghton Mifflin Harcourt Publishing Company • Image Credits: (bg) ©PhotoDisc/Getty Images; (t) ©Jamie Farrant/iStockphoto.com

The Write Way

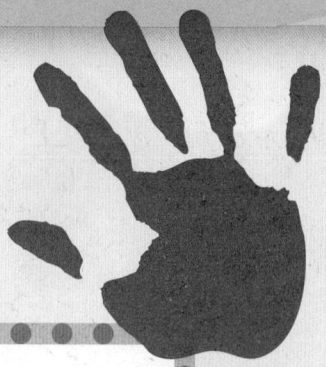

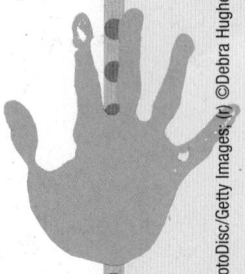

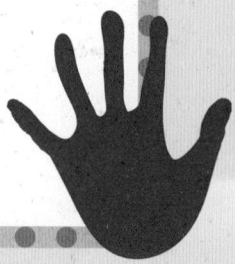

© Houghton Mifflin Harcourt Publishing Company • Image Credits: (bg) ©PhotoDisc/Getty Images; (t) ©Debra Hughes/Shutterstock

DIRECTIONS Choose one idea. • Draw to show how to classify objects by size. • Draw to show a graph. **Reflect** Be ready to tell about your drawing.

Name _____

Algebra • Classify and Count by Color

Essential Question How can you classify and count objects by color?

Learning Objective You will sort, classify, and count objects by the attribute of color.

Listen and Draw

not

DIRECTIONS Choose a color. Use that color crayon to color the clouds. Sort and classify a handful of shapes into a set of that color and a set of not that color. Draw and color the shapes.

© Houghton Mifflin Harcourt Publishing Company

Share and Show

1

red	blue
yellow	green

DIRECTIONS 1. Place shapes as shown. Sort and classify the shapes by the category of color. Draw and color the shapes in each category.

© Houghton Mifflin Harcourt Publishing Company

Name _____

2

1

red | blue

yellow | green

_____

_ _ _ _ _

_____

3

2

red | blue

yellow | green

_____

_ _ _ _ _

_____

4

3

red | blue

yellow | green

_____

_ _ _ _ _

_____

DIRECTIONS Look at the categories of color in Exercise 1. Count how many in each category. **2.** Circle the categories of color that have one shape. Write the number. **3.** Circle the category that has two shapes. Write the number. **4.** Circle the category that has three shapes. Write the number.

© Houghton Mifflin Harcourt Publishing Company

Problem Solving • Applications

5

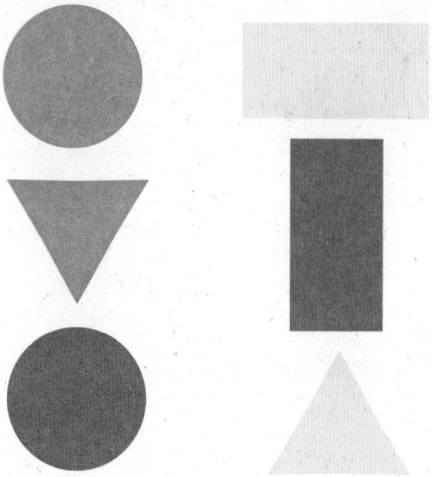

6

DIRECTIONS **5.** Ava placed her shapes as shown. How did she sort and classify her shapes? Draw one more shape in each category. **6.** Draw to show what you know about sorting and classifying by color.

HOME ACTIVITY • Provide your child with different colors of the same objects, such as straws, socks, or toys. Ask him or her to sort and classify the objects into two sets, a set of all one color and a set of all the other colors.

© Houghton Mifflin Harcourt Publishing Company

Name _____

Algebra • Classify and Count by Color

Learning Objective You will sort, classify, and count objects by the attribute of color.

1

yellow	red

2

3

yellow	red

_____

_____

DIRECTIONS 1. Place a yellow square, red triangle, red rectangle, yellow square, and red triangle at the top of the page as shown. Sort and classify the shapes by the category of color. Draw and color the shapes in each category. 2. Look at the categories in Exercise 1. Count how many in each category. Circle the category that has 3 shapes. Write the number.

© Houghton Mifflin Harcourt Publishing Company

Lesson Check

1

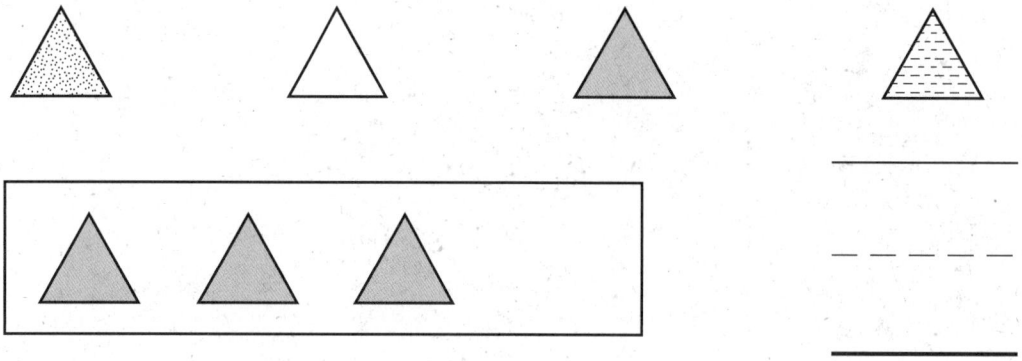

Spiral Review

2

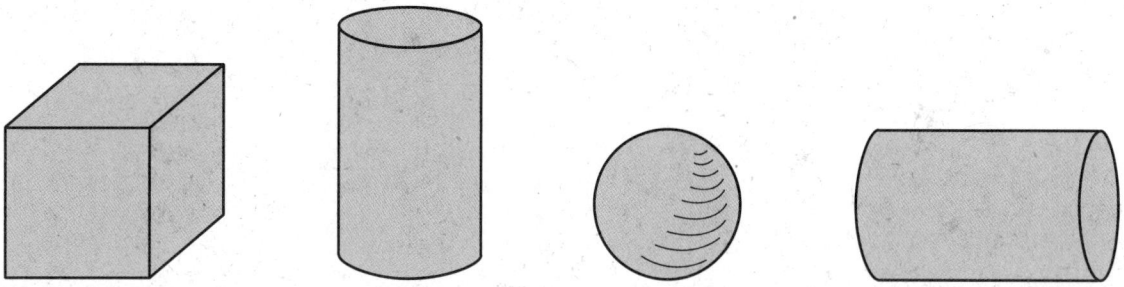

3

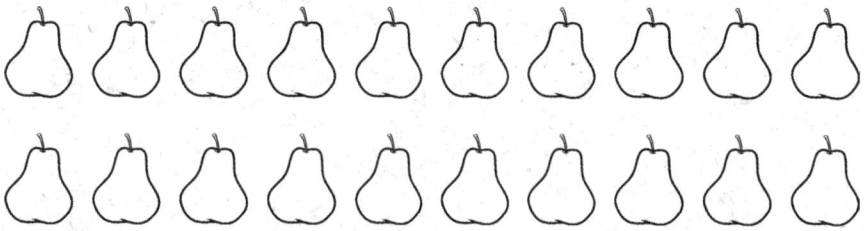

DIRECTIONS **1.** Look at the set of shapes. Which shape belongs in the same category? Draw that shape in the box and color it. How many shapes are in the category now? Write the number. **2.** Which shape does not stack? Mark an X on the shape. **3.** Count and tell how many pieces of fruit. Write the number.

FOR MORE PRACTICE GO TO THE **Personal Math Trainer**

© Houghton Mifflin Harcourt Publishing Company

Name _____

Algebra • Classify and Count by Shape

Essential Question How can you classify and count objects by shape?

Learning Objective You will sort, classify, and count objects by the attribute of shape.

Listen and Draw

	not

DIRECTIONS Choose a shape. Draw the shape at the top of each side. Sort and classify a handful of shapes into a set of the shape you chose and a set that is not that shape. Draw and color the shapes.

© Houghton Mifflin Harcourt Publishing Company

Share and Show

1

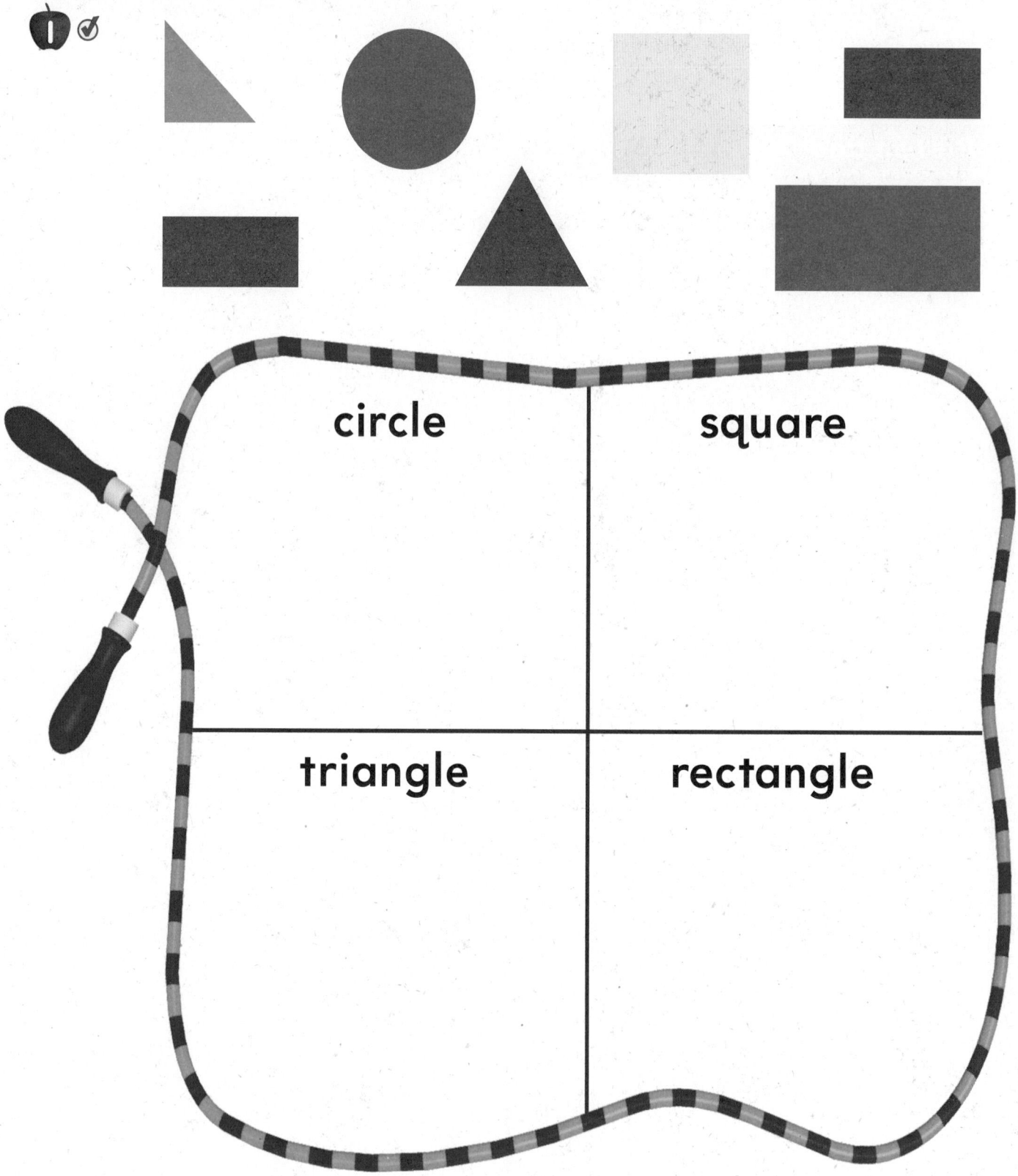

DIRECTIONS 1. Place shapes as shown. Sort and classify the shapes by the category of shape. Draw and color the shapes in each category.

© Houghton Mifflin Harcourt Publishing Company

Name _____

2

1

circle | square

triangle | rectangle

_____

_ _ _ _ _

_____

3

2

circle | square

triangle | rectangle

_____

_ _ _ _ _

_____

4

3

circle | square

triangle | rectangle

_____

_ _ _ _ _

_____

DIRECTIONS Look at the categories of shapes in Exercise 1. Count how many in each category. **2.** Circle the categories of shapes that have one shape. Write the number. **3.** Circle the category that has two shapes. Write the number. **4.** Circle the category that has three shapes. Write the number.

© Houghton Mifflin Harcourt Publishing Company

Problem Solving • Applications

WRITE Math

5

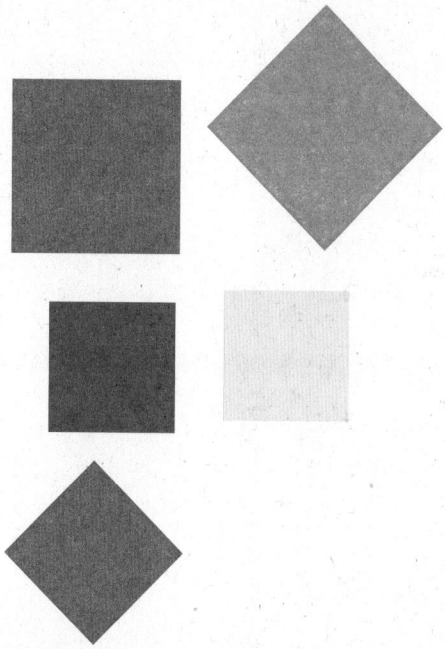

6

DIRECTIONS **5.** Brandon used his shapes. How did he sort and classify his shapes? Draw one more shape in each category. **6.** Using the same shapes, draw to show what you know about sorting and classifying by shape in a different way.

HOME ACTIVITY • Have your child sort objects in a house into categories of shape.

© Houghton Mifflin Harcourt Publishing Company

Name _____

Algebra • Classify and Count by Shape

Learning Objective You will sort, classify, and count objects by the attribute of shape.

1

triangle	circle

2

2

triangle	circle

_____

_____

_____

DIRECTIONS **1.** Place a green triangle, blue circle, red triangle, and blue circle at the top of the page as shown. Sort and classify the shapes by the category of shape. Draw and color the shapes in each category. **2.** Look at the categories in Exercise 1. Count how many in each category. Circle the categories that have two shapes. Write the number.

© Houghton Mifflin Harcourt Publishing Company

Lesson Check

1

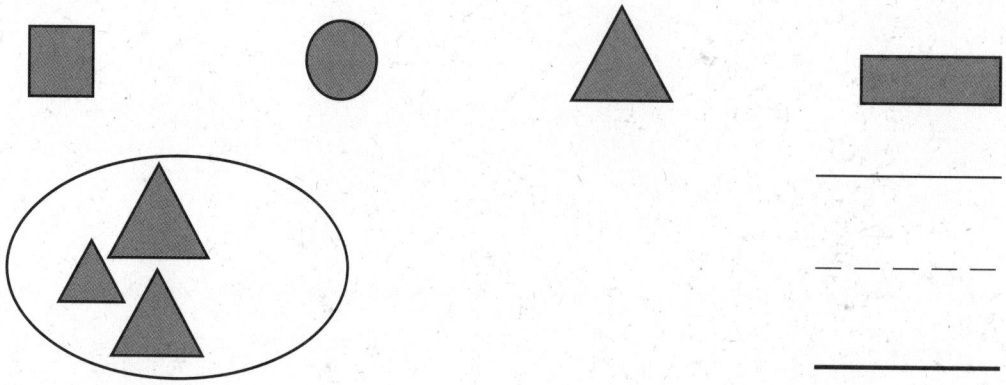

Spiral Review

2

3

5 = _____ + _____

DIRECTIONS **1.** Look at the set of shapes. Which shape belongs in the same category? Draw that shape in the oval. How many shapes are in the category now? Write the number. **2.** Find two crayons. Place one end of each crayon on the line. Compare the lengths. Draw the crayons. Say *longer than*, *shorter than*, or *about the same length* to describe the lengths. Circle both crayons if they are about the same length. Circle the longer crayon if one crayon is longer than the other. **3.** Complete the addition sentence to show the numbers that match the cube train.

FOR MORE PRACTICE GO TO THE Personal Math Trainer

© Houghton Mifflin Harcourt Publishing Company

Name _____

HANDS ON
Lesson 12.3

Algebra • Classify and Count by Size

Essential Question How can you classify and count objects by size?

Learning Objective You will sort, classify, and count objects by the attribute of size.

Listen and Draw

big	small

DIRECTIONS Sort and classify a handful of shapes by size. Draw and color the shapes.

© Houghton Mifflin Harcourt Publishing Company

Share and Show

1

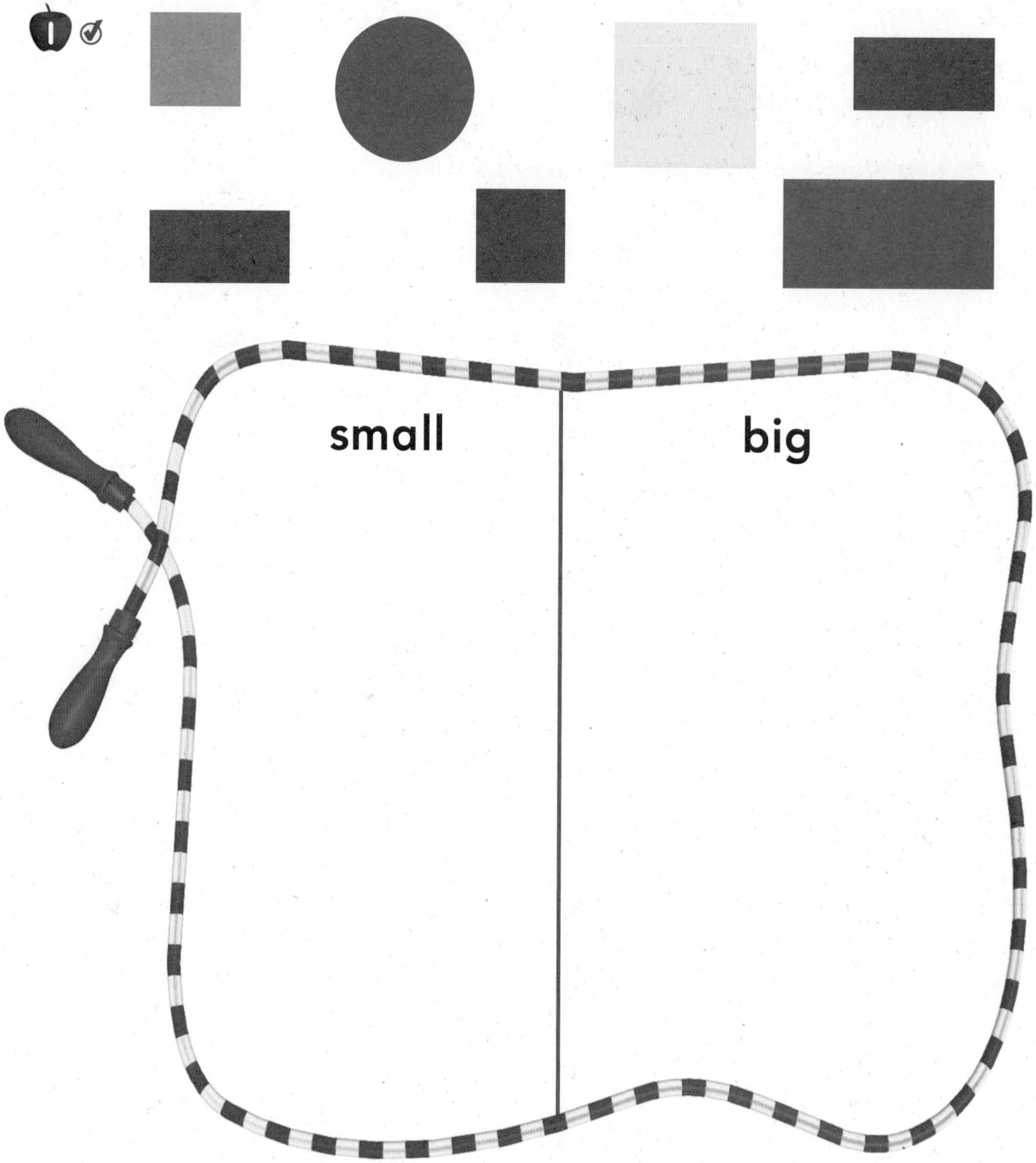

DIRECTIONS **1.** Place shapes as shown. Sort and classify the shapes by the category of size. Draw and color the shapes in each category.

© Houghton Mifflin Harcourt Publishing Company

Name _____

2

4

small

big

_____

_____

3

3

small

big

_____

_____

© Houghton Mifflin Harcourt Publishing Company

DIRECTIONS Look at the categories of size in Exercise 1. Count how many in each category. **2.** Circle the category that has four per category. Write the number. **3.** Circle the category that has three per category. Write the number.

HOME ACTIVITY • Have your child sort objects in a house into categories of size.

Mid-Chapter Checkpoint

Personal Math Trainer
Online Assessment and Intervention

Concepts and Skills

1

2

3 THINK SMARTER

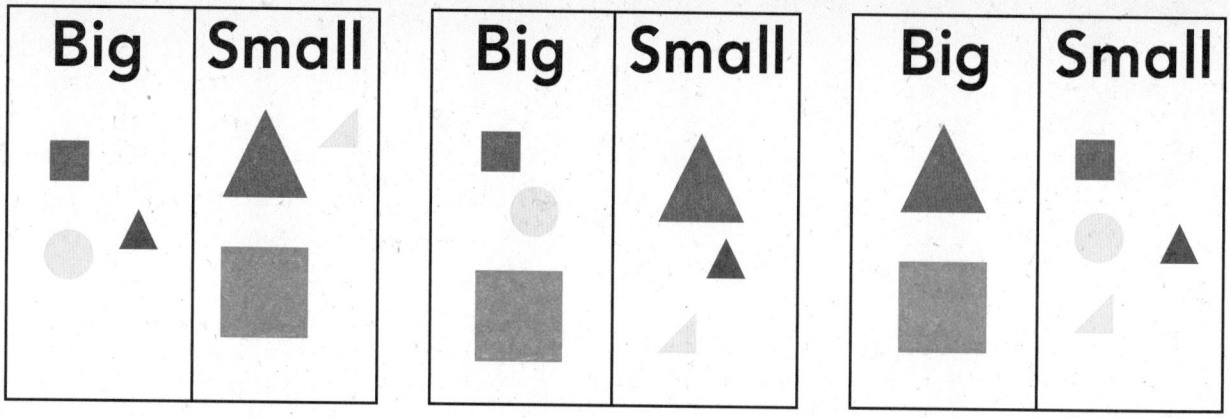

DIRECTIONS 1. Look at the set at the beginning of the row. Circle the shape that belongs in that set. 2. Look at the shape at the beginning of the row. Mark an X on the set in which the shape belongs. 3. Mark under the chart that shows the shapes correctly classified.

© Houghton Mifflin Harcourt Publishing Company

Name _____

Algebra • Classify and Count by Size

Learning Objective You will sort, classify, and count objects by the attribute of size.

1

small	big

2

small	big	
		_____
		_____

DIRECTIONS 1. Place a yellow square, blue circle, red rectangle, and blue rectangle at the top of the page as shown. Sort and classify the shapes by the category of size. Draw and color the shapes in each category. 2. Look at the categories in Exercise 1. Count how many in each category. Circle the category that has one per category. Write the number.

© Houghton Mifflin Harcourt Publishing Company

Lesson Check

1

small	big

Spiral Review

2

3

DIRECTIONS 1. Sort and classify the shapes by the category of size. Draw the shapes in each category. 2. How many flat surfaces does the cylinder have? Write the number. 3. Sarah makes a five-cube train. She takes the cube train apart to show how many cubes are gray. Trace and write to show the subtraction sentence for Sarah's cube train.

FOR MORE PRACTICE GO TO THE Personal Math Trainer

© Houghton Mifflin Harcourt Publishing Company

Name _____

Make a Concrete Graph

Essential Question How can you make a graph to count objects that have been classified into categories?

Learning Objective You will make a graph to count objects that have been classified into categories.

Listen and Draw

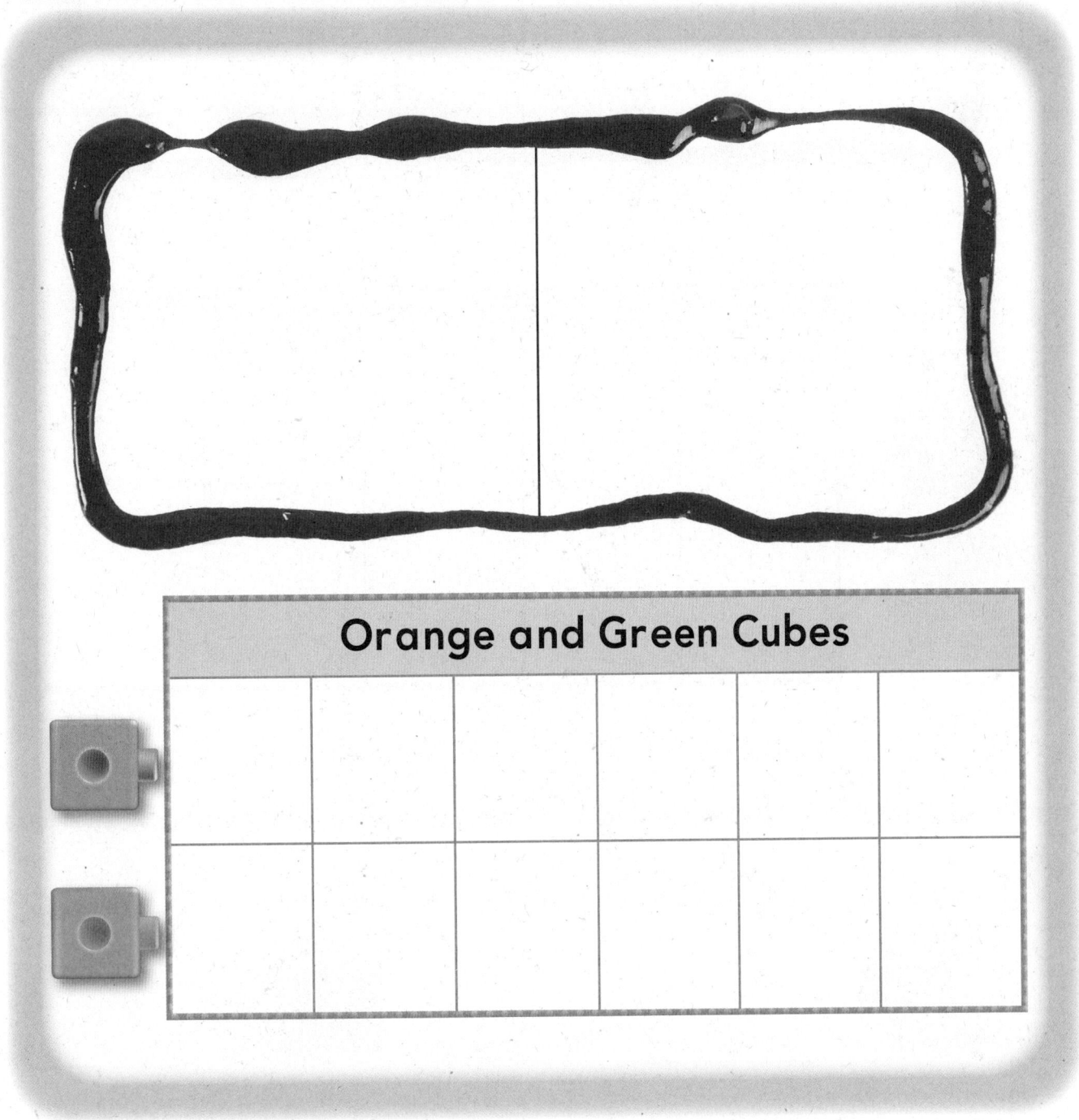

DIRECTIONS Place a handful of orange and green cubes on the workspace. Sort and classify the cubes by the category of color. Move the cubes to the graph by category. Draw and color the cubes. Tell a friend how many in each category.

© Houghton Mifflin Harcourt Publishing Company

Share and Show

1

2

Red and Blue Cubes				

3

_____

_____

_____

_____

_____

_____

DIRECTIONS 1. Place a handful of red and blue cubes on the workspace. Sort and classify the cubes by category. 2. Move the cubes to the graph. Draw and color the cubes. 3. Write how many of each cube.

© Houghton Mifflin Harcourt Publishing Company

Name _____

4

5

Green Circles and Triangles

6

_____

_____

_____

_____

_____

_____

DIRECTIONS **4.** Place a handful of green circles and triangles on the workspace. Sort and classify the shapes by category. **5.** Move the shapes to the graph. Draw and color the shapes. **6.** Write how many of each shape.

© Houghton Mifflin Harcourt Publishing Company

Problem Solving • Applications (Real World)

7

My Graph				

_____

_____

_____

_____

DIRECTIONS 7. Use five cubes of two colors. Color the cubes to show the categories. Draw and color to show what you know about making a graph with those cubes. How many are in each category? Write the numbers.

HOME ACTIVITY • Have your child tell about the graph that he or she made on this page.

© Houghton Mifflin Harcourt Publishing Company

Name _____

Make a Concrete Graph

Learning Objective You will make a graph to count objects that have been classified into categories.

1

2

Circles and Triangles					

3

_____

_____

_____

_____

_____

_____

DIRECTIONS **1.** Place a handful of green circles and triangles on the workspace. Sort and classify the shapes by category. **2.** Move the shapes to the graph. Draw and color the shapes. **3.** Write how many of each shape.

© Houghton Mifflin Harcourt Publishing Company

Lesson Check

1

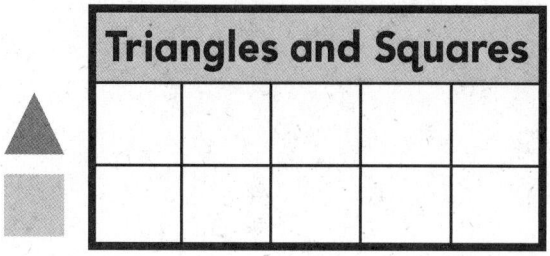

Spiral Review

2

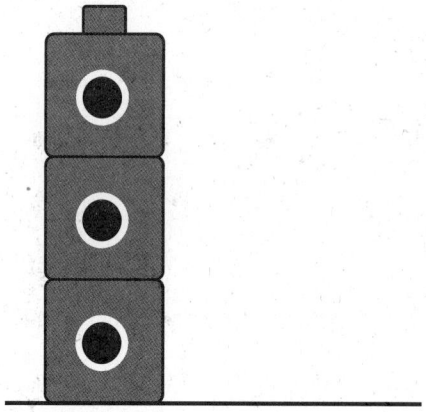

3

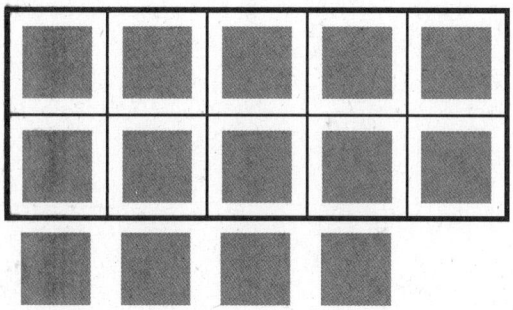

DIRECTIONS **1.** Look at the shapes. Draw and color the shapes in the graph. Write how many of each shape. **2.** Make a cube train that is about the same height as the cube train shown. Draw and color the cube train. **3.** How many tiles are there? Write the number.

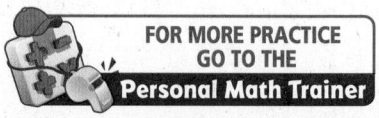

© Houghton Mifflin Harcourt Publishing Company

Name _____

Problem Solving • Read a Graph

Essential Question How can you read a graph to count objects that have been classified into categories?

Learning Objective You will read a graph and count objects that have been classified into categories to solve problems.

Unlock the Problem

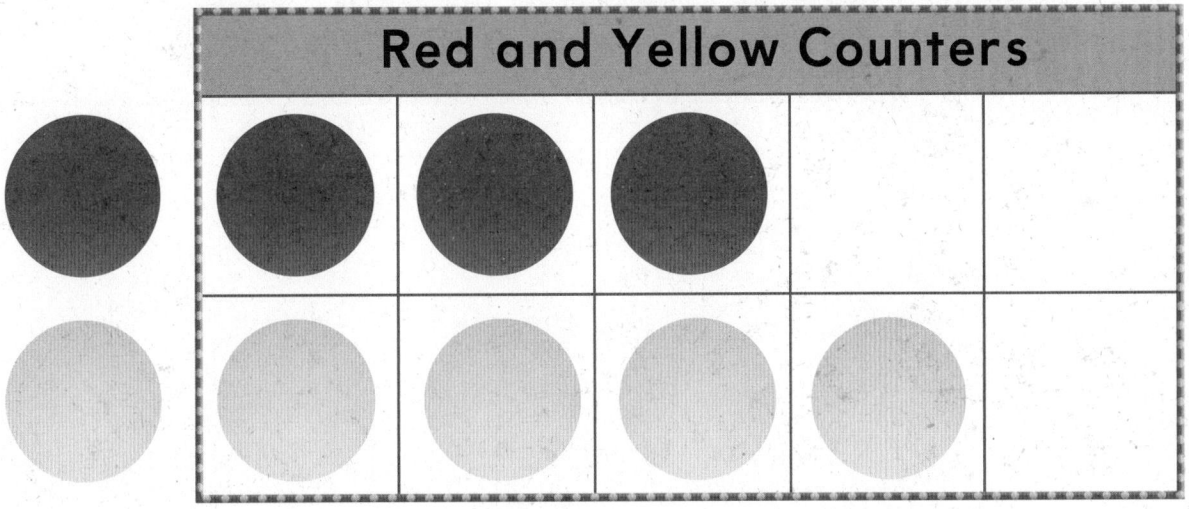

DIRECTIONS Erin made a graph of her counters. How many counters are in each category? Trace the numbers. Trace the circle to show which category has more counters.

© Houghton Mifflin Harcourt Publishing Company

Try Another Problem

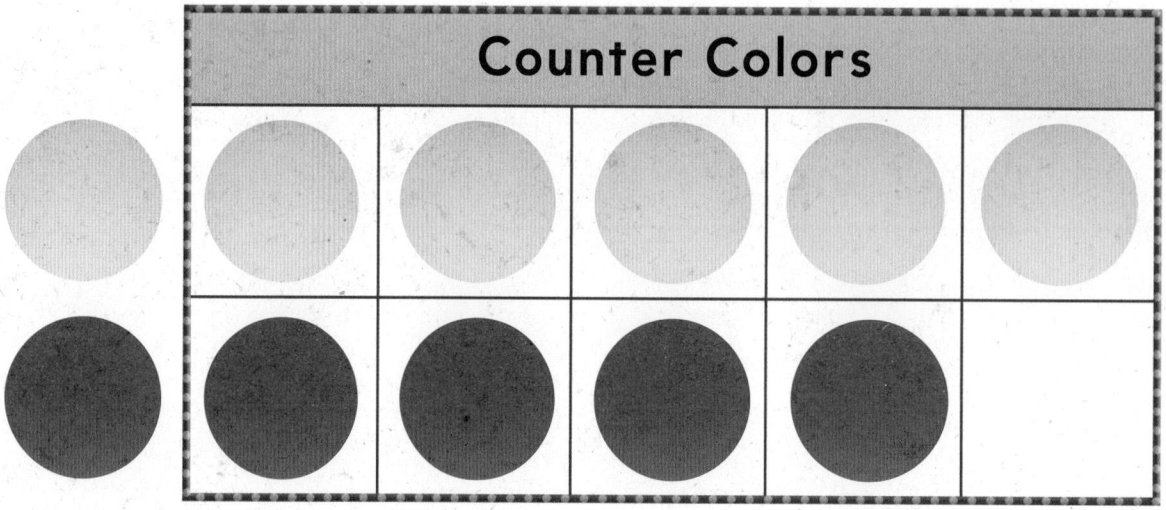

1

2

DIRECTIONS 1. Billy made a graph showing his counters. Color the counters to show his categories. How many counters are in each category? Write the numbers. 2. Circle the category that has more counters on the graph.

© Houghton Mifflin Harcourt Publishing Company

Name _____

Share and Show

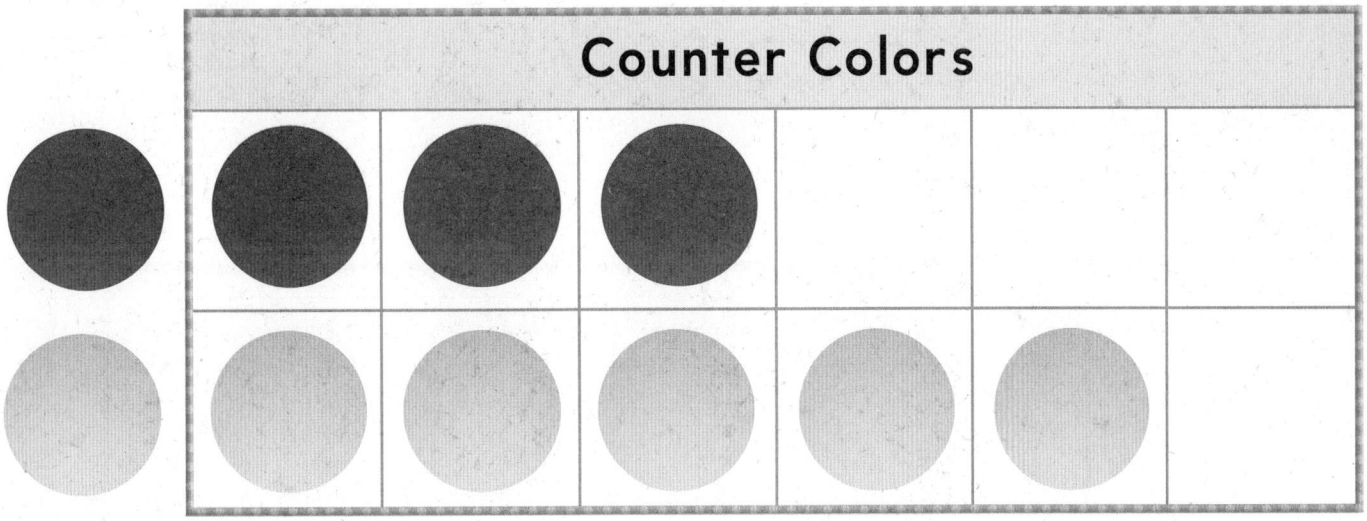

3 ✓

4 ✓

DIRECTIONS **3.** Rong made a graph of her counters. Color the counters to show her categories. How many counters are in each category? Write the numbers.
4. Circle the category that has fewer counters on the graph.

© Houghton Mifflin Harcourt Publishing Company

On Your Own Real World

WRITE Math

5

Cube Colors				

_____

_____

_____

_____

_____

_____

DIRECTIONS **5.** Brian has more blue cubes than red cubes. Draw and color to show his cubes on the graph. Count how many in each category. Write the numbers.

HOME ACTIVITY • Have your child tell about the graph he or she made on this page. Ask him or her which category has more cubes and which category has fewer cubes.

© Houghton Mifflin Harcourt Publishing Company

Name _____

Read a Graph

Learning Objective You will read a graph and count objects that have been classified into categories to solve problems.

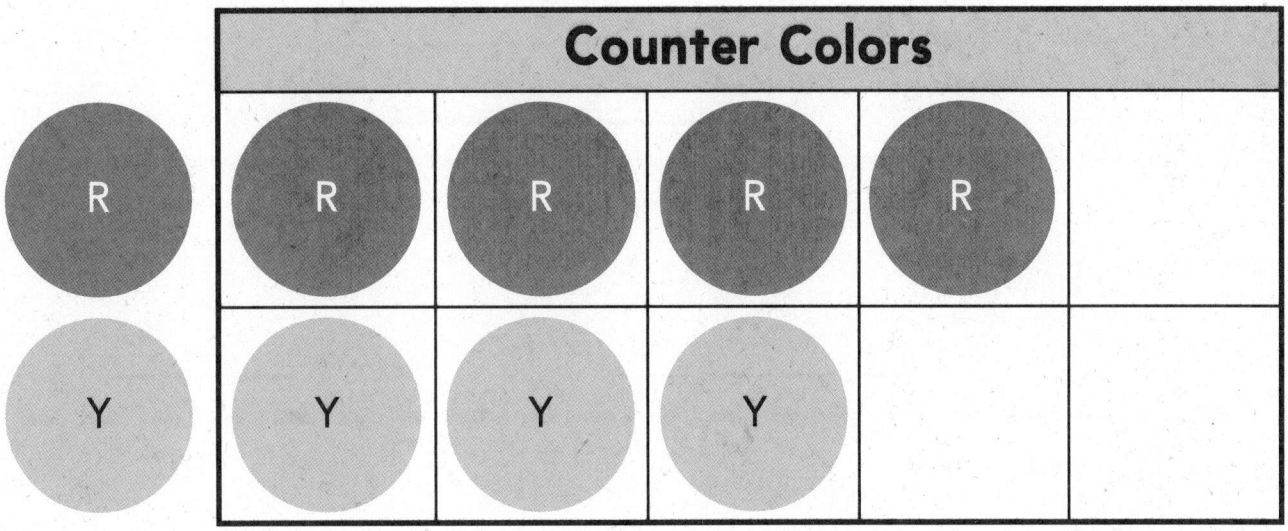

1

_____

_____

2

R

Y

DIRECTIONS 1. Color the counters to show the categories. R is for red, and Y is for yellow. How many counters are in each category? Write the numbers. 2. Circle the category that has more counters on the graph.

© Houghton Mifflin Harcourt Publishing Company

Lesson Check

1

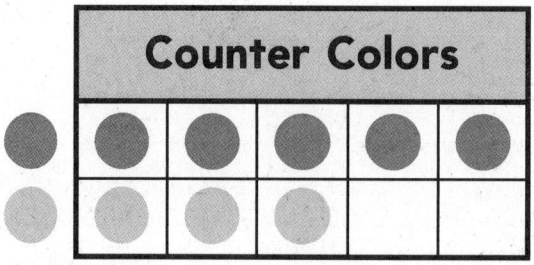

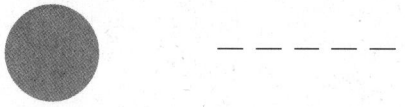

Spiral Review

2

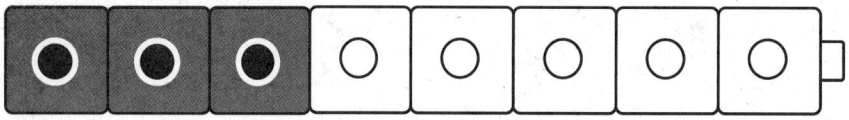

8 = ___ + ___

3

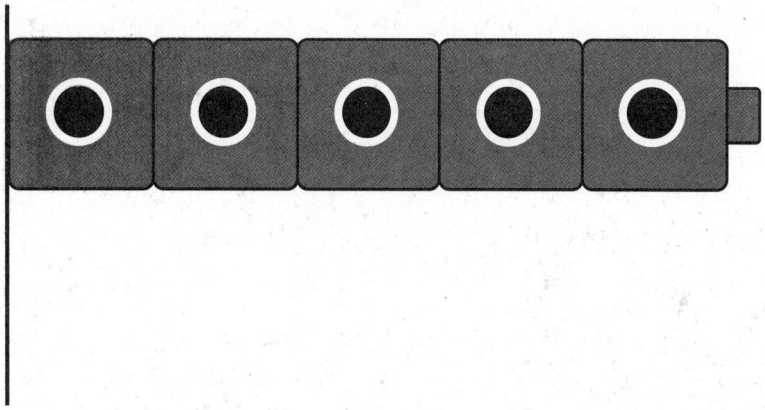

DIRECTIONS 1. How many counters are in each category? Write the numbers. Circle the category that has more counters. 2. Complete the addition sentence to show the numbers that match the cube train. 3. Make a cube train that is about the same length as the cube train shown. Draw and color the cube train.

© Houghton Mifflin Harcourt Publishing Company

Name _____

Chapter 12 Review/Test

1

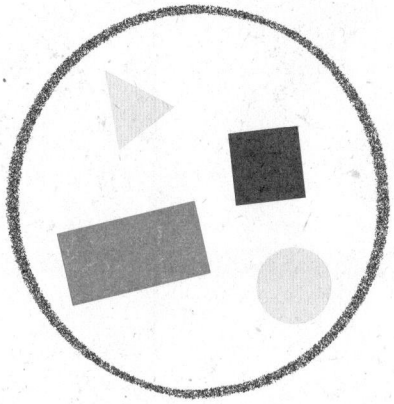

2

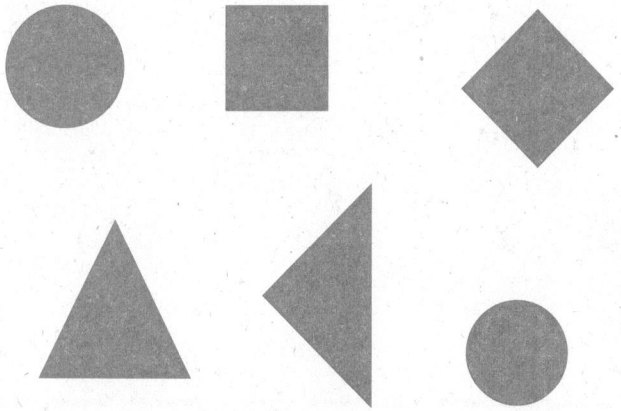

3

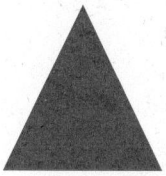

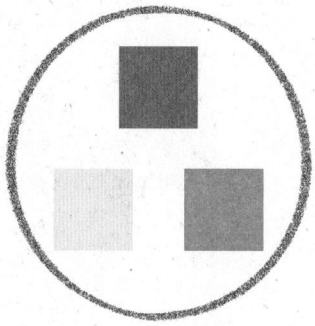

DIRECTIONS 1. Lin sorted some shapes into categories by color. Look at the shape at the beginning of the row. Mark an X on the category that shows where the shape belongs. 2. Draw and color a shape that belongs in this category. 3. Look at the shape at the beginning of the row. Mark under all of the categories the shape can belong.

© Houghton Mifflin Harcourt Publishing Company

4

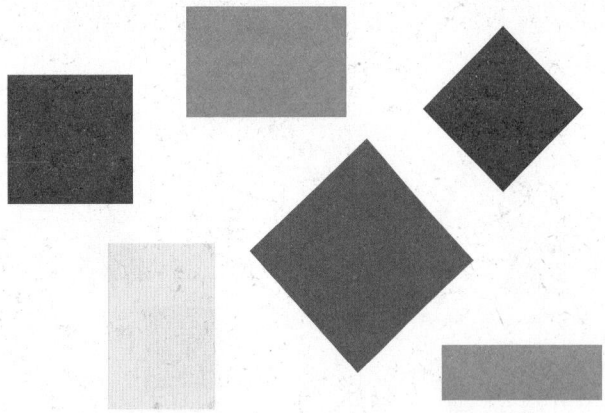

5 THINK SMARTER+

Personal Math Trainer

big _____

small _____

6

Big	Small

○

Big	Small

○

DIRECTIONS **4.** Draw and color a shape that belongs in this category. **5.** Mark an X on each big shape. Write how many big objects. Draw a circle around each of the small objects. Write how many small objects. **6.** Mark under the chart that shows the shapes correctly classified.

© Houghton Mifflin Harcourt Publishing Company

Name _____

Personal Math Trainer

7 THINK SMARTER+

Triangles and Circles				

_____ _____

_____ _____

8

Blue Squares and Circles					

DIRECTIONS **7.** Sort and classify the shapes by category. Draw each shape on the graph. Write how many of each shape. **8.** Jake sorted some shapes. Then he made a graph. Count how many shapes there are in each category. Mark an X on the category that has more shapes.

© Houghton Mifflin Harcourt Publishing Company

9

Chart A				

color	Yes ○	No ○
size	Yes ○	No ○
shape	Yes ○	No ○

10

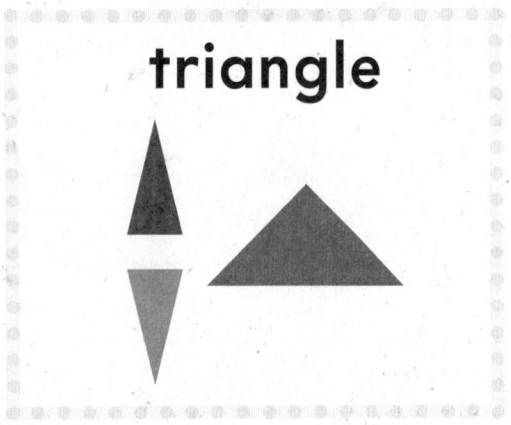

○

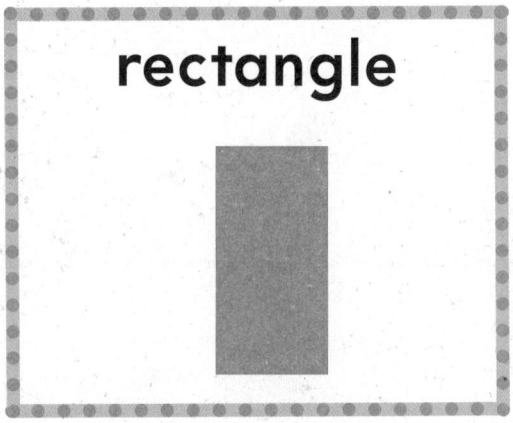

○

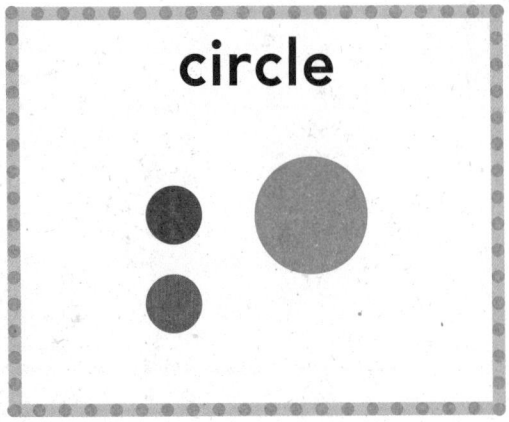

○

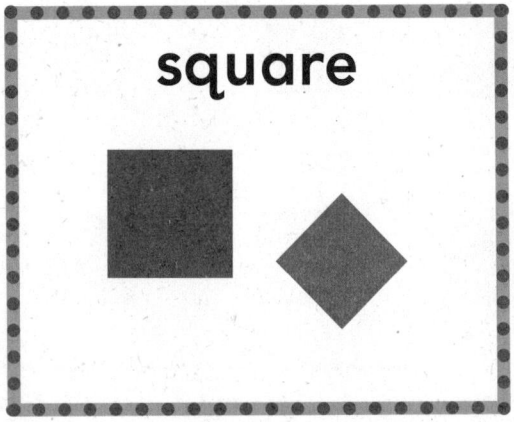

○

DIRECTIONS **9.** Is this chart sorted by color, size, and shape? Choose Yes or No. **10.** Choose all of the sets with the same number of objects.

© Houghton Mifflin Harcourt Publishing Company

Name _____

Our Senses

Develop Concepts

Use with *ScienceFusion* pages 1–4.

1

2

3

4

DIRECTIONS 1. Draw one object you can hear. 2. Draw two objects you can smell. 3. Draw three objects you can see. 4. Draw four objects you can taste.

© Houghton Mifflin Harcourt Publishing Company

Sum It Up!

see

smell

taste

touch

hear

© Houghton Mifflin Harcourt Publishing Company

DIRECTIONS Draw to show what you know about your senses using popcorn.

Name _____

Recycling Paper

Develop Concepts

Use with *ScienceFusion* pages 103–104.

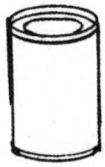

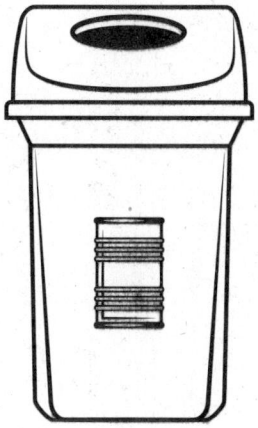

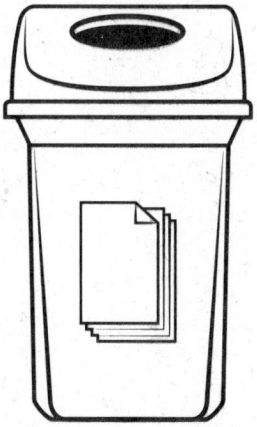

DIRECTIONS Draw a line from the object to its container.

© Houghton Mifflin Harcourt Publishing Company

Sum It Up!

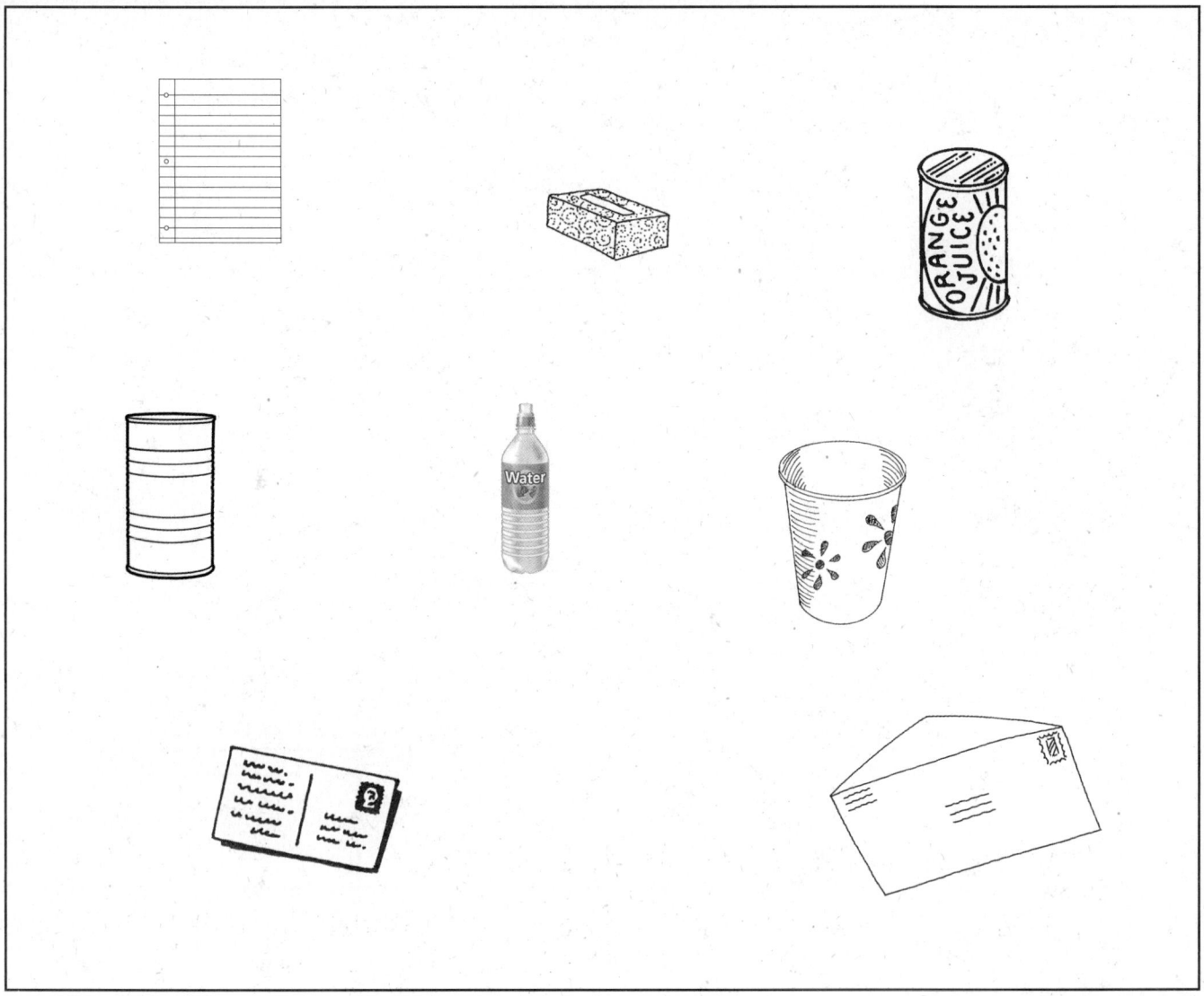

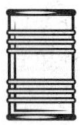

_____

_____

_____

_____

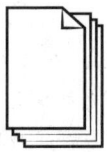

_____

_____

DIRECTIONS Count the metal cans, the objects made of paper, and the plastic bottles. Write how many of each object. Circle the number that is the greatest.

STEM 4

© Houghton Mifflin Harcourt Publishing Company

Name _____

Rocks

Develop Concepts

Use with *ScienceFusion* pages 63–66.

1 _____

_ _ _ _ _ _ _

_____ rocks

2 _____

_ _ _ _ _ _ _

I found _____ rocks.

DIRECTIONS 1. These rocks have different sizes, shapes, and textures. Count the rocks. Write how many. 2. Find some rocks. Write how many rocks you found.

© Houghton Mifflin Harcourt Publishing Company • (tl)©Artville/Getty Images; (tc) ©Thomas Northcut/Getty Images; (tr) ©funkyfood London - Paul Williams/Alamy; (bl) ©Getty Images/PhotoDisc

Sum It Up!

3 _____

_____ rocks in the sandbox

4 _____

_____ rocks outside the sandbox

5 _____

_____ rocks in all

DIRECTIONS 3. Count the rocks in the sandbox. Write how many. 4. Count the rocks outside the sandbox. Write how many. 5. Count all the rocks in the picture. Write how many.

© Houghton Mifflin Harcourt Publishing Company

Name _____

Living and Nonliving

Develop Concepts

Use with *ScienceFusion* pages 105–108.

1

2

3

DIRECTIONS 1. Draw a picture of a living thing. **2.** Draw a picture of a nonliving thing. **3.** Draw a picture of a basic need of a living thing.

© Houghton Mifflin Harcourt Publishing Company

Sum It Up!

_____ living things

_____ nonliving things

DIRECTIONS Circle each living thing. Mark an X on each nonliving thing. Write how many living things. Write how many nonliving things.

© Houghton Mifflin Harcourt Publishing Company

Name _____

Aquarium Design

Design It: Model Terrarium

Use with *ScienceFusion* pages 137–138.

5 + 3 = 8

DIRECTIONS Use two colors to color objects in the terrarium that models the addition sentence.

© Houghton Mifflin Harcourt Publishing Company

Develop Concepts

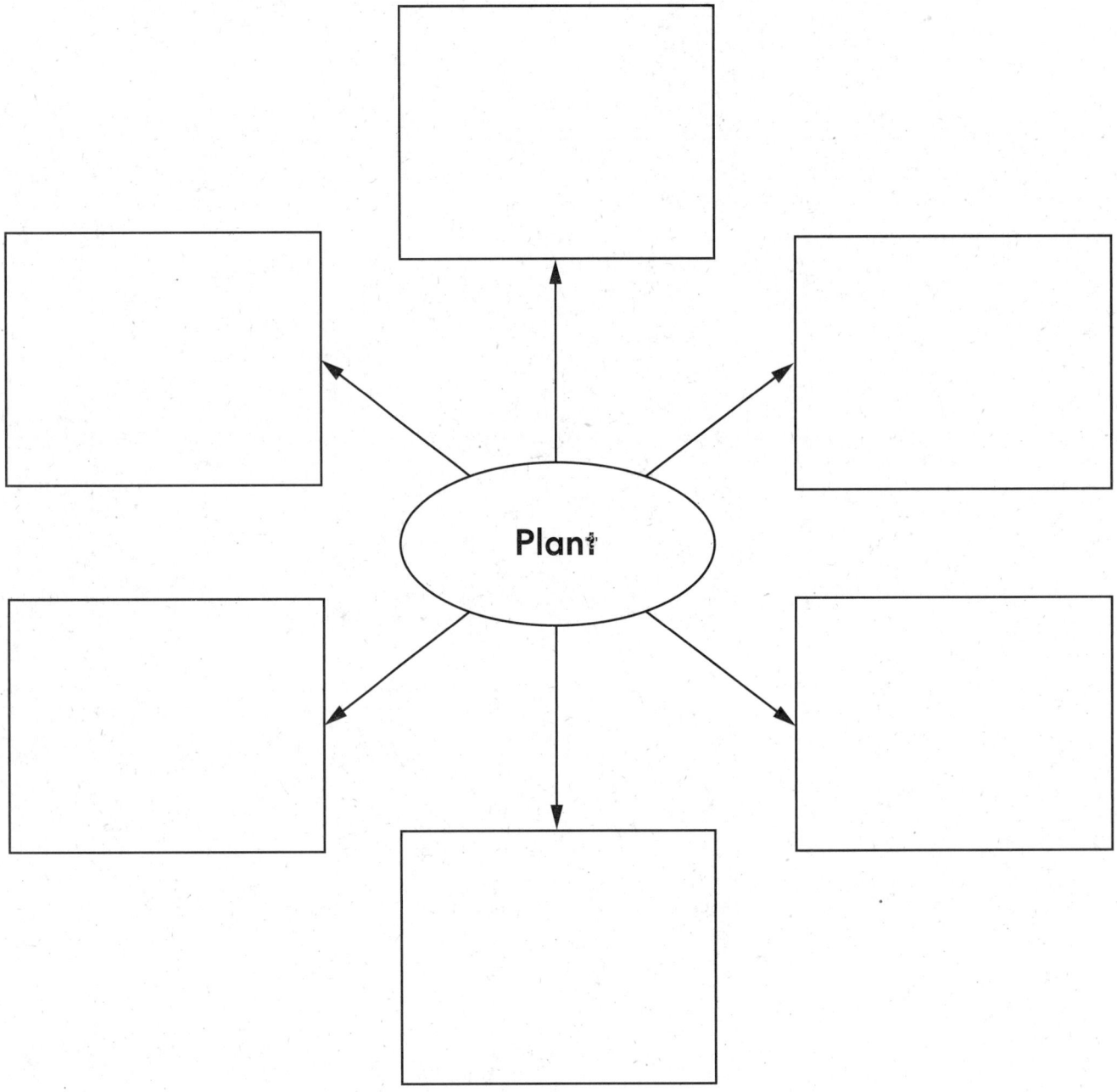

DIRECTIONS Describe the basic needs of a terrarium.

© Houghton Mifflin Harcourt Publishing Company

Name _____

Many Animals

Develop Concepts

Use with *ScienceFusion* pages 109–112.

Animals with Different Coverings

1

feathers	

2

scales	

3

fur	

DIRECTIONS 1–3. Count how many. Write the number.

© Houghton Mifflin Harcourt Publishing Company

Sum It Up!

4 _____

_____ animals with fur

_____

5 _____

_____ animals with feathers

_____

6 _____ - _____ = _____

DIRECTIONS **4.** Count the animals with fur. Write the number. **5.** Count the animals with feathers. Write the number. **6.** Complete the subtraction sentence that shows the difference between the two numbers.

© Houghton Mifflin Harcourt Publishing Company

Name _____

Plants Grow and Change

Develop Concepts

Use with *ScienceFusion* pages 133–136.

1

DIRECTIONS 1. Draw to show what this seedling might grow into.

© Houghton Mifflin Harcourt Publishing Company

Sum It Up!

2

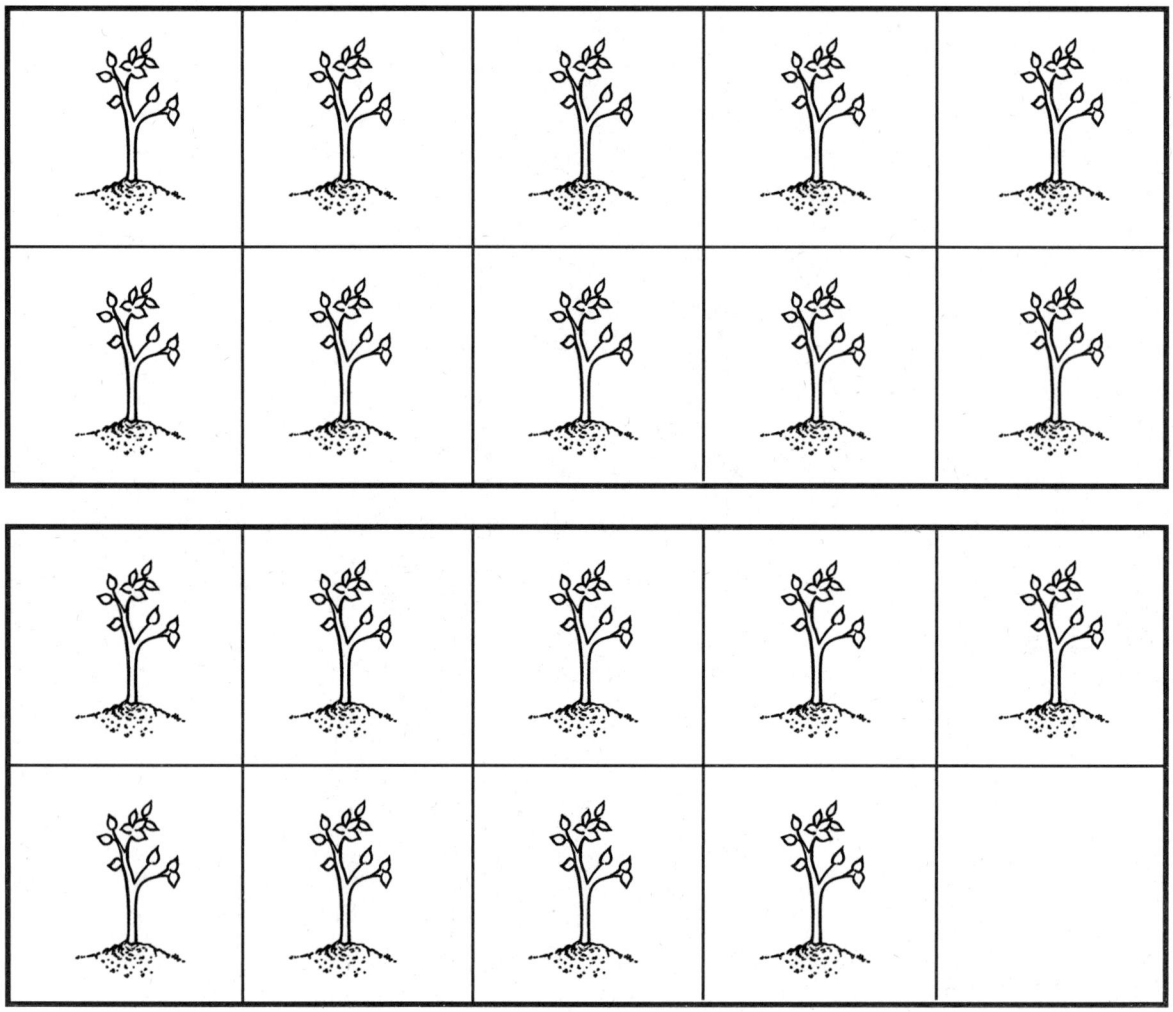

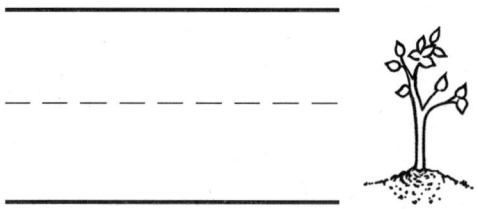

DIRECTIONS **2.** Count the seedlings. Write the number.

© Houghton Mifflin Harcourt Publishing Company

Name _____

Night Sky

Develop Concepts

Use with *ScienceFusion* pages 99–102.

day night

© Houghton Mifflin Harcourt Publishing Company

DIRECTIONS Circle the word that tells when we see stars in the sky.

Sum It Up!

_____

_ _ _ _ _ _ _ _ _

_____ stars

© Houghton Mifflin Harcourt Publishing Company

DIRECTIONS James counted stars in the sky. Circle sets of ten stars. Count the sets of stars by tens. Write how many.

Name _____

Matter

Develop Concepts

Use with *ScienceFusion* pages 23–26.

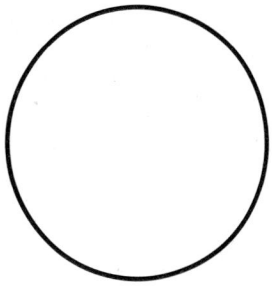

1

2

DIRECTIONS 1. Draw an object that is shaped like a square. **2.** Draw an object that is shaped like a circle.

© Houghton Mifflin Harcourt Publishing Company

Develop Concepts

3

DIRECTIONS **3.** Find which shapes are the same. Color all the shapes that are the same one color. Use as many colors as the types of shapes.

© Houghton Mifflin Harcourt Publishing Company

Name _____

Solving Problems

Develop Concepts

Use with *ScienceFusion* pages 13–16.

1

DIRECTIONS 1. Find objects that are shaped like the shapes in the chart. In each column, draw to show the things you found.

© Houghton Mifflin Harcourt Publishing Company

Sum It Up!

2

	Does it roll?	Does it stack?	Does it slide?

3

DIRECTIONS **2.** Look at the shape at the beginning of each row. Decide if it can roll, stack, or slide. Mark an X or insert a check mark in each space to tell if that shape can roll, stack, or slide. **3.** Draw to show an object that rolls and does not stack.

© Houghton Mifflin Harcourt Publishing Company

Name _____

Light

Develop Concepts

Use with *ScienceFusion* pages 33–36.

1

Morning

Afternoon

Evening

2

DIRECTIONS **1.** Look at the pictures. Circle one time of day.
2. Draw to show something you do at that time of the day.

© Houghton Mifflin Harcourt Publishing Company

Sum It Up!

3

Morning

Afternoon

Evening

© Houghton Mifflin Harcourt Publishing Company

DIRECTIONS **3.** Draw a line from the time of day to the shadow it may cause on the tree.

Name _____

Using Magnets

Develop Concepts

Use with *ScienceFusion* pages 61–62.

1

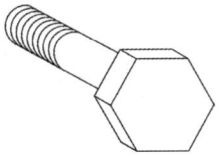

DIRECTIONS 1. Decide which objects the magnet will attract. Circle the objects the magnet will attract. Mark an X on objects the magnet will not attract.

© Houghton Mifflin Harcourt Publishing Company

Sum It Up!

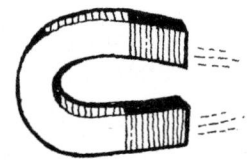

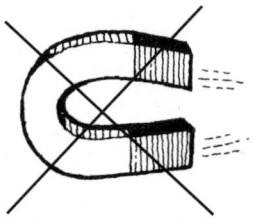

Magnets
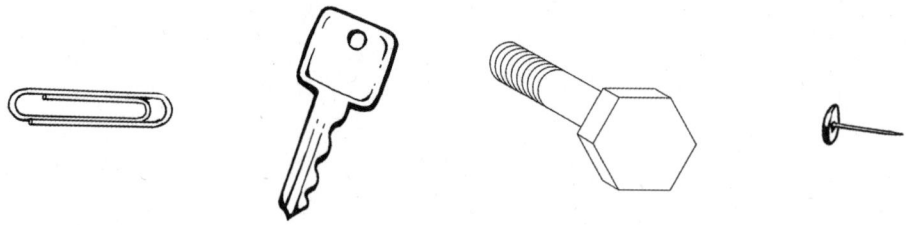
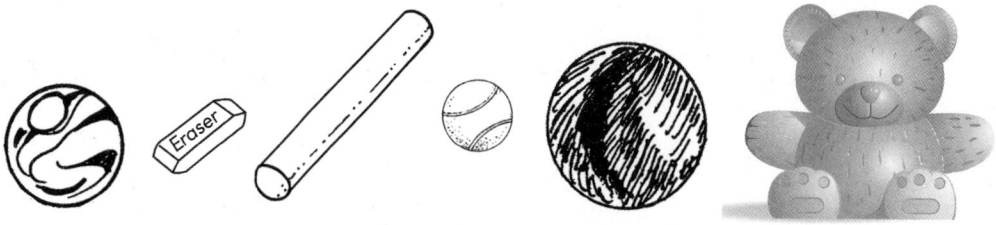

2 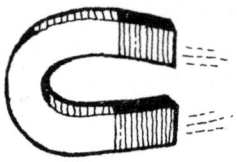

_____

_ _ _ _ _ _ _

_____

3 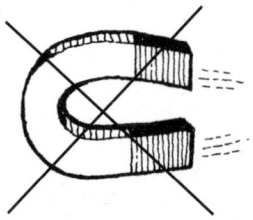

_____

_ _ _ _ _ _ _

_____

DIRECTIONS Look at the graph. **2.** How many objects does the magnet attract? Write the number. **3.** How many objects does the magnet not attract? Write the number.

© Houghton Mifflin Harcourt Publishing Company

Picture Glossary

above [arriba, encima]

The kite is **above** the rabbit.

add [sumar]

3 + 2 = 5

alike [igual]

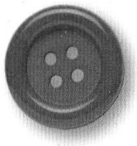

and [y]

and

2 + 2

behind [detrás]

The box is **behind** the girl.

below [debajo]

The rabbit is **below** the kite.

beside [al lado]

The tree is **beside** the bush.

© Houghton Mifflin Harcourt Publishing Company

big [grande]

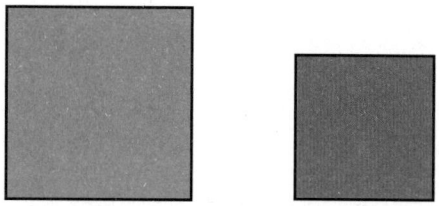

big

category [categoría]

fruits

toys

circle [círculo]

classify [clasificar]

apples

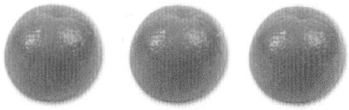

not apples

color [color]

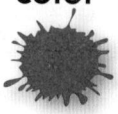

red
[rojo]

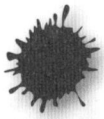

blue
[azul]

yellow
[amarillo]

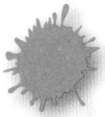

green
[verde]

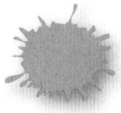

orange
[anaranjado]

compare [comparar]

cone [cono]

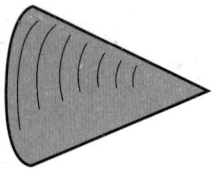

corner [esquina]

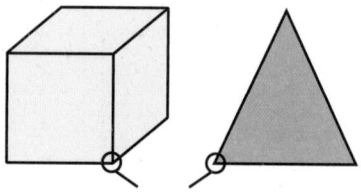

corner

© Houghton Mifflin Harcourt Publishing Company • Image Credits: (apples) ©Artville/Getty Images; (boat) ©D. Hurst/Alamy; (blue truck) ©C Squared Studios/PhotoDisc/Getty Images

cube [cubo]

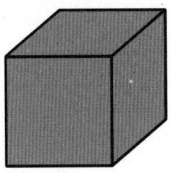

curve [curva]

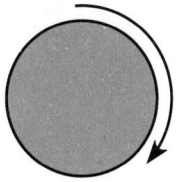

curved surface
[superficie curva]

Some solids have
a **curved surface.**

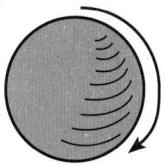

cylinder [cilindro]

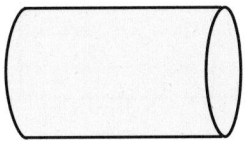

different [diferente]

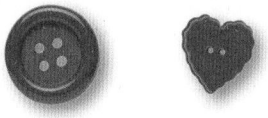

eight [ocho]

eighteen [dieciocho]

eleven [once]

fewer [menos]

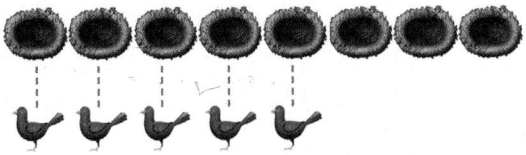

3 **fewer** birds

© Houghton Mifflin Harcourt Publishing Company

fifteen [quince]

fifty [cincuenta]

1	2	3	4	5	6	7	8	9	10
11	12	13	14	15	16	17	18	19	20
21	22	23	24	25	26	27	28	29	30
31	32	33	34	35	36	37	38	39	40
41	42	43	44	45	46	47	48	49	50

five [cinco]

flat [plano]

A circle is a **flat** shape.

flat surface [superficie plana]

Some solids have a flat **surface**.

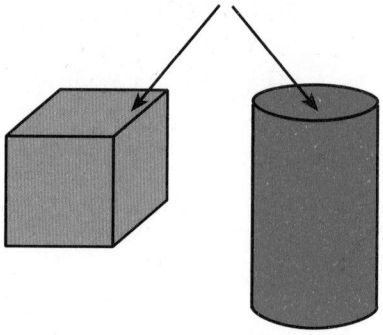

four [cuatro]

fourteen [catorce]

graph [gráfica]

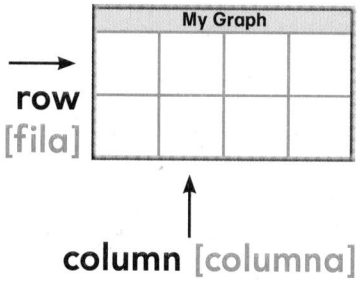

© Houghton Mifflin Harcourt Publishing Company

greater [mayor]

9 is greater than 6

heavier [más pesado]

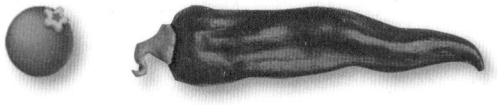

heavier

hexagon [hexágono]

in front of [delante de]

The box is **in front of** the girl.

is equal to [es igual a]

$3 + 2 = 5$

$3 + 2$ **is equal to** 5

larger [más grande]

2 3

A quantity of 3 is **larger** than a quantity of 2.

less [menor/menos]

9 is **less** than 11

lighter [más liviano]

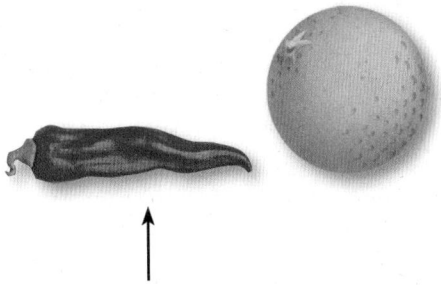

lighter

© Houghton Mifflin Harcourt Publishing Company

longer [más largo]

match [emparejar]

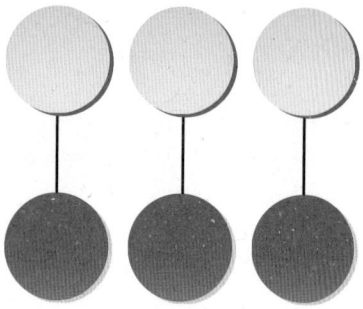

minus – [menos]

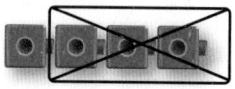

4 – 3 = 1

4 **minus** 3 is equal to 1

more [más]

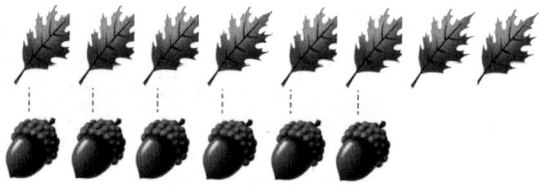

2 **more** leaves

next to [al lado de]

The bush is **next to** the tree.

nine [nueve]

nineteen [diecinueve]

one [uno]

© Houghton Mifflin Harcourt Publishing Company

one hundred [cien]

1	2	3	4	5	6	7	8	9	10
11	12	13	14	15	16	17	18	19	20
21	22	23	24	25	26	27	28	29	30
31	32	33	34	35	36	37	38	39	40
41	42	43	44	45	46	47	48	49	50
51	52	53	54	55	56	57	58	59	60
61	62	63	64	65	66	67	68	69	70
71	72	73	74	75	76	77	78	79	80
81	82	83	84	85	86	87	88	89	90
91	92	93	94	95	96	97	98	99	100

ones [unidades]

3 **ones**

pairs [pares]

3

3	0
2	1
1	2
0	3

number **pairs** for 3

plus + [más]

2 **plus** 1 is equal to 3

$2 + 1 = 3$

rectangle [rectángulo]

roll [rodar]

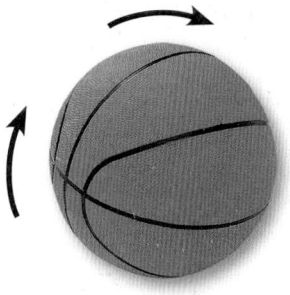

same height
[de la misma altura]

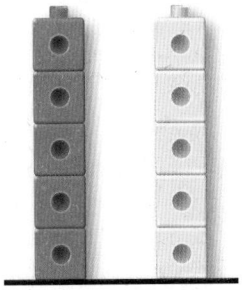

© Houghton Mifflin Harcourt Publishing Company

same length [del mismo largo]

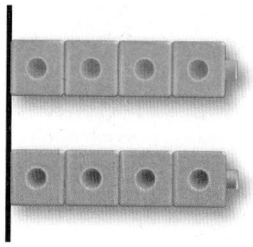

same number
[el mismo número]

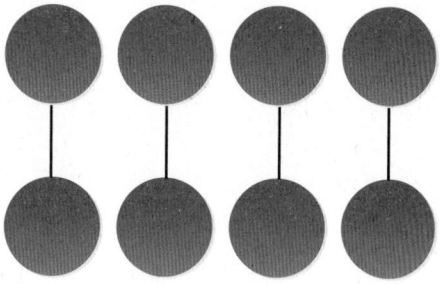

same weight [del mismo peso]

seven [siete]

seventeen [diecisiete]

shape [forma]

shorter [más corto]

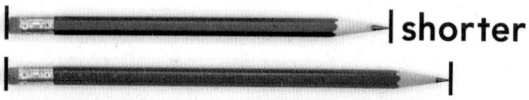

side [lado]

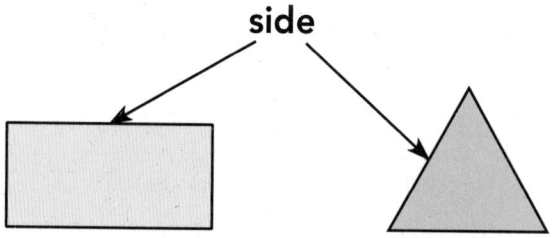

© Houghton Mifflin Harcourt Publishing Company

sides of equal length [lados del mismo largo]

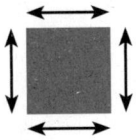

six [seis]

sixteen [dieciséis]

size [tamaño]

big

small

slide [deslizar]

small [pequeño]

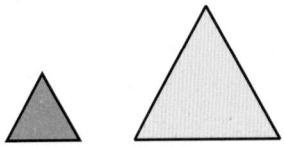

small

solid [sólido]

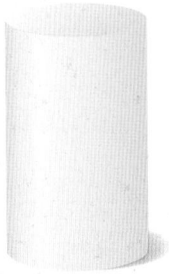

solid

A cylinder is a **solid** shape.

© Houghton Mifflin Harcourt Publishing Company • Image Credits: (tr) ©Eyewire/Getty Images

sphere [esfera]

square [cuadrado]

stack [apilar]

subtract [restar]

Subtract to find out how many are left.

taller [más alto]

taller

ten [diez]

tens [decenas]

1	2	3	4	5	6	7	8	9	10
11	12	13	14	15	16	17	18	19	20
21	22	23	24	25	26	27	28	29	30
31	32	33	34	35	36	37	38	39	40
41	42	43	44	45	46	47	48	49	50
51	52	53	54	55	56	57	58	59	60
61	62	63	64	65	66	67	68	69	70
71	72	73	74	75	76	77	78	79	80
81	82	83	84	85	86	87	88	89	90
91	92	93	94	95	96	97	98	99	100

↑ **tens**

© Houghton Mifflin Harcourt Publishing Company

thirteen [trece]

three [tres]

three-dimensional shapes
[figuras tridimensionales]

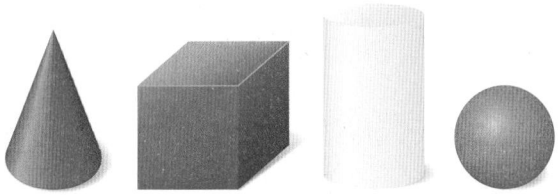

triangle [triángulo]

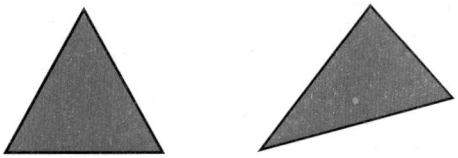

twelve [doce]

twenty [veinte]

two [dos]

two-dimensional shapes
[figuras bidimensionales]

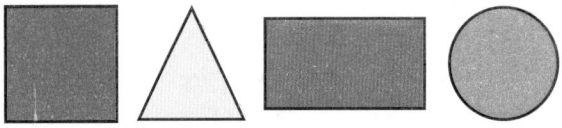

© Houghton Mifflin Harcourt Publishing Company

vertex [vértice]

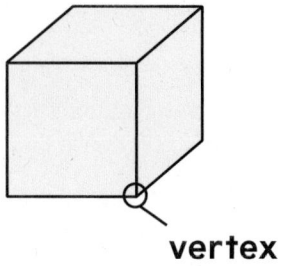

vertices [vértices]

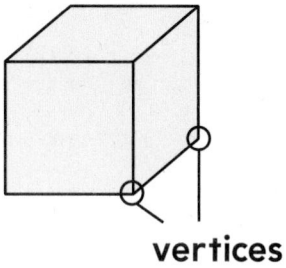

zero, none [cero, ninguno]

zero fish

© Houghton Mifflin Harcourt Publishing Company • Image Credits: (tr) ©C Squared Studios/PhotoDisc/Getty Images

Index

A

Above, 615–618
Activities
Games. *See* Games
Home. *See* Home Activity
Act Out Addition Problems, 243–246
Act Out Subtraction Problems, 323–326
Add
fluently within 5, 231–234, 243–246, 249–251, 261–264, 273–276
Addition
add to, 231–234
equations, 255–258, 261–264, 267–270, 273–276, 279–282, 285–288, 291–294, 297–300
is equal to, 243–244, 249, 255, 267–268, 273, 285, 297
model and draw, 249–251
number pairs, 273–276, 279–282, 285–288, 291–294, 297–300
plus, 237–240, 243–246, 249–251, 255–258, 261–264, 267–270, 273–276, 279–282, 285–288, 291–294, 297–300
problem solving, act out addition problems, 243–246
put together, 237–240
sentences, 255–258, 261–264, 267–270, 273–276, 279–282, 285–288, 291–294, 297–300
subtraction and, 347–350
ways to make ten, 193–196
word problems, 231–234, 237–240, 243–246, 249–251, 258, 264, 276, 282, 288, 294, 300
Add to, 231–234
Algebra
addition
model and draw problems, 249–251
number pairs, 273–276, 279–282, 285–288, 291–294, 297–300
sentences, 255–258, 261–264, 267–270
subtraction and, 347–350
classify
and count by color, 687–690
and count by shape, 693–696
and count by size, 699–701
compare two-dimensional shapes, 553–556
subtraction
addition and, 347–350
model and draw problems, 329–331
sentences, 335–338, 341–344
ways to make 5, 49–52
ways to make 10, 193–196
Alike, 553–556
Assessment
Chapter Review/Test, 73–76, 111–114, 173–176, 223–226, 303–306, 353–356, 421–424, 477–480, 565–568, 633–636, 679–682, 717–720
Mid-Chapter Checkpoint, 34, 96, 140, 202, 252, 332, 394, 450, 526, 600, 664, 702
Show What You Know, 10, 78, 116, 178, 228, 308, 358, 426, 490, 570, 646, 684

B

Behind, 627–630
Below, 615–618
Beside, 621–624
Big, 699–701

C

Category, 688–690, 693–696, 699, 701
Chapter Review/Test, 73–76, 111–114, 173–176, 223–226, 303–306, 353–356, 421–424, 477–480, 565–568, 633–636, 679–682, 717–720

© Houghton Mifflin Harcourt Publishing Company

Circle
curve, 499–502
describe, 499–502
identify and name, 493–496
sort, 493–496

Classify
and count by color, 687–690
and count by shape, 693–696
and count by size, 699–701

Color
sort by, 687–690

Compare
by counting
sets to 5, 105–108
sets to 10, 211–214
heights, 655–663, 673–676
lengths, 649–652, 673–676
by matching
sets to 5, 99–102
sets to 10, 205–208
numbers/sets
greater, 87–90
less, 93–95
same, 81–84
to five, 99–102, 105–108
to ten, 205–208, 211–214
to twenty, 447–449
two-dimensional shapes, 553–556
two numbers, 217–220
weights, 667–670, 673–676

Cone
curved surface, 597–599
flat surface, 598
identify, name, and describe, 597–599
sort, 597

Corners. *See* Vertices

Count
compare by, 105–108, 211–214
forward
to fifty, 453–456
to one hundred, 459–462, 465–468, 471–474
to twenty, 429–432, 435–438, 441–444
model and, 13–16, 25–28, 37–40, 67–70, 119–122, 131–134, 143–146, 155–158, 181–184, 361–364, 373–376, 385–388, 397–400, 409–412, 429–432
and write, 19–22, 31–33, 43–46, 67–70, 125–128, 137–139, 149–152, 161–164, 187–190, 367–369, 379–382, 385–388, 403–406, 415–418, 435–438
numbers. *See* Numbers
by ones, 453–456, 459–462
by tens, 465–468, 471–474

Cube
flat surfaces, 586
identify, name, and describe, 585–588
sort, 585–588

Curious George®, Curious About Math, 9, 77, 115, 177, 227, 307, 357, 425, 489, 569, 645, 683

Curve
of circle, 499–502
sort by, 553–556

Curved surface, 580, 592, 598

Cylinder
curved surface, 592
flat surfaces, 592
identify, name, and describe, 591–594
sort, 591–594

D

Data
classify and count, 687–690, 693–696, 699–701
graphs, concrete, 705–708, 711–714

Different, 553–556

E

Eight
count, 143–146, 149–152
model, 143–146
write, 149–152

© Houghton Mifflin Harcourt Publishing Company

Eighteen
count, 409–412, 415–418
model, 409–412
write, 415–418

Eleven
count, 361–364, 367–370
model, 361–364
write, 367–370

Equations
addition, 243–246, 249–251, 255–258, 261–264, 267–270, 273, 276, 279–282, 285–288, 291–294, 297–300
subtraction, 323–326, 329–331, 335–338, 341–344

Essential Question. In every Student Edition lesson. Some examples are: 13, 43, 311, 329, 687, 705

Expressions
addition, 231–234, 237–240
subtraction, 311–314, 317–320

F

Family Involvement
Family Note. *See* Family Note
Home Activity. *See* Home Activity

Fifteen
count, 385–388
draw a picture, 391–393
model, 385–388
use numbers to, 391–393
write, 385–388

Fifty, 453–456

Five
compare
numbers to, 81–84, 87–90, 93–95, 99–102, 105–108
by counting sets to, 105–108
by matching sets to, 99–102
count, 37–40, 43–46
draw, 37–40, 46
fluently add within, 231–234, 243–246, 249–251, 273–276
fluently subtract within, 311–314, 323–326, 329–331, 335–338
model, 37–40
ways to make, 49–52
write, 43–46

Five frames, 13–15, 25–27, 37–39, 81–82, 87–88, 93–94

Flat, 603–606, 609–612. *See also* Two-Dimensional Shapes.

Flat surface, 586, 592, 598

Four
count, 25–28, 31–33
draw, 25–28
model, 25–28
write, 31–33

Fourteen
count, 373–376, 379–382
model, 373–376
write, 379–382

G

Games
At the Farm, 686
Bus Stop, 12
Connecting Cube Challenge, 648
Counting to Blastoff, 80
Follow the Shapes, 572
Number Line Up, 118
Number Picture, 492
Pairs That Make 7, 230
Spin and Count!, 180
Spin for More, 310
Sweet and Sour Path, 360
Who Has More?, 428

Geometry, 481–488 *See* Shapes; Three-dimensional shapes; Two-dimensional shapes

Glossary, H1–H12

Graph, concrete, 705–708, 711–714

Greater, 87–90

Guided Practice. *See* Share and Show

H

Hands On, 13–19, 25–28, 37–40, 49–52, 55–58, 81–84, 87–90, 93–95, 119–122, 131–134, 143–146, 155–158, 181–184,

© Houghton Mifflin Harcourt Publishing Company

193–196, 237–240, 249–251, 273–276, 279–282, 285–288, 291–294, 297–300, 317–320, 329–331, 347–350, 361–364, 373–376, 385–388, 397–400, 409–412, 429–432, 553–556, 573–576, 579–582, 585–588, 591–594, 597–599, 609–612, 649–652, 655–658, 667–670, 687–690, 693–696, 699–701, 705–708

Heavier, 667–670

Heights
compare, 655–658, 673–676

Hexagon
identify and name, 541–544
describe, 547–550
sides, 547–550
vertices, 547–550

Home Activity, 16, 22, 28, 33, 40, 46, 52, 58, 64, 70, 84, 90, 95, 102, 108, 122, 128, 134, 139, 146, 152, 158, 164, 170, 184, 190, 196, 201, 208, 214, 220, 234, 240, 246, 258, 264, 270, 276, 282, 288, 294, 300, 314, 320, 326, 331, 338, 344, 350, 364, 370, 376, 382, 388, 393, 400, 406, 412, 418, 432, 438, 444, 449, 456, 462, 468, 474, 496, 502, 508, 514, 520, 525, 532, 538, 544, 550, 556, 562, 576, 582, 588, 594, 599, 606, 612, 618, 624, 630, 652, 658, 663, 670, 676, 690, 696, 701, 708, 714

Hundred
count by ones to, 459–462
count by tens to, 465–468

Hundred chart, 459–462, 465–468

I

In front of, 627–630

Is equal to, 243–248

L

Larger, 55–58

Lengths
compare, 649–652, 673–676

Less, 93–95

Lighter, 667–670

Listen and Draw
activity, 25, 87, 93, 131, 143, 155, 193, 199, 237, 249, 255, 273, 279, 285, 291, 297, 317, 329, 347, 361, 367, 373, 379, 385, 397, 403, 409, 415, 429, 435, 441, 453, 459, 465, 511, 523, 535, 547, 553, 573, 655, 687, 693, 699, 705
Real World, 13, 19, 31, 37, 43, 49, 55, 67, 81, 105, 119, 125, 137, 149, 161, 181, 187, 211, 217, 231, 261, 267, 311, 335, 341, 471, 493, 499, 505, 517, 529, 541, 579, 585, 591, 597, 609, 615, 621, 627, 649, 655, 667, 673

Longer, 649–652

M

Manipulatives and Materials
bead string, 364, 376, 388, 400, 412, 421, 432
cone, 597–600
connecting cubes, 310
counters, two-color, 50–52, 121, 133, 145, 157
Number and Symbol Tiles, 347
three-dimensional shapes, 573–576, 603–606, 609–612
two-dimensional shapes, 553–556, 603–606, 609–612

Matching
compare by, 99–102, 205–208

Math Processes and Practices In many lessons. Some examples are:
1. Problem Solving. In many lessons. Some examples are: 25, 37, 61, 167, 231, 243, 249, 261, 267, 311, 323, 329, 335, 341, 391, 673
2. Abstract and Quantitative Reasoning. In many lessons. Some examples are: 13, 19, 25, 31, 37, 43, 55, 61, 67, 87, 231, 237, 243, 249, 255, 261, 267, 273, 279, 285, 511, 523, 535, 547, 585, 591, 597, 687, 693, 699, 705

© Houghton Mifflin Harcourt Publishing Company

3. Use and Evaluate Logical Reasoning. In many lessons. Some examples are: 81, 87, 93, 99, 105, 167, 361, 373, 397, 409, 447, 609, 621, 627, 649, 655, 661, 667, 673
4. Mathematical Modeling. In many lessons. Some examples are: 49, 61, 99, 119, 167, 181, 193, 205, 237, 243, 249, 317, 323, 329, 391, 447, 541, 603, 615, 621, 627
5. Use Mathematical Tools. In many lessons. Some examples are: 55, 81, 87, 93, 99, 119, 131, 143, 155, 181, 205, 237, 317, 347, 385, 429, 447, 493, 499, 505, 517, 529, 541, 553, 559, 573, 579, 585, 591, 597
6. Use Precise Mathematical Language. In many lessons. Some examples are: 105, 211, 217, 429, 465, 493, 499, 505, 517, 529, 573, 579, 585, 591, 597, 621, 627, 649, 655, 661, 667, 673, 687, 693, 699, 705, 711
7. See Structure. In many lessons. Some examples are: 49, 55, 119, 131, 143, 155, 193, 255, 273, 279, 285, 291, 297, 361, 367, 373, 379, 385, 397, 511, 517, 523, 529, 535, 541, 547, 553, 559, 573, 579, 603
8. Generalize. In many lessons. Some examples are: 131, 143, 155, 205, 211, 217, 255, 347, 367, 379, 403, 415, 453, 459, 465, 471, 511, 523, 535, 547, 553, 559, 609, 705, 711

Math Story, 1–8, 481–488, 637–644

Measurement
heights, compare, 655–658, 637–644
lengths, compare, 649–652, 673–676
weights, compare, 667–670, 673–676

Mid-Chapter Checkpoint, 34, 96, 140, 202, 252, 332, 394, 450, 526, 600, 664, 702

Minus, 311–314, 317–320, 323–326, 329–332, 335–338, 341–344, 347–350

Modeling
addition, 249–251, 273–276, 279–282, 285–288, 291–294, 297–300
numbers. *See* Numbers
put together, 237–240
shapes, 609–612
subtraction, 329–331
take apart, 317–320, 329–331
take from, 311–314, 323–326, 336–338, 341–344

N

Next to, 621–624

Nine
compare to, 167–170
count, 155–158, 161–164
model, 155–158
write, 161–164

Nineteen
compare, 409–412, 415–418
count, 409–412, 415–418
model, 409–412
write, 415–418

Numbers
compare. *See* Compare
eight, 143–146, 149–152, 285–288
eighteen, 409–412, 415–418
eleven, 361–364, 367–370
fifteen, 385–388, 391–394
fifty, 453–456
five, 37–40, 43–46, 273–276
four, 25–28, 31–33
fourteen, 373–376, 379–382
to nine, 167–170
nine, 155–158, 161–164, 291–294
nineteen, 409–412, 415–418
one, 13–16, 19–22
to one hundred, 459–462, 465–468
order. *See* Order
pairs of, 273–276, 279–282, 285–288, 291–294, 297–300
same, 55–58, 81–84
seven, 131–134, 137–139, 279–282
seventeen, 397–400, 403–406
six, 119–122, 125–128, 279–282
sixteen, 397–400, 403–406

© Houghton Mifflin Harcourt Publishing Company

ten, 181–184, 187–190, 199–201, 205–208, 211–214, 297–300
three, 25–28, 31–33
twelve, 361–364, 367–370
twenty, 429–432, 435–438, 441–444
two, 13–16, 19–22
use to 15, 391–393
ways to make 5, 49–52
ways to make 10, 193–196
write, 19–22, 31–33, 43–46, 67–70, 125–128, 137–139, 149–152, 161–164, 187–190, 367–370, 379–382, 385–388, 403–406, 415–418, 435–438
zero, 61–64, 67–70

O

One/Ones
count, 13–16, 19–22, 361–364
draw, 13–16, 22
model, 13–16, 361–364
write, 19–22

On Your Own. *See* Problem Solving

Order
numbers
to five, 55–58
to ten, 199–202
to twenty, 441–444

P

Pair, 49–52

Personal Math Trainer. In all Student Edition lessons. Some examples are: 10, 75, 76, 78, 113, 114, 116, 175, 176, 178, 225, 226, 228, 304, 305, 308, 353, 356, 358, 422, 423, 426, 479, 480, 490, 566, 568, 570, 633, 634, 646, 680, 681, 684, 718, 719

Picture Glossary. *See* Glossary

Plus, 237–240, 243–246, 249–251, 255–258, 261–264, 267–270, 273–276, 279–282, 285–288, 297–300

Position words
above, 615–618
behind, 627–630
below, 615–618
beside, 621–624
in front of, 627–630
next to, 621–624

Practice and Homework. In every Student Edition lesson. Some examples are: 185–186, 247–248, 321–322, 445–446, 515–516, 601–602, 671–672

Problem Solving
activity, 22, 46, 52, 58, 184, 190, 196, 270, 344, 350, 462, 468, 496, 502, 508, 514, 520, 532, 538, 556, 576, 690, 696, 708
On Your Own, 64, 170, 208, 562, 606
Real World activity, 16, 28, 40, 70, 84, 90, 108, 122, 128, 134, 146, 152, 158, 164, 214, 220, 234, 240, 258, 264, 276, 282, 288, 294, 300, 314, 320, 338, 364, 370, 376, 382, 388, 400, 406, 412, 418, 432, 438, 444, 456, 474, 544, 550, 582, 588, 594, 612, 618, 624, 630, 652, 658, 670, 676, 714
Real World On Your Own, 102, 246, 326
Real World Unlock the Problem, 61, 99, 167, 243, 323, 391, 603, 661
strategies
act out addition problems, 243–245
act out subtraction problems, 323–325
draw a picture, 167–170, 391–393, 559–562, 661–663
make a model, 61–64, 99–102, 205–208, 447–449
Unlock the Problem, 205, 447, 559

Put Together, 237–240, 249–251, 255–258

R

Reading
numbers. *See* Numbers

© Houghton Mifflin Harcourt Publishing Company

Real World
Listen and Draw, 13, 19, 31, 37, 43, 49, 55, 67, 81, 105, 119, 125, 137, 149, 161, 181, 187, 211, 217, 231, 237, 255, 261, 267, 273, 279, 285, 291, 297, 311, 317, 335, 341, 453, 471, 493, 499, 505, 517, 529, 541, 547, 579, 585, 591, 597, 609, 615, 621, 627, 649, 655, 667, 673, 705
On Your Own, 102, 246, 326
Problem Solving, 16, 28, 40, 70, 84, 90, 108, 122, 128, 134, 146, 152, 158, 164, 214, 220, 234, 240, 258, 264, 276, 282, 288, 294, 300, 314, 320, 338, 364, 370, 376, 382, 388, 400, 406, 412, 418, 432, 438, 444, 456, 474, 544, 550, 582, 588, 594, 612, 618, 624, 630, 652, 658, 670, 676, 708, 714
Unlock the Problem, 61, 99, 167, 243, 323, 391, 603, 658

Rectangle
describe, 535–538
identify and name, 529–532
sides, 535–538
sort, 529–532
vertices, 535–538

Roll, 573–576

Same length, 649–652

Same height, 655–658

Same number, 81–84

Same weight, 667–673

Sentences
number
addition, 255–258, 261–264, 267–270
subtraction, 335–338, 341–344

Sets
add to, 231–234
compare
fewer, 93–95
more, 87–90
same number, 81–84
put together, 237–240
take apart, 317–320
take from, 311–314

Seven
count, 131–134, 137–139
model, 131–134
write, 137–139

Seventeen
count, 397–400, 403–406
model, 397–400
write, 403–406

Shape(s) Three-dimensional shapes, 573–612;
Two-dimensional shapes, 489–564
combine, 559–562
flat, 603–606
model, 609–612
solid, 603–606
sort by, 693–696

Share and Show. In every Student Edition lesson. Some examples are: 14, 44, 312, 330, 688, 700, 706

Shorter than, 649–652, 657

Show What You Know, 10, 78, 116, 178, 228, 308, 358, 426, 490, 570, 646, 684

Sides
hexagon, 547–550
number of, 511–514
rectangle, 535–538
sides of equal length, 511–514
square, 511–514
triangle, 523–525
sides of equal length, 511–514
number of, 511–514

Six
count, 119–122, 125–128
model, 119–122
write, 125–128

Sixteen
count, 397–400, 403–406
model, 397–400
write, 403–406

Size
sort by, 699–701

Slide, 573–576

Small, 699–701

© Houghton Mifflin Harcourt Publishing Company

Solid, 603–606, 609–612. *See also* Three-dimensional shapes

Sort
circles, 493–496
by color, 687–690
rectangles, 529–532
by shape, 693–696
by size, 699–701
squares, 505–508
three-dimensional shapes, 603–606
triangles, 517–520
two-dimensional shapes, 553–556, 603–606

Sphere
curved surface, 580
identify, name, and describe, 579–582
sort, 579–580

Square
describe, 511–514
identify and name, 505–508
sides, 511–514
sort, 505–508
vertices, 511–514

Strategies. *See* Problem Solving

Subtract
fluently within 5, 311–314, 323–326, 329–331, 335–338

Subtraction
addition and, 347–350
equations, 335–338, 341–344, 347–350
minus, 317–320, 323–326, 331, 332, 335–338, 341–344, 347–350
model and draw, 329–331
problem solving strategy, act out
subtraction problems, 323–326
subtraction sentences, 335–338, 341–344
take apart, 317–320, 329–331
take away, 311–313
take from, 311–314, 323–326, 335–338, 341–344
word problems, 311–314, 317–320, 323–326, 335–338, 341–344, 347–350

Symbols. *See* **Minus,** Plus, Is equal to

T

Take apart, 317–320, 329–331

Take from, 311–314, 323–326, 335–338, 341–344

Taller, 655–656

Ten frames, 119, 132, 144, 156, 181–183, 200–201, 237–239, 317–319, 354, 362–363, 374–375, 385–387, 398–399, 404–405, 410–411, 416–417, 442–443

Ten(s)
compare
by counting sets to ten, 211–214
by matching sets to ten, 205–208
two numbers, 217–220
count, 181–184, 187–190, 199–201, 465–468
to, 199–201
forward to, 199–201
order to, 199–201
model, 181–184
ways to make, 193–196
write, 187–190

Test Prep
Mid-Chapter Checkpoint, 34, 96, 140, 202, 252, 332, 394, 450, 526, 600, 664, 702

Think Smarter. In all Student Edition chapters. Some examples are 34, 96, 140, 202, 252, 332, 394, 450, 526, 600, 664, 702

Think Smarter +. In all Student Edition lessons. Some examples are: 75, 76, 113, 114, 175, 176, 225, 226, 304, 305, 353, 356, 422, 423, 479, 480, 566, 568, 633, 634, 680, 681, 718, 719

Thirteen
count, 373–376, 379–382
model, 373–376
write, 379–382

Three
count, 25–28, 31–33
draw, 25–28
model, 25–28
write, 31–33

© Houghton Mifflin Harcourt Publishing Company

Three-dimensional shapes
cone, 597–599
cube, 585–588
cylinder, 591–594
model, 609–612
roll, 573–576
slide, 573–576
solid, 603–606, 609–612
sort, 573–576
sphere, 579–582
stack, 573–576

Triangle
combine, 559–560
describe, 523–525
identify and name, 517–520
sides, 523–525
sort, 517–520
vertices, 523–525

Try Another Problem, 62, 100, 168, 206, 244, 324, 392, 448, 560, 604, 712

Twelve
count, 361–364, 367–370
model, 361–364
write, 367–370

Twenty
compare numbers to, 447–449
count, 429–432, 435–438, 441–444
model, 429–432
order, 441–444
write, 435–438

Two
count, 13–16, 19–22
draw, 13–16
model, 13–16
write, 19–22

Two-dimensional shapes
circle, 493–496, 499–502
combine, 559–562
flat, 609–612
hexagon, 541–544, 547–550
model, 609–612
rectangle, 529–532, 535–538
square, 505–508, 511–514
triangle, 517–520, 523–525

U

Unlock the Problem, 205, 447, 559
Real World, 61, 99, 167, 243, 323, 391, 603, 623

V

Vertex/Vertices
hexagon, 547–550
rectangle, 535–538
square, 511–514
triangle, 523–525

Vocabulary
Builder, 11, 79, 117, 179, 229, 309, 359, 427, 491, 571, 647, 685
Chapter Vocabulary Cards
Vocabulary Game

W

Weights
compare, 667–670, 673–679

Write
numbers. *See* Numbers
Write Math. *See* Write Math

Write Math, 16, 22, 28, 40, 46, 52, 58, 64, 70, 84, 90, 102, 108, 122, 128, 134, 146, 152, 158, 164, 170, 184, 190, 196, 208, 214, 220, 234, 240, 246, 258, 264, 270, 276, 282, 288, 294, 300, 314, 320, 326, 338, 344, 350, 364, 370, 376, 382, 388, 400, 406, 412, 418, 432, 438, 444, 456, 474, 496, 502, 508, 514, 520, 532, 538, 544, 550, 556, 562, 576, 582, 588, 594, 606, 612, 618, 624, 630, 652, 658, 670, 676, 690, 696, 708

Z

Zero
count, 67–70
draw, 70
model, 61–64
write, 67–70

© Houghton Mifflin Harcourt Publishing Company